THE DARTMOUTH PROPRIETY:
Land Ownership in the Township Before 1800

An Honors Thesis
Presented to the Faculty of the History Department
of Southeastern Massachusetts University

by Sally M. Aldrich

May 1987

ISBN: 978-0-578-33791-3
First Printing: 2021

Printed in the United States of America

The term "Dartmouth" invites confusion. "Dartmouth" from 1664 until 1787 encompassed the present towns of Westport, Dartmouth, Acushnet and Fairhaven and the present City of New Bedford. It also included part of Tiverton and Little Compton, until the line was redrawn between Rhode Island and Massachusetts in 1746. In 1787, the eastern part of Dartmouth was set off as the separate town of New Bedford, including the areas which comprised the later towns of Fairhaven and Acushnet. The western part of Dartmouth became the separate town of Westport in the same year. Thereafter, the original territory was referred to as "the ancient Propriety of Dartmouth" or simply "Old Dartmouth," and "Dartmouth" referred to the bounds and entity which comprise the current incorporated town. In the historical context of the following chapters, "Dartmouth" refers to whichever legal entity existed at the time the events discussed were taking place. However, in these few introductory words and in Chapter I, the term is used specifically to address the history of the present town of Dartmouth.

Although Dartmouth is one of the earliest white settlements in New England, the Town's records are in a state of terrible disarray and the land records of the Proprietors for the first 75 years were destroyed by fire in 1725. This loss, coupled with the lack of references to Dartmouth in other works of New England colonial history, make it exceedingly difficult to reconstruct what really went on in the town during the crucial years of its settlement. However, this difficulty may be overcome through a study of legal matters relating to the land, and by sifting through the surviving records. From this study, a better understanding into what was taking place in Dartmouth emerges.

To my knowledge, little effort has been made to preserve, catalogue, or interpret the workings of the town government. The exception is that on the occasion of New Bedford's centennial, that city copied over records "of particular interest" to it, which have since been microfilmed. These consisted of town meeting records and vital statistics from 1674 to 1787 and some highway layouts neither indexed nor labeled. Entirely separate from the Proprietors' records, the early town meeting records are rather brief, limited to the election of officers, but the later ones enlighten the reader as to the town's attitude toward many subjects. A team of researchers with a computer and a great deal of time could come up with some very interesting analyses using this information. Unfortunately, such a project is beyond the scope of my present endeavor. In this work, I have concentrated on a legal history of the early land ownership with some social, economic and political commentary. Along the way, I hope to stimulate interest and provide some source material on Dartmouth for those who may want to delve further into the history of the town.

There are two aspects of the development of land ownership in Dartmouth. First, there is the history of how the undivided or common lands were parceled out by the Proprietors, who held sole legal title to all lands in Dartmouth at the time the town was settled in the mid-17th century. The chief source for this information is the Record of Meetings of Proprietors from 1725/6 to 1821, which exists in one original volume in the Bristol County (Southern District) Registry of Deeds. When the Massachusetts General Court passed legislation to authorize the preservation of the town's early land records in 1867, this volume was not included. I found it necessary to transcribe the original manuscript into a personal typed copy, modernizing the spelling and punctuation for readability. These minutes chronicle the Proprietors' efforts to deal with the situation arising from the tragic loss of their pre-1726 records and also their attempts to finish apportioning the common lands to individuals.

In 1867, four other Proprietors' books of records were copied over into two manuscript volumes. These aim (unsuccessfully) to reconstruct the record of land titles derived from the shares held by the original Purchasers of Dartmouth in 1652. The entries in these volumes are, at best, jumbled, contradictory, repetitive, and not properly indexed. Ultimately, the Proprietors and everyone else had to rely on surveyors' field notes in journals made by Benjamin Crane and his successors, who officially surveyed the town starting in 1710. These field notes, which form the basis of all land titles in the area today, were preserved in printed form in 1910.

The other aspect of land ownership is the history of the devolution of the divided lands after they were set off to individuals. Transfers during life are reflected in actual deeds recorded in the Bristol County (Southern District) Registry of Deeds, and transfers at death are found in wills and probate inventories filed in the Bristol County Probate Court. Although these vital records do not tell us much about the non-landowning residents of the community, they do provide insight for understanding those men of means who were likely to be pivotal players in the affairs of the town.

Works mentioning Dartmouth, to the extent known to me, are listed in the bibliography. The Old Dartmouth Historical Society Sketches are most valuable. There are other sources as well. The records of actions concerning Dartmouth taken by the government of New Plimoth are available. Old maps are enlightening. As late as 1871, for example, a map of Dartmouth illustrates the geographic isolation of farmsteads, the numerous scattered schools and meetinghouses, and the small burial grounds which dotted the township. Although Quaker values repressed town pride and left graves unmarked, the reoccurrence of family names in deeds point to a continuity and homogeneity, which suggest limited immigration into the town. Some emigration occurred to adjoining cities like New Bedford and Fall River as well as a drain of population in the general westward expansion of the country. From a number of secondary works about land tenure, farming, Quaker religious life, and growth in other towns in New England, information can be gleaned indirectly about Dartmouth.

What is found in these pages is but a small contribution to the greater task of bringing town history to life. In this work, I have usually modernized spelling in quoted materials for clarity, but I have left dates exactly as I found them. Readers should be aware that under the old calendar the new year began on March 25 until 1752, when the Gregorian calendar adopted the present practice of beginning the year on January 1. The preservation of the surviving records should become a priority issue for area historians, particularly with regard to the Proprietors' records. These should be indexed by computer so they can be analyzed further. If I have succeeded in laying some groundwork in these pages, the importance of such an undertaking will be self-evident.

For acknowledgments, I would like to mention (posthumously) Henry B. Worth, whose interest in land history preceded mine. I am particularly grateful to Paul Cyr and Elaine Silva of the New Bedford Free Public Library staff, who have rendered valuable assistance. Special thanks go to the SMU History Committee, consisting of Martin J. Butler, John M. Werly, and Kevin J. Hargreaves, who have graciously consented to read this work.

CONTENTS

APPENDIX 1: Map of the Warwick Patent

APPENDIX 2: Old Comer Reserved Tracts

APPENDIX 3: Indian Deed of 1652

APPENDIX 4: List of Proprietors of Dartmouth in 1652

APPENDIX 5: Map of the Three Dartmouth Villages

APPENDIX 6: Confirmatory Deed from William Bradford in 1694

APPENDIX 7: A. Map of Highways (1620-1675)
            B. Map of Highways and Industries (1675-1775)

APPENDIX 8: Map of Marsh Meadow

APPENDIX 9: British Royal Navy Chart

APPENDIX 10: Massachusetts Tax Valuation List of 1771

APPENDIX 11: United States Census of 1790

APPENDIX 12: Letter of James B. Congdon to Bristol County Commissioners (1867)

APPENDIX 13: Map of Southern Bristol County (1871)

I. INTRODUCTION

Many local historians write about "visible history." They concern themselves with when and where their area was settled, who chose to settle there and why. Historians venerate houses left standing and cherish old artifacts as sacred relics from our ancestors' lives. They talk about life in "the good old days" and eulogize distinguished persons of the community who left their mark. They build monuments of local pride to commemorate local events. Reminiscences by octogenarians give us anecdotes which remind us of common human foibles and comment on famous and infamous personages who affected the community by their residency or touched the community by the happenstance of their passage through. All of these records have an important place in our lives and have their value in helping us understand the past and identify with our roots.[1]

But what of the "invisible" history, the things so taken for granted as commonplace and unexceptional that they are overlooked or ignored? In the first historical work of the area, published in 1858, Daniel Ricketson remarked in his final pages, "I have said but little about the agricultural interest of the township, which . . . is nevertheless of no small importance to the inhabitants."[2] Succeeding histories have done little to fill this void.

The land itself, what is built upon it, and who lives there, are indeed all visible, but the implications of land ownership have remained largely invisible to most of us three centuries later due to unfamiliarity with methods of landholding and lost, mutilated, and difficult to interpret records. Land is the basis of wealth, security and stability; the institutions governing land ownership give the community its foundation. Legal, cultural, religious and economic values control how we look at land, how we utilize it, and what we say about it. The Indians' concepts of land owning were at variance with those of white settlers, yet each group envisioned the land serving its particular needs. The impact of these two cultures upon the land within the original town of Dartmouth provides a rewarding field to investigate because (1) it has not been done before, and (2) it is uniquely different from the accepted view of landholding in colonial New England. Who got it, how much, how it was used, how it passed from neighbor to neighbor and from one generation to the next, and the inferences which might be drawn from that information are all subjects of investigation.

Within the current bounds of Dartmouth, from the mid 17th century, when white settlers supplanted Indians, until the mid-20th century, life in the quiet, agricultural township changed little. It was enormous geographically, yet it remained sparsely populated. The scattered homesteads and saltwater farms, with several more concentrated communities around the mill sites, apparently drew little attention from the outside world. Farming was predominant in Dartmouth, as elsewhere in New England, and there was no rapid change to provoke debate. However, Dartmouth was not a typical New England town. There was no town common nor central clustered settlement. It was bypassed by major roads linking other New England regions. The non-navigable streams which sliced its interior proved an impediment to land transportation. Without a large navigable river or a commodious harbor, Dartmouth's geographic makeup caused it to be overlooked in commercial exploitation. Nevertheless, the presence of the sea was felt in less assuming ways --- for coastal transportation, fishing, saltmaking, shipbuilding, and the like.

The history of Dartmouth has been virtually ignored in the annals of Massachusetts history, past and present, except for an occasional reference to the devastation wrought upon the township during King Philip's War. Even that reference is often reproachful in tone, because Dartmouth had refused to consolidate into a "proper" Christian settlement with a garrison defense against Indian attack.[3] The Colony of New Plimoth, of which Dartmouth was legally a part, was absorbed into the Colony of Massachusetts Bay in 1691. Thereafter, power and leadership shifted to Puritan Boston and other thriving communities to the north, relegating Plymouth to a secondary position, an economic backwater in the rising tide of Massachusetts mercantile prosperity.

For her part, Plymouth, whose descendants migrated into the fertile lands of Duxbury and Scituate and other areas to the north, was never happy to acknowledge her stepchild, Dartmouth. Few Plymouth Purchasers decided to settle in this region, cut off from Plymouth by a difficult overland trek and the treacherous Cape Cod waters.[4] Nature dictated that Dartmouth should draw from its nearest western neighboring settlements of any size, Newport and Portsmouth, Rhode Island, and Dartmouth maintained commercial and genealogical ties with these communities for a long time afterward. Sailing to Newport was one-third the distance to Plymouth, and infinitely more comfortable. As a consequence, Dartmouth was separated geographically, and thanks to the Quaker influence, religiously and genealogically, though not legally, from the government of New Plimoth. There was little common ground, with either Plymouth or the rest of Massachusetts, which was ruled by Puritans who viewed Quakers as a threat to their ordered building of a "city upon a hill." Dartmouth actually voted to become part of Rhode Island in 1741, but Massachusetts refused to let the town go.[5]

Since Bedford Village soon eclipsed the rest of Dartmouth in growth and prosperity, breaking away in 1787 to form a separate town and eventually becoming the City of New Bedford, historic attention focused upon the growth of that whaling center. New Bedford had the large population, the good harbor, the fine buildings and whaleships, the wealth to support enterprise and culture, the exotic ties with the West Indies, the Pacific and Far East, and the prominent citizens who made a name for themselves at home and abroad. 19th century and early 20th century historians idolized the civic and cultural achievements of their prominent men and concerned themselves with "aristocratic history" rather than the more "commonplace" world outside the city. They mentioned New Bedford's common origins as part of Old Dartmouth only to reinforce claims of antiquity.[6]

The areas which became Fairhaven and Acushnet were included in the setoff to New Bedford in 1787, and in the same year the western territory of Old Dartmouth was set off as Westport. Bereft of much of her area, the present town of Dartmouth continued to remain largely unnoticed until the middle of this century. Now, as we approach the end of the twentieth century and in a time when the land is undergoing accelerating change, the urgency to preserve the past grows.

Scrutinizing the history of land ownership, one reaches the inescapable conclusion that the town really takes its character from the period 1660 to roughly 1800. The 17th century marked the time when the Indian way of life vanished from southern New England. Arriving English settlers transformed the landscape, using new methods of agriculture to implement priorities different from those held by the native population for millennia. But while Dartmouth participated in the same ecological changes occurring elsewhere in New England, in many ways the township's history diverged from that of other

New England towns. In particular, the ancient Propriety of Dartmouth derived its existence from a unique unfolding of events in the 17th century, and over the 18th century the Propriety took a course which very likely was little anticipated at its inception. Modern land ownership is clearly the result of a fascinating and obscure evolution which preceded it. Since the history of English settlement in the region is bound up with events which occurred at least a half century before the town of Dartmouth came into existence, it is to a much earlier era that we now turn.

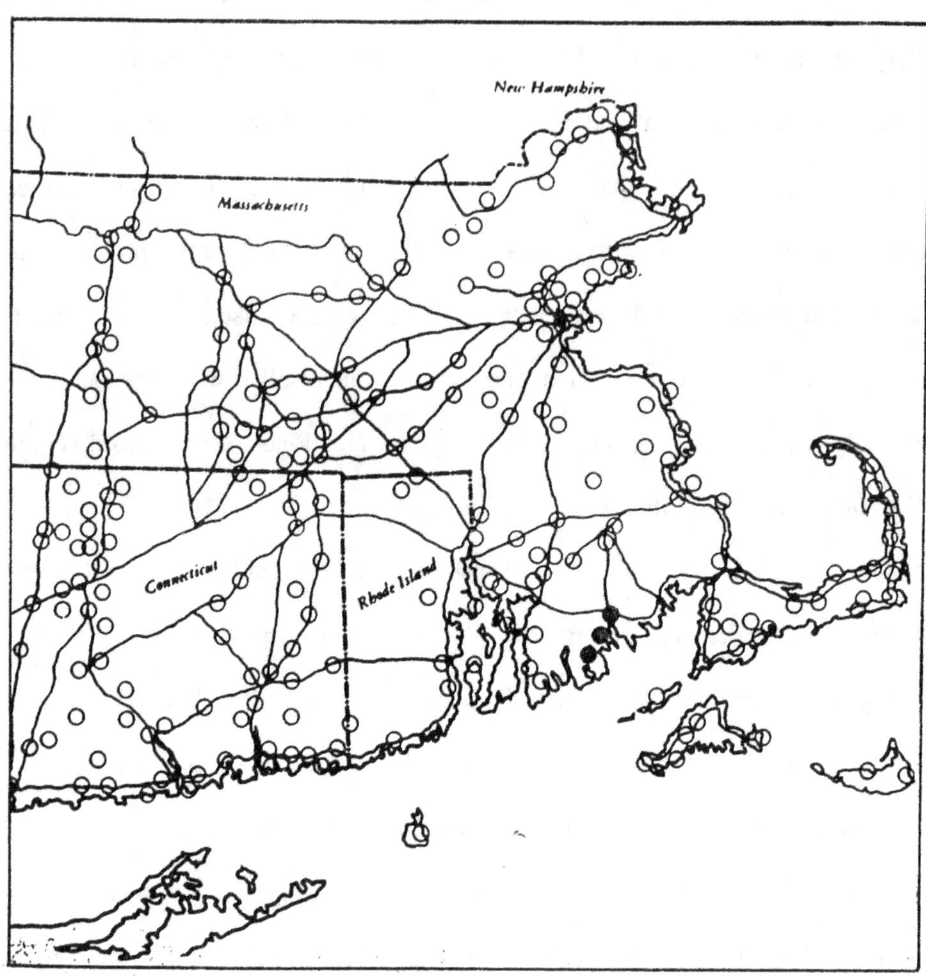

Indian villages and major routes of travel in 1600.

II. FIRST INHABITANTS

The map opposite is not a modern highway map, although it could easily serve that purpose; rather, it designates Indian villages and the major routes of travel connecting them, compiled for the year 1600.[1] It immediately dispels the notion that America was a virgin wilderness awaiting the Biblical injunction of "subdue the earth," which white men sought to fulfill. America was not settled by white men in the 17th century; it was *resettled*.[2] Native Americans, whom we misname "Indians," had lived in New England for nine or ten millennia.[3] Several branches of the Algonquin nation had populated the region for about 1,000 years.[4] Estimates of their number in 1600 range from 60,000 to 100,000 for southern New England, or perhaps 287 people per hundred square miles.[5] By contrast, there were 93,000 white inhabitants by 1700.[6]

The Indian tribes of southern New England were not nomads, but well-settled, agricultural peoples.[7] The Massachusetts, people of the Great Blue Hill, occupied the Boston area, a hub of activity, then as now. The Narragansetts lived on the western shores and islands of Rhode Island, the Sakonnets on the southeastern shore of Narragansett Bay, and the Nausets on Cape Cod and the Islands.[8] The geographic area currently comprising Bristol and Plymouth Counties was inhabited by the Pokanoket Indians, more commonly known as the Wampanoags. At the time of English settlement, the dwelling place of their chief sachem Ousamequin, or "Massasoit" to the English, was on the west side of Mount Hope Bay in what is now Bristol and Warren, Rhode Island. The map shows a concentration of Wampanoag villages along the Taunton River, in the Middleboro area, and east of the Sakonnet River. The three (darkened) circles in the area which came to be known as Old Dartmouth denote the sites of local tribal groups--the Acushenas, Ponagansetts and Coaksetts.[9] These sites were later occupied by the three English villages of Cushnet, Ponaganset, and Coakset in Dartmouth township.

Indian tribes were headed by a chief sachem, either male or female, and tribal custom had the force of law. The chief consulted his council on important matters and tried to achieve full public endorsement for decisions. Tribal boundaries, traditional and mutually respected, were defined by physical features, such as streams or hills.[10] In addition to the village site, each southern New England tribe had fields cultivated with maize, beans, squash, pumpkins and Jerusalem artichokes, a local fishing place, and more distant hunting grounds. Fishing spots at inland falls and shellfish beds on the coast were neutral ground, open to all tribes.[11] Indian dwellings were simply constructed of bent poles covered with thatch, mats or bark, with a smoke hole at the top.[12]

Each family could cultivate as much land for its own use as it wanted and also would be expected to help with lands cultivated in common to support the chief and to provide for tribal hospitality. Each family owned its own house, household goods, clothing, weapons, implements and tools, ornaments, and dogs. Held in common were berry fields, deer pastures, groves of nut trees, and the natural resources which would furnish the raw materials for dugout canoes, houses, baskets, tools and firewood. The sachem was trustee for the tribe of lakes, streams and other territory held for the common benefit and would not transfer it without tribal consultation and concurrence.[13]

It is beyond the scope of this paper to explore the diverse viewpoints held by scholars on whether Indians' recognized private land ownership, but they clearly did have a concept of land tenure. While there may have been tribal variations, the most widely supported conclusion is that land tenure was based on use and occupancy. Tenure became especially important when land came under cultivation, which was certainly the case in southern New England long before 1600. Within its recognized territory, the tribe moved seasonally to different sites and abandoned exhausted cornfields for the years necessary for the soil to regain fertility, before re-occupying the site. Basically, land was the communal asset of the tribe, and each member took from it as needed for the term of his life. One did not purchase, sell, gift or devise the land, in the European sense, although it was apparently the custom to allow the offspring of a deceased person to continue to cultivate the same plot their parent had tended.[14]

The Indians of southern New England chose their places of settlement near bodies of water for the same reasons that white settlers would later find these places so attractive: easy transportation, an abundance of fish, and a more temperate climate favorable to agriculture. For the Wampanoags, the Taunton River watershed and the Mount Hope Bay area were ideal. These sites were accessible to the sea and to inland fresh water ponds, and the "light" soil was easily cultivated.[15] Berries, grapes and nuts grew abundantly.[16] Between planting and harvesting, there was time for short trips to the seashore for fishing, clamming, lobstering, playing games, and general summer relaxation. They left enormous shell heaps on all the necks jutting into Buzzards Bay as evidence of their summer sojourns.

To clear the land for planting and easier hunting, the Indians used stone axes and fire. Undergrowth and pine trees burned easily.[17] Large hardwood trees could be killed by stripping off the bark and girdling them, letting the stumps rot in the ground after the dead trees keeled over.[18] Women knew that when the budding leaves of the white oak reached the size of a mouse's ear, it was time to scoop the earth into hills, fertilize it with alewives, and plant corn.[19] Bean seeds would be added to the hills so that the sprouts could climb up the corn stalks, and later squashes and pumpkins would be planted between the hills to keep down the weeds.[20] Then the children would guard the seeds from the birds and keep the dogs from digging up the fish. Tobacco was a crop planted separately and tended by the men. "Drinking" tobacco, as smoking a pipe was called, was integral to tribal hospitality; tobacco was also used as a painkiller and as a snakebite antidote.[21]

Indians had a very balanced diet which made them tall and healthy.[22] They had a longer lifespan than Europeans. Their teeth were excellent, and their children were well formed and did not suffer from rickets or malnutrition.[23] They raised a surplus of crops which they stored in large underground pits, and on numerous occasions white settlers on the verge of starvation sought food from them.[24]

Brereton, who accompanied Englishman Bartholomew Gosnold to Cuttyhunk in 1602 called the Indian envoys who came from the Dartmouth mainland "exceeding courteous, gentle of disposition, and well- conditioned; . . . for shape of body and lovely favour, I thinke they excell all the people of America." He further described the men as having "stature much higher than we; of complexion or colour, much like a darke Olive; their eie-browes and haire black, which they weare long, tied up behind in knots."[25] The women were "fat and very well favoured" and he concluded that as a people the Indians have "a perfect constitution of body, active, strong, healthfull, and very wittie."[26]

The healthful and self-sufficient existence of the Indians of southern New England was to last only another decade after Gosnold's departure. Their isolation on the North American continent had given them no defenses against European diseases. As increasing numbers of fishermen and explorers visited the Atlantic coast, illnesses from which Europeans, with their stronger immunity, could recover, wrought havoc among the Indians. Although the Narragansetts to the west escaped the worst of it, the Wampanoags and other tribes to the east and north were especially hard hit. Epidemics raged from 1614 to 1617, devastating their villages. Whether it was smallpox, measles, scarlet fever or bubonic plague is in dispute among scholars, but the effects were clear.[27] Perhaps as many as 80% to 90% of the population died.[28] From Penobscot Bay in Maine to Narragansett Bay in Rhode Island, for twenty miles inland, the land was depopulated.[29] Especially around the area of Boston harbor, bones and skulls lay everywhere, as the survivors became too ill to bury the dead.[30]

When Captain Thomas Dermer sailed along the Plymouth coast in 1619, he found "antient plantations, not long since populous, now utterly void."[31] When the Pilgrims went ashore at the spot they named Plymouth in 1620, they decided to "set on the mainland . . . on a high ground, where there is a great deal of land cleared, and hath been planted with corn three or four years ago."[32] The Pilgrims were, in fact, settling on the abandoned Indian village of Patuxet. An excellent first-hand account was published under the title *Mourt's Relation* in 1622.[33]

Although neighboring Indians kept watch on them from a distance during the winter, three months passed before the English made formal contact with them. In March they met Squanto, "the only native of Patuxet, where we now inhabit."[34] Squanto had escaped the fate of the rest by reason of his having been kidnapped in 1614 and taken to England. Five years later he returned to find his village empty.[35]

In the summer of 1621, the English decided upon an expedition to Pokanoket, "the habitation of the great King MASSASOIT." Although they had had a reasonably cordial meeting when Massasoit visited in the spring, the English remained wary of the Indians. Their mission was "partly to know where to find them [the savages] if occasion served, as also to see their strength, [and to] discover the country."[36] They also intended to "make satisfaction for some conceived injuries," for they had helped themselves to corn stores on Cape Cod upon first landing there, "finding no inhabitants but some graves of dead new buried."[37] The rightful owners, who had fled into the woods, now demanded restitution.

Stephen Hopkins and Edward Winslow were chosen emissaries by Governor Bradford, to be accompanied by Squanto on the journey. They traveled to Nemasket (Middleboro), and when they reached the Taunton River, observed:

> The head of this river is reported to be not far from the place of our abode; upon it are and have been many towns, it being a good length. The ground is very good on both sides, it being for the most part cleared. Thousands of men have lived there, which died in a great plague not long since. . . .[38]

They passed over a land depopulated. In the memorable phraseology of historian Francis Jennings, America was a widow rather than a virgin.[39]

Twenty years previously, Gosnold's chroniclers had landed on Dartmouth's southern shores and had sung the praises of "the goodliest continent that we ever saw," but Gosnold had failed to convince any of his crew to remain in a strange new world filled with Indians, even to man a trading post.[40] By 1620 the Indians were greatly diminished in number, and the survivors were especially vulnerable, at a time when the English were ready to begin colonizing in earnest. In *Mourt's Relation*, the report of the journey to Massasoit did not fail to assess the real estate potential. After mentioning the plague, the writer added, " . . . and pity it was and is to see so many goodly fields, and so well seated, without men to dress and manure the same."[41] He remarked that the cleared fields were becoming overgrown with weeds for lack of cultivation. He also noted the good stands of oak, walnut, fir, beech and chestnut "yet the trees stand not thick, but a man may well ride a horse amongst them."[42]

To English eyes the land appeared to be theirs for the taking. Like a good real estate agent, upon his return to Plymouth, Edward Winslow lost no time in sending favorable word back home. His letter states: "I make no question but men might live as contented here as in any part of the world. . . . The country wanteth only industrious men to employ, for it would grieve your hearts if, as I, you had seen so many miles together by goodly rivers uninhabited. . . ."[43]

Gosnold's men had landed on the south coast and the Plymouth travelers had passed just to the north of the area which would, about half a century later, become incorporated as a township under the name of "Dartmouth." How the town came into being is inextricably interwoven with the history of the little colony of "Saints" and "Strangers" who came to the New World in 1620 and staked out Plymouth Plantation.[44]

III. CHARTER RIGHTS

The harvest reaped by the Pilgrims and other English settlers in the 17th century was sown much earlier by the maritime energies of Drake, Hawkins, Pring, Gorges, Smith, Hobson, Dermer and Gosnold.[1] Among European nations, discovery was often the basis of claim to a new territory; but, to use the common expressions, "possession was nine-tenths of the law" and "might made right." Actual settlements were far more effective in perfecting claims to the New World than empty pronouncements, and land was ultimately held by the sword.[2] Recognition by other European nations was a key objective. Europeans took Indian deeds not necessarily in acknowledgment of Indian sovereignty but to use as legal evidence against each other.[3] Christians gave little thought to "heathen," i.e., Indian, occupation. As Jennings put it, "For Europeans, the issue was not <u>whether</u> they should rule [over the Indians], but <u>which</u> of them should do it."[4] If Europeans claimed sovereignty based on five principles -- papal donation, first discovery, sustained possession, voluntary self-subjection by the natives, and armed conquest, it could be argued that the last four were utilized by the English to one degree or another in the vicinity of Dartmouth from the time of Gosnold's discovery in 1602 to King Philip's War in 1676.

Gosnold's reports to England following his 1602 voyage encouraged interest in settlement in America. After war with Spain ended in 1604, England was free to claim wide areas of the North American coast, despite overlapping Spanish claims. By the middle of the first decade of the 17th century, the English consensus was that collective efforts might succeed where earlier one-man expeditions had failed.[5] A succession of English colonial charters followed, containing three dimensions, in priority, (1) territorial demarcation or "the space concept," (2) the power to govern, and (3) rights in land.

In 1606, King James I issued the First Charter of Virginia to two trading companies formed by groups of Englishmen from London and Plymouth, respectively. They shared the terms of the charter but were assigned different localities for settlement.[6]

The London Company was empowered to establish its colony of Southern Virginia between parallels 34° and 41° north latitude (South Carolina to Connecticut) in any place not already "actually possessed by any Christian Prince or People."[7] The Plymouth Company was empowered to establish its colony of Northern Virginia between 38° and 45° (Chesapeake Bay to Northern Maine). Between 38° and 41° (Chesapeake and Connecticut), either company could settle, as long as its colony was at least 100 miles distant from the other.[8] Each grant included islands within 100 miles of the coast, but no definitive inland boundary, except to state that settlement was to be "along the coast." Once a colony had sited itself, it could claim territorial rights 50 miles up and 50 miles down the coast and 100 miles inland, establishing territorial rights 100 miles each in length and depth or 10,000 square miles total area, plus all the islands.[9] This First Charter did not extend infinitely westward.

Of the legal terms of the royal Virginia Charter of 1606, the inclusion of one particular provision was instrumental in causing it to fail. The king retained control of land grants. The colony was governed by a royal council of 13 members, who served at the king's pleasure and remained in England, supervising a local council "on site." While the local council could nominate persons to receive land, it was the king and his royal council who made the final decisions, and perhaps more importantly, carried out the transfers.[10]

In April 1607 the London Company, which had undertaken its own provisioning by selling stock, established its territorial claim at Jamestown, Virginia. Those who had invested in the expedition and came themselves to the New World were called "Planters," and those investors who remained in England allowing their representatives to watch over their interests were known as "Adventurers."[11]

The actual founding of the Jamestown Colony proved just how unworkable the First Charter was for purposes of establishing a permanent occupation of the land, rather than merely manning a trading outpost. These new residents wanted title to their lands and guarantees of their political rights and responsibilities in an immediate and enduring relationship with their governing body.[12] Consequently, the Second Charter, issued in 1609, gave a newly created corporation, known as the Virginia Company, the power to grant land directly to the settlers without consulting the king and to govern the colony virtually autonomously.[13] This Second Charter also greatly expanded the Virginia colony's territorial limits west to the Pacific Ocean and severed the connection between the London (or Southern Virginia) Company and the Plymouth (or Northern Virginia) Company. A Third Charter was issued to Southern Virginia in 1612 expanding its patent to include the Bermuda Islands to the east, the territory south to 30° and the territory north back to the original 41°, which had been lost under the Second Charter.[14] Although the Virginia charters did not survive the early 1620's, the Second Charter, with its land-granting and liberal political provisions became the prototype of many later charters influencing American history, including the one issued in 1620 to the Council of New England.[15]

Meanwhile, the Plymouth Company, which held the other portion of the 1606 First Charter, had the right to settle "Northern Virginia" between Chesapeake Bay and Northern Maine and held exclusive patent to areas from Connecticut northward. Unfortunately, their efforts to capitalize on the fishing and fur trade with a settlement called Popham at the mouth of the Kennebec River in Maine in 1607 ended in failure. The London Company of Southern Virginia stepped forward, eager to absorb the interest of any stockholders in the failed Popham venture who still wanted to invest in North America. Further interest in colonizing Northern Virginia might have disappeared had not Captain John Smith traversed the northern coast in 1614 and published enthusiastic reports in London in 1616. Smith is credited with naming "New England," but no new attempts at settlement followed for a few years.[16]

In 1620, the group of English Separatists who had settled in Leyden, Holland, in 1609 decided to emigrate to America. This congregation, later to be called by us "Pilgrims," arrived at that decision, in the words of William Bradford, "not out of any newfangledness or other suchlike giddy humor by which men are oftentimes transported to their great hurt and danger, but for sundry weighty and solid reasons . . . ."[17] Those reasons were, in the order Bradford enumerated them, (1) a desire for economic opportunity denied them in Holland, (2) a desire to preserve their nationality, language, and "pure" way of life for their children, who were being corrupted by such Dutch frivolities as merrymaking on the Sabbath, (3) a feeling of insecurity with the approaching end of the Dutch truce with Spain, and (4) "lastly . . . not least" the desire for "propagating and advancing the gospel of the Kingdom of Christ in those remote parts of the world; yea, though they [the Pilgrims] should be but even as stepping-stones unto others for the performing of so great a work."[18]

The advantages and difficulties of coming to the New World, and to which part of it, were indeed carefully explored in Bradford's narrative.[19] They rejected Guiana as too tropical, and they were persuaded by Thomas Weston, an English promoter, not to pursue a Dutch patent to settle in New York.[20] Instead, Weston promised to find English investors to underwrite a settlement under the auspices of the Southern Virginia charter. In February 1620 a patent for a "Particular Plantation" was issued by the Virginia Company to John Peirce, a Weston associate.[21] A "Particular Plantation" patent, being the most liberal kind, gave promise that the Separatists would have their sought-after personal autonomy under their religious leaders. Between 1617 and 1624, Virginia issued 44 such patents, also known as "Hundreds," some of which "colonies within a colony" were actually founded.[22] The Separatists intended to settle near the Hudson River, which at that time was still within the northern sphere of Southern Virginia, being south of the 41° parallel.[23]

On July 1, 1620, the Separatists signed a seven-year agreement for their provisioning, in which they were forced to concede to the harsh demands of Weston and his associate Merchant Adventurers.[24] The details of how "Strangers" joined the "Saints," their delayed departure, the arduous sea crossing, and their arrival in a strange new world are well known.

Their decision to stay where they landed in New England created the legal problem of being physically outside their patent.[25] Nine months previous, the Plymouth Company of Northern Virginia had begun negotiating for a new patent with a fishing monopoly in New England. The Separatists had known about this, but having deposed of their goods and committed themselves to emigrating, they were unable to await the outcome. A New England charter was finally issued without a fishing monopoly in November 1620, while the *Mayflower* was at sea. It followed the model of the Second Charter of Virginia regarding land rights and political discretion, and gave jurisdiction of the area between latitudes 40° and 48° (Philadelphia to Canada) and from Atlantic to Pacific to a corporation which became known as the Council for New England.[26]

Under the new charter, the Pilgrims would have been "squatters" even on the Hudson River. Of course, they had no knowledge that the patent had actually been granted until much later, but their intended settlement in Massachusetts, clearly north of 41°, was the impetus for the signing of the

"Mayflower Compact," to regulate their colony in the absence of <u>any</u> English charter.[27] Opposition by Southern Virginia to any curtailment of its fishing rights in northern waters caused the New England charter to come under repeated attacks and clouded its future.[28] In 1621, the Colony of New Plymouth secured a vague patent from the Council of New England, confirming their right to remain where they were. A similar patent was procured for them in 1622 by the same John Peirce who had obtained their unused 1620 Southern Virginia patent.[29]

In any event, the Pilgrims were left alone to struggle for survival in the New World. They appear to have been ill-used by Weston and their own agent, Isaac Allerton, during those early years; the extensive wrangling is chronicled throughout Bradford's narrative.[30] In 1627, Bradford and the other Plymouth "Planters" bought out the "Adventurers" for £1800, to be paid at the rate of £200 yearly, with a "forfeit" of 30 shillings a week for any late payments.[31]

The Governor and Council of "Planters" on this side of the Atlantic now had to apportion the assets among the *Mayflower* survivors and those who had come to the settlement in the intervening years because they were all expected to help pay off the debt. Bradford reported that, in a decision reached by the whole body of freemen, both first arrivals and newcomers (before 1627) would be "enrolled for purchasers; single free men to have a single share, and every father of a family to be allowed to purchase so many shares as he had persons in his family," excluding servants. Trade would be managed in common and its profits would be applied first to the debt, with the deficiency made up by the purchasers according to their proportion.[32] The details of how the chattels, house lots and the first 20 acres of tillage near the village were apportioned need not concern us here. The Purchasers or Old Comers, as they were henceforth known, did eventually pay off the debt, expand the settlement, and welcome more new arrivals to the colony in ensuing years.

In January 1629/30, William Bradford and his associates, on behalf of the Purchasers or Old Comers, received the important "Warwick Patent," so-called because it had been signed by the Right Honorable Robert Earle of Warwick for the Council for New England.[33] After reciting the 1620 charter to the Council, the patent noted that Bradford and his associates had founded New Plymouth at their own expense and had not only survived but prospered, so that the present number of inhabitants had increased to almost 300 (not all Purchasers, of course). In consideration of that achievement, the patent granted permanent title to a tract of land extending from the Cohasset River on the north to the Narragansett River on the west, plus Cape Cod and all the islands. This is roughly the area of Bristol, Plymouth, Barnstable, Dukes and Nantucket Counties in Massachusetts plus the eastern part of Rhode Island. The patent specifically mentioned Pokanoket, Massasoit's home, as its northwest corner (see Appendix 1 for rough boundaries).[34] The grant also included a second tract 15 miles each side of the Kennebec River (in Maine) to enhance trading and fishing opportunities.

The land was "to be holden of his Majestie of England, his heirs and successors, as of his manor of East Greenwich in the County of Kent in free and common socage and not in capite nor by knights service."[35] This "easy tenure," referred to as "free and common socage" was the most sought-after form of tenure when English colonists petitioned for land grants and deserves some further explanation.

It is well known that William the Conqueror confiscated the holdings of the defeated English King Harold in 1066 and took an inventory of the kingdom by means of the Domesday Book. He parceled out these lands to his noblemen, who held them of him in a tenure known as "in capite" or "in chief," meaning that there was no intermediary. They owed him "knights service" and other feudal duties. These nobles, in turn, made lesser grants to others and the whole chain of tenure was known as feudalism. During succeeding centuries, the feudal relationships were modified and more clearly defined, and many duties were commuted into fixed monetary payments. When the idea of inheriting the land came to fruition in England, primogeniture became the dominant form of inheritance.[36]

It is less widely known that certain parts of England never developed the feudal system of land holding. The custom of land tenure in East Greenwich in the County of Kent maintained the ancient Saxon form on the manor there. The salient features of this "common law" tenure were that there were only <u>freemen</u>, not villeins, occupying the land, that they paid a fixed, monetary rent, often nominal, rather than performing services for their lord, and that all children inherited property, providing sons with a livelihood and daughters with a dowry.[37]

When giving charters, the tenure of "free and common socage" was a concession by the king for ventures which entailed a high degree of risk, which, if successful, would directly or indirectly enrich the

Crown.[38] Many American charters had this form of tenure, but others did not. Royal or provincial colonies in New Hampshire, New York, New Jersey, North and South Carolina, Georgia, and even in Virginia after the revocation of its early charters did not have East Greenwich tenure. Pennsylvania, Delaware and Maryland were held by "Lord Proprietors," whose lands were under feudal tenure, held of the Crown by the sword. Sir Fernando Gorges claimed parts of northern New England under feudal tenure until 1639. Like Plymouth, Massachusetts Bay, Rhode Island Plantations and Connecticut had corporate charters with East Greenwich tenure. It is difficult to generalize on this exceedingly complex subject, particularly because the granting and revocation of 17th century charters were so common and greatly influenced by the tremendous turmoil enveloping the English monarchy until stability returned after the Glorious Revolution of 1689.[39]

In any event, the Warwick Patent provided for all subsequent deeds creating private ownership in southeastern Massachusetts to be issued under tenure of "free and common socage." There were other conditions in the patent quite common to all colonial charters. In the 1620 Council for New England charter, the monarchy had reserved to itself the right to receive payment for one-fifth part of all gold and silver mined anywhere in the territory. Consequently, the Council passed on the same reservation in the Warwick Patent, to which it added a reservation of an additional one-fifth part to itself. This never proved to be a burden, of course.[40] Finally, the Warwick Patentees of Plymouth Colony were given the right "to frame and make orders, ordinances and constitutions for the ordering, disposing, and governing of our persons, and distributing the lands"—in other words, self-government.[41]

All this, of course, they had done and would do, charter or no charter, until the American Revolution. In later years, Plymouth never sought to have the Warwick Patent confirmed by the changing heads of government in England. Although Massachusetts Bay had received confirmation, their charter was revoked in 1684; and two years later, King James II installed Sir Edmund Andros in the colony with unlimited powers to restore royal jurisdiction. The attempts of Andros to invalidate all land titles unless they were confirmed with payment of a feudal quitrent of 25 shillings six pence per 100 acres ended in failure, and he was removed in 1689, soon after the Glorious Revolution. The land rights which the colonists had refused to give up were confirmed under the Second Charter of Massachusetts of 1691, which incorporated all of Plymouth Colony into Massachusetts. Naturally, similar royal intervention was attempted in the times leading up to the American Revolution with no more success.[42]

Public notice of the Warwick Patent was placed in the book of *Laws* of the Plymouth Colony Records.[43] In addition to reciting the background of the founding of the colony and giving the legal terms of the charter, to further validate their claims, the authors have included two rationalizations which deserve mention. First, there was the "vacancy argument" that they had settled "at a place called by the natives . . . Patuxet . . . all which land being void of Inhabitants."

Second, there was the more complex "allegiance allegation." This stated that after "entering into a league of peace" with Massasoit, the latter "freely gave them [the Plymouth colonists] all the lands adjacent, to them and their heirs forever, acknowledging himself content to become the subject of our Sovereign Lord King" in exchange for "taking protection of us."[44] *Mourt's Relation* contained what has often been characterized as "the first American mutual security pact," made during Plymouth's first encounter with Massasoit in March 1621. The terms of the peace treaty were that (1) no Indian would harm the English, (2) if any did, the offender(s) would be punished under English law, (3) Indians and English would not steal each other's tools, (4) each would aid the other in time of war, (5) Massasoit would notify his neighbors of the existence of the treaty to forestall war, and (6) weapons would be left behind when they visited each other.[45] There were approximately 30 tribes in the Wampanoag Indian Federation led by Massasoit, bound by the terms of the treaty, which held up for more than half a century until King Philip's War.

Few would dispute that the Wampanoags made peace with the English because they had been decimated by disease, saw little necessity to oppose English occupation of the unoccupied Plymouth lands, and recognized the benefits of an alliance as protection against the stronger Narragansetts to the west. However, to suggest that Massasoit by this treaty gave them the land and became the king's subjects, neither of which is mentioned in the treaty, is gross English overstatement geared to rationalize usurpation of the land through validation of the patent.

Both these arguments had already appeared in *Mourt's Relation* in the final chapter, "Reasons and Considerations touching the lawfulness of removing out of England into the parts of America."[46] The "vacancy argument" was neatly turned into the "civilization rationale":

> Their [the Indian heathens'] land is spacious and void. . . . They are not industrious, neither have art, science, skill or faculty to use either the land or the commodities of it, but all spoils, rots, and is marred for want of manuring, gathering, ordering, etc. . . . so is it lawful now to take a land which none useth, and make use of it.[47]

The "allegiance allegation" is couched in terms of "true, Christian love":

> The emperor [Massasoit], by a joint consent, hath promised and appointed us to live at peace where we will in all his dominions, taking what place we will, and as much land as we will, and bringing as many people as we will . . . because we are servants of James, King of England, whose the land (as he confesseth) is; second, because he hath found us just, honest, kind and peaceable, and so loves our company. [48]

Such English ethnocentrism, in both cases, speaks for itself!

Under the Warwick Patent, as far as the English were concerned, title to the land was secure, and the colony expanded apace during the 1630's. As new settlers arrived, they increased the ratio of landless freemen to Old Comers, who held title in common to all the lands which had not been set off to individuals. These newcomers began to agitate for a share of the abundant undistributed land and to resent the fact that the decisions for parceling out that land rested with the Governor and his assistants. In 1638, a proposal was agreed to by Old Comers and New Comers alike to pay William Bradford and his associates £300 to reimburse their personal expenses in procuring the Warwick Patent. The Old Comers were to reserve several tracts of land for themselves in exchange for surrendering the Warwick Patent to the body of freemen of the colony.[49] The General Court approved the arrangement in March 1639/40 and confirmed the location of the parcels in December 1640. Surrender of the Warwick Patent to the body of freemen occurred in March 1640/1.[50]

The three tracts reserved by Bradford and his associates are shown on the map in Appendix 2.[51] The first was on Cape Cod; the third was in the Rehoboth area. The second parcel comprised all of Old Dartmouth (Acushnet, Fairhaven, New Bedford, Dartmouth, and Westport). Although the map appears to include Little Compton and Tiverton, Rhode Island, in "Reserved Tract No. 2," in actuality, the

description read as follows:

> . . . [from] a place called Acoughcus [Acoaxet or Westport River], which lieth
> in the bottom of the bay [Buzzards Bay] adjoining to the west side of Point
> Peril [Gooseberry Neck], and two miles to the western side of the said river, to
> another place called Acushnet River, which entereth at the western end of
> Nacata [Sconticut Neck], and two miles to the eastward thereof, and to extend
> eight miles up into the country.[52]

Consequently, not more than a small slice of Little Compton or Tiverton was officially part of this

reserved tract. However, it must be borne in mind that boundaries were never clearly defined in the early

years of English settlement (nor necessarily in later years) and became the source of repeated litigation.

Eleven years passed. At its June 1652 session held at New Plymouth, the General Court remarked

"that whereas the Purchasers and Old Comers were granted formerly two or three tracts of land . . . which

they never yet for diverse causes enjoyed," during that time part of the land had been given away "to other

plantations."[53] Consequently, the General Court, gave the Purchasers and Old Comers court approval,

under a deadline of 14 months, to take a deed from the Indians to extinguish Indian rights to the tracts.

The order "to take up their particular proportions of land within the precincts" of their chosen tract was a

clear move by the Court to urge settlement of the land as soon as possible.[54]

A copy of the famous "deed" dated November 29, 1652 from Wasomequin [Massasoit] and his son

Wamsutta, on behalf of the Indians, to John Winslow and John Cooke, on behalf of the English

Purchasers of Old Dartmouth, appears in Appendix 3.[55] The deed was unusual in that it was signed first

by the English grantees and then Wamsutta made his mark— Massasoit apparently did not sign at all.

Most deeds are signed only by the seller and are but the evidence of a completed event in which the

consideration (money or other value) has been paid by the buyer and acknowledged by the seller in full

satisfaction and delivery of the premises.[56] The 1652 deed had the look of a treaty and took the form of

an agreement not yet carried out. It called for the future payment of goods by the English and the

withdrawal of Indians from the territory within one year.

The territory conveyed matched the "Reserved Tract No. 2" except that between 1641 and 1652,

the Old Comers started claiming an eastern boundary *three* rather than two miles east of the Acushnet

River and the western boundary specifically followed the west branch of the Westport (Acooksett) River from the Harbor north. Both east and west boundaries extended inland to the north "to go so high that the English may not be annoyed by the hunting of the Indians in any sort of their cattle."

The deed was recorded in 1654, which coincided with an order of the General Court passed June 1654, establishing a procedure for the recording of deeds with the town clerk of the town where the land was situated. Of five witnesses appointed by the town, any three could certify a claim and order a deed recorded as a public document. After two years from the date of recording, if no one had objected to it in the meantime, the deed automatically became "sufficient evidence for the future." Since there was no town of Dartmouth at the time, the deed to Dartmouth lands was recorded with the Plymouth town clerk. Registering deeds in this fashion was an American innovation, and the lack of English precedent probably contributed to the poor quality of records to be found in most early recording systems. The system was modified a number of times, and the place of recording was soon moved to the county seat.[57]

In the early part of the 17th century, the English King James I laid claim to much of the North American coast and was able to validate those claims by effecting enduring settlements in a number of places, including at Plymouth. Through the granting of charters, colonists recognized that they held their lands by tenure from the English Crown. Plymouth colonists were not able to utilize any of the Virginia charters, but they showed resourcefulness in self-government by signing the "Mayflower Compact" and in survival by making a lasting peace treaty with the Indians. Their status was later confirmed under East Greenwich tenure through receipt of the Warwick Patent. In 1640/1, Dartmouth was one of three tracts given to the Old Comers in exchange for a termination of their former exclusive rights to the rest of the Plymouth Colony lands. In 1652, the English sought to extinguish Wampanoag title by recording a deed. Only in this century are we in a position to appreciate the ethnocentric attitudes taken by Europeans toward Indian land tenure, but even 300 years ago the changes being wrought in the landscape by the new settlers were unmistakable.

IV. CHANGING USE

Dartmouth was Massasoit's last sale. In the first set of Indian deeds, the Titiquet Purchase of 1637 and the Cohannet Purchase of 1638, the English obtained the lands of Taunton, Easton, Norton, Mansfield, Dighton, Berkley and Raynham, all in Massachusetts.[1] In the second set of Indian deeds in 1641, the English obtained Rehoboth, Seekonk, Swansea and the Attleboros in Massachusetts and Pawtucket, Providence, Barrington and Cumberland in Rhode Island.[2] The purchase of Dartmouth followed in 1652, but by 1657 Massasoit refused further deeds. By this time, there were only ancient Assonet, Dighton and Mount Hope left in Indian control. In 1659, Assonet, which became Fall River and Freetown, was "extorted" from Massasoit's son, Wamsutta, to discharge "a liquor debt owed to one John Barns" from two years earlier.[3] According to the publication, *Our County and Its People*, "Massasoit had long refused to part with this part of his domain . . . and his son respected his father's wishes as long as he could withstand the pressure."[4]

Massasoit died about 1662, and Wamsutta died soon afterward.[5] Massasoit's other son, Metacomet, or "Philip" to the English, now became chief sachem of the Wampanoags. He was forced to confirm the bounds of the Dartmouth purchase in 1665.[6] By 1675, he reversed his father's and brother's policy of accommodation and waged "King Philip's War" in a tragic and unsuccessful attempt to drive out the English and restore the land to the Indians.[7]

King Philip's feelings, expressed shortly before the war, are best described in his own words:

> The English who came first to this country were but a handful of people,
> forlorn, poor and distressed. My father was then sachem, he relieved their
> distresses in the most kind and hospitable manner. He gave them land to plant
> and build upon. . .they flourished and increased. By various means they got
> possessed of a great part of his territory. But he still remained their friend till
> he died. My elder brother [Wamsutta or Alexander] became sachem. . .He was
> seized and confined and thereby thrown into illness and died. Soon after I
> became sachem they disarmed all my people. . .Their land was taken. . . But a
> small part of the dominion of my ancestors remains. I am determined not to
> live until I have no country.[8]

Although the "price" paid for the Dartmouth lands in 1652 has often been characterized by English writers as only a handful of trade goods or described sneeringly as a mere pittance, the goods traded were those of great value to the Indians. The English provided goods not easily obtainable from nature; and while the Indians could easily have done without them, as they had done for centuries, the items listed in the deed were all especially useful acquisitions (see Appendix 3).

The goods fell into three categories. Of clothing items, there were 30 yards of cloth, 15 pairs of breeches, 8 blankets, 8 moose skins, 8 pairs of stockings and shoes, and one cloak. By the mid-17th century, the Indian hunting grounds had been curtailed and deer and other animals were no longer plentiful. Preparation of skins was a long and tedious task and to obtain moose skins required a journey far to the north. Cloth was lighter, cooler in summer, and more versatile, especially by the bolt. All of the clothing items offered protection against mosquitoes in summer and the close-fitting ones offered warmth in winter. In particular, the stockings insulated against injury from briars, branches and poison ivy while traveling, and the shoes would make winter walking drier and more comfortable.

Of iron implements, there were 15 axes, 15 hoes, two kettles, and one iron pot. Without question, an English ax was superior in utility to one chiseled from stone, bone or beaver teeth. Hoes were especially important in cultivating cornhills, and an iron one surpassed in strength a clam shell bound on the end of a stick. An iron kettle or pot would not crack or burn as a clay or wood cooking vessel might, and was thus more durable.

The third category, which could be deemed "hospitality items," consisted of £2 wampum and 10 shillings of "another commodity" thought to be either tobacco or rum. The shell beads known as wampum were made by grinding two types of shells into cylindrical shapes, smoothing and polishing them, and piercing them to be strung on rawhide. The black ones made from quahog shells were valued at twice the white ones made from the mouths of periwinkle. Before the advent of English trading, wampum beads were used solely for decoration and as convenient prizes to wager in games. They were also an essential ingredient to bind diplomatic arrangements between tribes; the exchange of gifts, such as wampum belts, was an expected part of the ceremony.[9] Trade with the English caused wampum to acquire a standard currency: three black or six white ones equaled one English penny and a standard measurement was 60 beads on a one-foot string.[10] Tobacco was also a requisite part of any tribal

ceremony, and it bears more likelihood of being the other "commodity" than rum, given the participation

of Bradford's associates in negotiating this agreement.[11]

All of the abovementioned items were designed for peace, not war; they offered physical comfort

and utility in daily living, crop cultivation, cooking, land clearing, and social obligations. They were

trade goods on which Indians were increasingly dependent due to overhunting of furbearing animals and

encroachment by white settlers. They were also items of status among Indians. European diseases had

brought about "demographic collapse," disruptions of the longstanding social, ecological and economic

relationships between tribes of Indians.[12] The severe reduction of the Wampanoag population had

weakened their ability to make strong political alliances with other Indian tribes. Wampum, in particular,

was a status symbol, both personally and for the tribe.

It is intriguing to speculate on how the Indians apportioned the payment. The hospitality items

were probably added to the common tribal store, but the clothing and utensils were personal property and

most likely were divided among tribal leaders. Did eight men each get two yards of cloth, one blanket,

one moose skin, one pair of breeches, one pair of shoes and stockings, one ax and one hoe, while seven

less-esteemed men got only two yards of cloth, a pair of breeches, an ax and a hoe? Perhaps Massasoit

himself got the cloak and his wife the iron pot. That still left two kettles; such wares were usually the

property of women, and they may have participated in the allotment. Certainly, the goods were

distributed among more than a few, as it was not Indian custom to horde possessions, and the decision to

allow the English to move onto Dartmouth lands would have been reached in tribal consultation.[13]

Yet the question must be asked: Was it really Wampanoag intention to <u>convey</u> the Dartmouth

lands? Since the people had not recovered from the 1614-1617 decimation nor the smallpox epidemic

which struck in the 1630's, one could argue that they did not need all that land. Or perhaps they feared

the Narragansets to the west and sought English protection. Or perhaps, in a choice between the Taunton

River valley and Dartmouth, they preferred to relinquish Dartmouth. Or perhaps they hoped to

accommodate the English, whose guns and diseases they feared, not expecting their numbers to increase the way they did. Probably all these theories have their element of truth or could be construed to support English rationalizations as old as those in *Mourt's Relation*.

However, the most plausible explanation of all, from the Indian perspective on land ownership, is that the "price paid" was but consideration for the acknowledgment of a diplomatic treaty between the parties that the Indians would allow the English to use the land. Unwittingly, they signed away their rights in perpetuity in a totally English document.[14] While the Indians may have understood treaties and usufruct rights, it is unlikely that they understood deeds creating permanent, exclusive and individual property rights. Even the Taunton River valley, which clearly was more important to the Wampanoags than Dartmouth, was lost to the natives; the watershed was coveted more intensely than Dartmouth by white men from the first. The Indians were overpowered by the numbers of white men and their superior weapons. They were also defeated by the English unwillingness to accord them equal diplomatic status. In contrast to the much stronger western tribes, (such as the Iroquois), the Algonquin tribes, and especially the Wampanoags, were particularly vulnerable.

The Wampanoags did not choose the Dartmouth region for their seat of power, but numbers of them dwelt here, and others came seasonally to take advantage of seaside abundance, as people do today. These native Americans had undoubtedly adapted to geophysical and ecological changes in their environment over the centuries, but they were little prepared for the onslaught in the 17th century of European settlers, who wrought such dramatic changes on the landscape. Contact with the first Europeans decimated their numbers and left their land vacant for white settlers to claim. Without Indian help, the early settlers in Plymouth Colony would have perished. With the survival of the new immigrants, the way of life for the Indian survivors was forever changed.

English colonists (and other Europeans) brought with them to the New World their concepts of value and scarcity from the Old World and then modified them to meet the conditions they found in their new places of settlement. One of the primary ways in which they differed in their conception of their en-vironment from that held by Indians was that, from the time of European exploration, the New World was viewed as a list of merchantable commodities. For inhabitants, Indian and white, the land was the resource to furnish basic individual needs upon which survival depended. However, Indians had few "needs," while white settlers had "infinite needs."[15] White settlers looked to accumulate wealth not merely for personal status and security, but also for export and profit. As Carl Sauer noted, the new Americans were never willing to distinguish between "yield" and "loot."[16] Moreover, the infinitely large and relatively unoccupied American landscape fueled their wildest dreams.

The other English concept was "fixity," rooted perhaps in individualistic capitalist ideology. The new settlers in New England marked off their lands and bounded them with miles and miles of fences. They claimed more than just the right to use the land. They claimed ownership to everything within its bounds to the exclusion of all others. In a world where labor was scarce, land abundance and all it contained became their chief source of wealth.[17]

Since English colonists to southern New England settled on the cleared lands of former Indian habitation, they did not need to clear great forests in order to have a place to build their homes and plant their first fields. Routine Indian burning of the undergrowth had made many areas parklike, with stands of large, widely-spaced trees towering over ground carpeted with grass and herbage.[18] These fires had destroyed fleas, other vermin, and plant diseases and created good pasturage for deer, turkey, and quail.[19] Since fire did not respect property lines, the colonists had to restrict wide-scale burning once permanent buildings were erected.[20]

Compared to England, which had been largely deforested by the 17th century, there was an abundance of timber, as well as land, available in southern New England. The new white settlers built full-timbered rather than half-timbered houses and larger houses than they left behind in England. They built barns and sheds to house their animals. At first, they built wood fences, being faster than growing living hedges and easier to erect than stone walls. The first fences were either timbers laid horizontally in zigzag fashion (worm fences) or stakes driven into the ground in compact vertical formation (picket fences). Stumps and fallen logs were also utilized, and later fences were made of cedar rails. All wood fences eventually rotted and were replaced with stone walls, which took more labor initially, but saved on timber, got rid of field stones, and were sturdier and more durable, requiring minimal maintenance.

To heat their houses, the typical New England household burned 30 to 40 cords of firewood each year.[21] The Indians also loved big fires to keep warm in winter and moved their villages when wood was scarce. Roger Williams reported that the Indians asked and then answered their own question:

> Why come the *Englishmen* hither? and measuring others by themselves, they
> say, 'It is because you want *firing*,' for they, having burnt up the *wood* in one
> place . . . they are faine to follow the *wood*; and so remove to a fresh new
> place for the *woods* sake.[22]

But the white settlers consumed far more timber than the Indians. Between 1630 and 1800, New England settlers burned more than 260 million cords of firewood in their fireplaces, and in 1800 were burning 18 times more wood for fuel than using it for lumber.[23]

Nevertheless, timber for shipbuilding, especially the export of masts, was a vital industry and a major cash crop. Sawmills for both local consumption and export were the nuclei of settlements in wooded areas. Their activities were seasonal because they relied upon the availability of water power. The milling of oak lumber cost twice as much as pine because it was a harder wood to saw. Because the average water-powered saw mill could only produce several hundred feet of lumber per day, the choicest timber was used first and there was a great deal of waste.[24] Timber was also the raw ingredient for charcoal needed in the iron forges.

Southern New England had an abundance of oaks, hickories, chestnuts, and pines growing on its uplands.[25] On the edges of the many swamps and bogs in southern New England, untouched by Indian fires, grew white oaks, red maples, and most importantly, <u>Atlantic white cedars</u>.[26] The white cedar trees were in very high demand by the English because cedar shingles for roofs and clapboards and cedar fence posts and railings were light in weight and resistant to decay. Towns like Boston would pay a high price for any surplus local settlers could produce. The problem was that white cedars, once cut, were unable to reproduce themselves and were replaced in the swamps by red maples.[27] The huge white pines, the best source of ships masts, also did not reproduce. Other types of pine trees produced rosin, pitch and tar valuable to the shipbuilding industry.[28] White oaks were good at reproducing themselves, but were increasingly overcut.[29]

The worst destroyers of timber were not the lumbermen, but the farmers.[30] After cutting for housebuilding, barnbuilding and fencing, their next concern was to clear land for tillage and pasture. With such a shortage of labor, the easiest way to get rid of trees was to girdle them as the Indians had done. They stripped the bark off for about three feet up from the ground, which killed the tree. No new foliage blocked the sunlight from reaching the ground, where crops could be planted between the trunks. Eventually, the tree toppled over and its stump rotted. The method was time consuming, messy, wasteful of timber, and dangerous for farmers working underneath. Later in the 18th century, trees were felled with an axe in late summer, and the following May, the stumps burned to kill the roots.[31]

English settlers had envisioned fields of wheat and barley waving across the New England landscape, but those crops fared far more poorly than native corn.[32] The first settlers in New England would have perished if the Indians had not taught them how to cultivate this mainstay of their own diet. Corn produced excellent yield but was an "exhausting" crop, which affected a field's fertility in just a few years. It was a crop more suited to Indian hoe agriculture than to the huge plowed fields of the English.[33] The English used fish, seaweed, and animal manure as fertilizers, but in order to feed their livestock they needed to cultivate much greater areas than did the Indians.

The two distinguishing characteristics of English agriculture imported to New England were the use of the plow and keeping domesticated grazing animals.[34] The plow allowed for tillage of a much greater area with less manpower and effort, but it also disturbed the soil and caused irreversible ecological change to the environment. The plow also required the importation of oxen and horses, which even more drastically changed the environment.[35] Indians hunted deer, moose and beaver seasonally, but they did not "own" these animals until they were killed. The English owned their domesticated animals all the time, but they were not always able to control them. Dogs were native to the area and were owned by Indians. Horses, sheep, goats, swine, cattle and cats were unknown to the Indians and imported by the English.[36]

Imported domesticated animals were extremely valuable to the English settlers. Hogs reproduced well, ate anything, could hold their own against bears and wolves, and provided a winter supply of meat. Cattle produced not only meat, but hides for leather, and milch cows were the source of milk, cheese and butter. Oxen provided the animal power for farm work; horses were usually reserved for personal transportation and military matters. Sheep were vulnerable to predators and hard on pastureland, but provided wool for cloth making and mutton to eat. These livestock also represented a cash crop, because of the demand for provisioning ships and for sale to plantations in the West Indies.

Animal crowding became a bigger problem than human crowding.[37] A shortage of labor meant that fewer persons were available to herd the animals, so initially it was easier to enclose crops and allow the animals to run loose, foraging for their own food. They were branded or notched in the ear to mark their ownership. The Indians were quick to point out that if the English owned their animals, they should be responsible for Indian crop damage. However, the stance taken by the colonial courts was that only if the animal got through a sound fence would the animal owner be liable for damages to the crop owner.[38] Fence viewers were among the first officials appointed by the towns. Later, it became necessary to enclose animals, at least while crops were in the fields. The fence was "the most visible symbol of an 'improved' landscape," which clearly demarked private property.[39] The English denied that the Indians had property rights equivalent to their own because the latter did not enclose the land or own cattle.[40] The English attitude toward animals caused a fenced landscape, a planned program to eliminate natural predators like wolves, the need for wide country roads to take the animals to market, and increasing acres of pasturage to feed them.[41]

The best source of natural food for cattle were the meadow grasses which grew wild and abundantly in the marshes along the edges of rivers and around the heads of harbors. The marsh grasses growing on "salt meadow" and "fresh meadow" were mowed and stored as hay used for bedding and supplemented by corn as winter fodder for the animals. While the native marsh grasses were poor in quality compared to English varieties, they were important because they were ready to be harvested and because the animal population very rapidly outstripped the food supply, and every available source was needed. When cattle grazed on natural meadows, they left in their dung European seeds brought across the ocean in their feed. Gradually native grasses were supplanted by European varieties, and soon the English planted bluegrass, timothy and clover intentionally.[42]

Clearly, vast ecological changes occurred with the arrival of European settlers between 1600 and 1800. These were arguably as important as the Industrial Revolution of the 19th century, although a far more subtle transformation of the landscape. By 1800, southern New England was devoid of beaver, deer, bear, turkey, and wolf, but contained hordes of domesticated grazing animals, new pests and diseases. Beaver dams had been replaced with mill dams. Fixed property rights were symbolized by permanent homesteads and farm buildings and endless fences. The use of the plow allowed extensive tillage but often resulted in soil exhaustion due to poor husbandry and a whole new crop of weeds. The great oaks and white pines were gone, cedar was scarce, and hickory was fast disappearing because of the demand for fuel. Deforestation had caused more erratic climatic temperatures, and water and wind erosion.[43]

There is every reason to believe that the same ecological changes occurring elsewhere in New England were happening to the areas of Dartmouth into which English settlers moved. Since the population density remained extremely low compared to other areas of New England, the changes were no doubt less drastic, but still they did take place.

Farmsteads appeared on the coastal necks (Smith Neck, Sconticut Neck) and along the banks of the major rivers (Acushnet, Apponagansett, Paskamansett, and both branches of the Acoakset [Westport]). They settled at good mill sites (Russells Mills, Smith Mills, Head of Westport, Head of Acushnet). They mixed Indian names freely with new English names, but the three main villages retained their Indian names of Cushnet, Ponaganset, and Coakset. Within each village, the homesteads were widely scattered.

The Massachusetts Tax Valuation List of 1771, reproduced in Appendix 10, gives information on less than one-half the holdings those individuals in the township rated for tax purposes, since 9 of the 17 pages turned in by the town assessors have not survived. There were 407 names tallied on the available list, and according to the notes annexed to the end, there were 553 rateable polls (persons with taxable property) and 126 polls not rateable on the missing pages. Still, on the assumption that what survives is representative of the whole, some conclusions can be drawn, even without sophisticated computer analysis.

The taxed individuals may not necessarily have been a landowner or a houseowner, but for purposes of the following comments, he has been referred to as a "household." The average household owned one horse and two oxen. There were 844 head of cattle divided among the 80% of households who owned them, but about one-third of these owned only one. One household owned 15, ten households owned seven to nine, and the remaining two-thirds owned between two and six. By contrast, only 50% owned sheep and goats, but they shared a total of 3,514 animals. One household had 120 and another owned 100, but the average holding was a flock of 17. The 531 swine were owned by 67% of households. One household had eight and two had seven, but the rest had six or less, the average being only two.

Only 62% of households had fields for tillage. Of 1,055 acres, the average holding was a little over four acres. The importance of animals and the need to feed them is self-evident by the separate categories contained in the tax list for acreage and tonnage in pasture, saltmarsh, upland mowing land and fresh meadow. Dartmouth was more fortunate than inland towns in possessing so much shoreline and so many small rivers to provide natural meadow. Furthermore, the necks and islands were ideal for enclosing animals with a minimum of labor.

These figures support the conclusion that Dartmouth relied more on animal production than crop production within the first century of the town's history and that sheep were the most numerous herds. On the other hand, woodlots are not mentioned at all in the tax lists, although they undoubtedly were numerous.

It is hoped that an understanding of these ecological changes occurring in Dartmouth and the cultural values which they represented has provided a foundation to help the reader put the following discussions concerning the Dartmouth Propriety, which was the legal entity for landholding in the town, into a clearer context.

V. THE PROPRIETY

The Propriety of Dartmouth was a corporate form of ownership of the land. When "Reserved Tract No. 2" was received by William Bradford and the other Old Comers in 1641, the land was held in "undivided" ownership or "in common." On March 7, 1652/3, the Old Comers met in Plymouth and agreed that certain of them would take their shares in Dartmouth rather than in the other two reserved tracts.[1] John Winslow, for example, who had signed the Indian deed, did not choose to take a share in Dartmouth.[2] A list of names was prepared of those who would become the Proprietors; each Proprietor's proportionate interest in the whole was evidenced by "shares" (the names appear in Appendix 4). Before the list was officially recorded in the Plymouth Colony records, it was lost and a replacement had to be made from memory. When the original list surfaced in 1660, it was certified and recorded, and the one made from memory was annulled. [3]

In describing the Dartmouth Propriety, the closest analogy is to that of a modern business corporation in which those who invest in the company are called "stockholders" or "shareholders," and their evidence of ownership is a certificate representing shares in the company. Shareholders' control of the company's operations is limited to the clout wielded by their votes at shareholders' meetings, duly called, where majority normally rules. The corporation, as a legal entity separate from its shareholders, has the right to sue and be sued, and to make profits or suffer losses all by itself. Shareholders participate in the profits of the business in the form of dividends and are shielded from personal liability in the event of losses. The shareholders dispose of their investment at gain or loss by selling their stock on the open market or by receiving their proportionate share of assets in a liquidation.

Similarly, the Propriety of Dartmouth had shareholders, held formal meetings, voted dividends of land, sued and was sued. Its sole asset was non-income-producing land. Instead of the directors who take care of the modern corporation's ordinary business operations, the Propriety chose a clerk to record minutes and votes, chose agents to act in their behalf on urgent business, and empowered committees to carry out specific votes, such as land divisions, with the help of a surveyor. However, in contrast to a modern corporation, the Proprietors never operated under any adopted set of by-laws; each procedural vote passed by majority vote at a duly called meeting had the force and effect of a by-law until rescinded or superceded.[4] The Clerk of the Propriety kept Books of Records, and in December 1725, when Thomas Hathaway held that position, a fire at his house resulted in the burning of the records.[5] This tragic loss caused not only inconvenience and confusion, but actually influenced the future course of events regarding development of land ownership in Dartmouth.

It cannot be emphasized strongly enough that the Dartmouth Propriety was totally distinct from the Township of Dartmouth, which was incorporated in June 1664 by an act of the Plymouth General Court. The township consisted of its inhabitants. Those inhabitants who were freemen of a particular age and suitable estate, after taking the oath of fidelity, were entitled to vote at town meetings. However, a qualified voter was not required to be a landowner; his personal wealth could make him eligible to vote. Conversely, no inhabitant was entitled to a land allotment by virtue of his residency in the town, and the Propriety never granted any for that reason.

The town and the Propriety were separate entities and neither controlled the other. The Propriety originally owned all the real estate and, by majority vote at Proprietors' meetings, decided how much land and in what manner it should be allotted. However, the land was laid out only to shareholders who had either received their right as a Plymouth Old Comer or had purchased their right from an Old Comer or subsequent shareholder. Although the General Court gave towns the authority to admit and exclude persons wishing to be inhabitants, it had no power to require the Proprietors to admit or exclude new shareholders. The Propriety had no power to exclude any shareholder from a rightful claim purchased privately from a previous owner. Proprietors were prominent in town affairs not because they were Proprietors, but because they were the most numerous, affluent, and influential inhabitants. The Propriety, for its part, abstained from any participation in the functioning of the town, other than shared jurisdiction in laying out highways.

From an examination of the public records, there is no evidence that any land was ever given by the Proprietors to the town for the town's use except for roads. Moreover, the Propriety never gave the town any land for the purpose of redistribution to inhabitants. With the exception of a quarter-acre lot donated by William Sanford in 1751 on which to put the townhouse, the only way the town could acquire land was to buy it like everyone else. Before 1800, the town appears to have done so only once. In 1786, the town paid Michael (or Micah) Parker £12 for 18 acres adjacent to the Freetown line.[6]

When the list of Proprietors was prepared in Plymouth in 1652/3, there were 34 shares held by 36 owners. Four Proprietors held half-shares and the other 32 held full shares (Appendix 4). There were only three women, who were all widows of Plymouth Old Comers. A full share or any fraction of a share could be bought or sold among individuals without restriction at any time after the creation of the Propriety. The most common fractions were 1/2, 1/4, 1/8, 1/16, and 1/32; all of these fractions fit a recognizable progression of split-interests in which multiples of two and four are common factors. Those who held any part of a share were proportional owners in common with all the other Proprietors, originally in all the territory of Dartmouth, and unless they had sold all their rights in the Propriety in the meantime, even after 1800 they or their heirs owned a proportional interest in the considerable amount of remaining undivided land.

About twenty years after the founding of the town, four Proprietors were empowered by the Propriety to act as agents for the others in arranging for the building of a grist mill. In June 1684, "articles of agreement" were reached between Ralph Allen, Samuel Hicks, John Russell, and Arthur Hathaway, acting for the Proprietors, and George Badcock and Henry Tucker, who were to receive a thirty-fifth share of the Propriety for their services in building a mill in the place later called Smith Mills. The agreement was ratified at a Proprietors' meeting the following February by a majority of those present.[7] This became known as "the Mill Share."[8]

However, the Soule family, which for many years retained ownership of the 1/34th part originally belonging to George Soule of Duxbury, objected to "the Mill Share." Sometime between 1684 and 1726, the Soules were able to have their protest successfully decided by arbitration. In November 1726, when the Proprietors were trying to rebuild their records lost in the tragic 1725 fire, they ratified and confirmed "the Mill Share" as the thirty-fifth part of the Propriety, stipulating "the Soules' share only being the thirty-fourth part."[9] In other words, all the other Proprietors agreed to reduce their claim in the common land to accommodate an extra share for the mill except the Soules, who permanently retained their original percentage in the Propriety.

Proprietors' meetings were called when holders or "subscribers" totaling a prescribed number of shares requested the Clerk of the Propriety to issue a warrant or notification for all the Proprietors to meet at a specified place and time. In 1753, the prescribed number of shares was lowered from "five whole shares" to "three whole shares."[10] Shares became diluted as soon as the Propriety was created, but no warrants survived the 1725 fire to provide information on the applicants' shareholdings during the early history of the Propriety. However, in 1735, for example, subscribers signed with fractional shares from 1/2 to 1/16.[11]

Meetings were held at the "townhouse" (town hall) until 1793, and thereafter at private houses.[12] If the Clerk refused to call a meeting upon a proper application for it, the subscribers appealed to a Justice of the Peace for Bristol County, who ordered the Clerk or some other person to issue the warrant.[13] It would appear that initially notice was given personally to all Proprietors. This must have been cumbersome, given the size of the township and the difficulty of travel, not to mention the trouble of notifying absent Proprietors. On July 19, 1726, the Propriety voted that adequate notice would be given if the warrant were simply posted 14 days in advance of the meeting in an unspecified but conspicuous place in each of the three villages of Cushnet, Ponaganset, and Coakset (Appendix 5 outlines the village areas).[14] No vote counts or numbers attending meetings are reported in the records to allow us to track the Proprietors' attendance records over time, but notice by posting appears to have been adequate for quorum purposes. Thus it is reasonable to conclude that absentee Proprietorship did not pose an impediment to holding meetings. No protest over the notice procedure was ever entered in the minutes, although there were protests over votes by bare majority of those present.[15]

The warrant specified in detail the business to come before the meeting. The numbered items in the warrant were similarly numbered in the minutes recorded by the Clerk as votes passed, matters voted down, and business not voted. The warrants are invaluable in giving the current issues facing the Propriety framed in their historical context and in disclosing the rationale behind the proposed vote. Unfortunately, the Clerk recording the disposition provided little commentary of the discussions which must have occurred prior to each vote being taken. A Moderator was always chosen to coordinate the meeting, and if the business was not concluded on the first day, the meeting would be adjourned until all matters had been addressed.[16] The fire in 1725, of course, destroyed all the original minutes of meetings for the prior period. When they met in 1726, the Proprietors voted to seek attested copies, which had been extracted from the original minutes by some interested party, so that they could be re-entered into the records, ratified and confirmed.[17] These, together with the applications for later warrants, the warrants themselves, and the minutes from 1725 to 1800 (and an isolated meeting in 1821) constitute all that is available to piece together the story of how the Proprietors conducted their corporate business.[18]

In order to set off land from common ownership into individual ownership, the Proprietors passed votes declaring divisions of a certain number of acres, based upon a whole share, of a particular type of land. The three categories of land were upland, natural meadow (salt or fresh), and cedar swamp. Entitlement to participate in the divisions was strictly limited to Proprietors and had no relationship to residency in the town. The initial division was 200 acres of upland for each whole share. Its date is unknown except that it must have occurred by 1660, since a few families had settled at the head of the Acushnet River by that date. A second division of 400 acres of upland was granted in March 1682, and a third division of an additional 200 acres of upland followed in January 1694. Reference to these first three divisions can be found only in old deeds, since all references in the surviving Proprietors' records are to the later act which consolidated the three divisions.[19] In 1710, all the earlier votes were consolidated into "one special act of eight hundred acres to one whole share of upland and thirty-six acres to a share of natural meadow."[20] The meadow allotment must have been made with the initial grant of upland because there are deeds as early as 1680. Of course, if a Proprietor held only a one-quarter share, his entitlement was only 200 acres of upland and nine acres of meadow in this consolidated division. In June 1713, the Proprietors voted an additional 400 acres of upland, and later (date unclear but before 1730) another 300 acres was added, bringing the total upland allotment to 1,500 per share.[21] Each Proprietor had also received 16 acres of cedar swamp in May 1713, completing the three categories.[22] Thus, the final amount any Proprietor could claim by virtue of holding one whole share in the Propriety was 1,500 acres of upland (never consolidated into one act and always itemized as "the 800 acre division," "the 400 acre division," and the "300 acre division") plus 36 acres of natural salt or fresh meadow, and 16 acres of cedar swamp. The total acreage to be set off into Proprietors' individual ownership, based on 35 full shares, computed to 52,500 acres of upland, 1260 acres of natural meadow, and 560 acres of cedar swamp in a township with roughly twice that acreage.[23] The other one-half of the township remained in common ownership by the Propriety.

In order to take possession of the acreage to which the individual Proprietor was entitled by virtue of his claim in any of the divisions, he would "pitch upon" (stake a claim upon) the land he wanted. The method of "pitching" is not described in the Proprietors' records. There must have been some means of identification left on the land itself, as there were definite rules to be followed if two Proprietors "pitched" on the same parcel. Expediency would seem to require marking in some manner the rough boundaries of the area claimed, but no clue is revealed in the records as to whether and how this was done. It is possible that the land had to be actually "improved" with buildings and/or clearing of fields. In any event, the Proprietor "entered his pitch" with the surveyor empowered by the Propriety to receive such claims. Certainly a layman's version of the location and approximately acreage was given by the claimant to the surveyor so that the latter could plan to do the official layout.

In May 1713, for the selection of meadow, the Propriety voted that if "several persons happen to pitch upon one tract, they shall divide it among them by lot" with the proviso that those already holding meadow adjoining, "then they may have their part or parts joining thereto."[24] Also in this vote, beaches were classified as meadow.[25] The remaining undivided meadow in each village— Cushnet, Ponaganset, and Coakset— was to "be set out to each village" and the surveyor would convene the Proprietors belonging to that village to "lot for choice," with each taking "his part on one side or end of that tract where he pitched."[26] Any Proprietor who failed to attend the drawing would be relegated to drawing last. The division of meadows was ordered to be completed before the 400 acre division of upland commenced, but the stipulation was not followed.[27]

The Proprietors' vote for the 400 acre division provided that each Proprietor had one month from the third Tuesday of June 1713 to "bring in his pitch to the surveyor" and the surveyor was instructed not to begin laying out the tracts "until all have notice that have pitched on any one place . . . and whereas any may be disappointed of their pitch that they may have liberty to enter a new pitch forthwith."[28] The layouts were delayed for two months from the date of the vote to allow the pitches to be made. The surveyor and his assistants were empowered to settle conflicting claims; but that arrangement must have proved inadequate, because over a year later, in August 1714, the Proprietors voted "that where any difference shall prove so difficult that the surveyor cannot determine it, that then the persons contending shall cast lots. . . ."[29]

Casting lots was also the initial procedure for allotting cedar swamp acreage in 1713, "and where any refuse to draw . . . the Clerk shall draw for them."[30] Most of the cedar swamps were in the northern part of the town and provided building materials for local consumption and a cash crop for export. Since the cut cedar was gone forever, the swamps were left with inapplicable names in later years.

When new land was laid out to an individual, a surveyor and his assistants, or the Proprietors' committee, gave the owner a "return of survey." This was the equivalent of a deed from the Propriety for what had formerly been common land. The return was dated as of the date the work was done. The acreage and the category (upland, meadow, cedar swamp) were stated and to whom it was laid out. Usually there was allowance for "mean," stony, rocky, or barren land and often there was allowance for a way which would later be laid out through it. The approximate location was given, followed by a precise metes and bounds description, and then a recapitulation of how it was bounded on the north, east, south and west, i.e., by the names of abutters, landmarks, or bodies of water. Often it was bounded on one or more sides by other undivided or common land. The land was "qualified" by a "sample" (identified in the following paragraph) and charged to a particular Proprietor's or Purchaser's right for a particular division. Finally, the authority of those giving the return of survey was recited and the return was signed and delivered to the grantee, with a copy intended to be recorded in the Proprietors' Books of Records.[31]

A sample of land was selected for each division except the cedar swamp. All land laid out for each particular division was measured against the sample for quality, and the quantity of acreage was adjusted accordingly. For the 800 acre division of upland, the sample was "Abraham Tucker's homestead and the land that belongs to it." The Tucker homestead no doubt was northeast of the intersection of Tucker and Russells Mills Roads. Although the homestead had been laid out previously, it was officially re-surveyed in October 1710, and with some alteration and enlargement over the original layout, it was qualified for 280 2/3 acres "with allowance for rocky land and boggy swamp."[32] This land became the standard for all the early homesteads claimed in the 800. For the meadows, the sample was "Samuel Hixes meadow that lies at the foot of his homestead."[33] For the 400 acre division of upland, the sample was "Philip Taber's farm that lies on the north side of John Taber's homestead and joining to the Tiverton line."[34] This land is most likely in the present town of Adamsville, Rhode Island. The 300 acre division also used land of Philip Taber, but this time it was "Philip Taber's land that lies between George Lawton's homestead and Stoney Brook and on the South side of the Country Road," probably at the Head of Westport.[35] All of these places were so well known to the Proprietors that in later returns of surveys the language merely read "qualified by the sample."[36] While the field notes have been preserved, unfortunately none of the plot plans made by the surveyors have ever been found. If they ever turn up, they may solve some longtime mysteries concerning the location of various parcels.[37]

It is undisputable from the returns of surveys entered into the Proprietors' records that in most instances, very small acreage was "returned" in contrast to the size of the divisions to which Proprietors were entitled. The homesteads, laid out first, were inclined to be larger than later returns. There is no "average" parcel, but it is surprising that there is rarely a return of more than 100 acres and there are innumerable ones for less than 10 acres. Furthermore, Proprietors took their parcels all over the township.

For example, Peleg Slocum's homestead and his largest holdings were on Slocum's Neck, but he also had nine acres on the south side of Hathaway Road, 300 acres over by Tiverton, 25 acres on the west side of Clark's Cove, some acreage west of Russells Mills, meadow on both sides of Padanaram Harbor, several islands in the Paskamansett River, over 17 acres of cedar swamp in the "Ponaganset Great Swamp," and a number of other unidentified tracts. These returns represent only what was laid out by virtue of his fractional sharerights in the common lands, which he had bought from a number of individuals. He also bought extensive acreage already laid out to others, which would have been entered in the returns under those former owners' names.[38]

What was the distinction between a "Proprietor" and a "Purchaser"? The Old Comers of Plymouth were called "Purchasers" because they were the ones who had bought out the Merchant Adventurers in 1627. In reference to the Indian deed, the grantees were called "Purchasers," Those Old Comers who decided to take a share of Dartmouth became "Proprietors." Whether a Proprietor chose to settle within the bounds of Dartmouth or not, he was always at liberty to sell off part or all of his share, both divided and undivided land. Those who later purchased land or shares from original Proprietors were also called "Purchasers." In the Proprietors' records, the term "Proprietors and Purchasers" is used consistently throughout to identify a shareholder. For simplicity, we shall refer to any shareholder as a Proprietor, whether he was an original Proprietor or a later Purchaser.

A Proprietor became the sole owner of all the acreage for which he held a "return of survey." This was "divided land." He could sell part or all of that acreage to anyone without any fraction of the share he still held in the undivided land. If the buyer were already a Proprietor, he would not increase his claim in the undivided land as a result of the purchase. If he were not a Proprietor, he would not become one by purchasing divided land.

If the Proprietor sold only his claim in the undivided lands, the deed would specify, as for example, in a 1693 deed from Samuel Hicks to Thomas Taber, Jr.:

> all that my full quarter part of one whole share of the now undivided lands,
> both upland and meadow land situate, lying and being within the township of
> Dartmouth aforesaid with all my right and interest in or unto the said quarter
> part of one whole share, with all and singular the rights, privileges and
> appurtenances to said lands belonging or in any wise appurtaining.[39]

Shares were fragmented early in the history of the Propriety. A 1693 deed from John Palmer to Joseph Allen sold one-half of one-half of three-quarters of a whole share, excluding 27 acres of upland and 3 acres of meadow (already sold out of his interest in the share).[40]

A special difficulty arose for the Proprietors when a Proprietor sold both divided and undivided land at once. For example, Thomas Cornell of Portsmouth sold to Richard Cadman of Portsmouth 82 acres of upland and 6 acres of meadow and one-third part of a share of undivided lands of Dartmouth "together with all and singular the houses, barns, fences, commons, liberties, ways, highways, privileges, and appurtenances."[41] The specified acreage did not equal one-third of any Proprietors' division. In fact, there was frequently no relationship between what was sold in each category.

All of this inconsistency caused Christopher Gifford to pose the question to the Proprietors in 1733: "Suppose AB hath one whole share and sells to CD 100 acres, who shall have the privilege of a vote on said 100 acres, the donor or donee?"[42] How, indeed, would the Proprietors keep track of voter eligibility? Land transactions between private individuals were recorded in Plymouth before 1685 and in the Bristol County Registry of Deeds in Taunton after 1685, which was the date Plymouth County was split into three counties (Bristol, Barnstable and Plymouth).[43] Probate records, containing transfers by wills and inheritance, were kept at Plymouth until the Andros regime temporarily moved them to Boston from 1686 to 1692. After 1692, probate records for Bristol County residents were the province of the Probate Court in Taunton. The Proprietors Books of Records contained the acts of the Proprietors voting the divisions, the returns of survey, the claims of shareholders, and all related matters concerning the undivided lands. In addition to the destruction of three-quarters of a century of Proprietors' records, there were additional problems. Many did not seek to have the land allotted to them under each division laid out, and when they did, not all had their returns of survey entered into the Proprietors' records. Therefore, it was not just a matter of who owned how much of a share for voting purposes, but also a matter of not knowing how much of the share had been filled up in each division and there were, after all, five divisions, three in upland and one each of meadow and cedar swamp.

If the Proprietors had taken the easy way out, they would have followed the land development pattern of Assonet. The 26 purchasers of Assonet simply "gridded" out their territory into 26 numbered lots for which they drew lots. All the land was immediately divided along the grid lines and set off to individuals. That solved the problem of shares and claims in the undivided lands--there weren't any.[44]

Dartmouth, of course, had a more varied landscape, with many small streams, several major rivers and long peninsulas. It was so lacking in homogeneity that gridding never would have worked. The land area was immense, more than enough to accommodate all the Proprietors. Nevertheless, litigation involving the land was common from the beginning. In particular, there were some who wanted an early outright division.

In October 1684, Zachariah Allen, William Wood, George Soule, and Ebenezer Allen sued the rest of the Proprietors for £500 damages claiming that their demand (with others) to have all the land divided amongst the Proprietors had been rejected at a Proprietors' meeting held the previous month. The General Court at Plymouth entered judgment for the Proprietor defendants. One year later, the claimants, augmented by Nathaniel Soule and Joseph Allen, tried again, this time asking for £800 damages, and disclosing that they represented a total of 4 1/4 shares (less 30 acres). The Plymouth Court dismissed this suit for lack of evidence. The following March, the same six plaintiffs brought an identical suit which was again dismissed. A final suit for £1000 was brought only by the two Soules, and this time the Allens and Wood were added to 96 other Proprietors as defendants. Judgment was again for the Proprietor defendants and confirmed on appeal.[45]

Emery, in *The Lands of Old Dartmouth*, gave an alphabetized list of the names of 128 Dartmouth Proprietors involved in these suits from 1684 to 1694. It was Emery's opinion that this litigation was what led to the procuring of the confirmatory deed in 1694 from Major William Bradford, son of Governor William Bradford, the Pilgrim, but he did not elaborate except to note that Major Bradford was Deputy Governor and sat on at least the second suit, so that he would have been familiar with the facts in the case.[46]

The 1694 deed (Appendix 6) recited the history of settlement in Plymouth, the granting of the Warwick Patent, and the description of the Dartmouth tract (Reserved Tract No. 2) conveyed to the Proprietors "which now seems by some to be questioned as to the legal conveyance." By this 1694 instrument, Major Bradford confirmed the conveyance, receiving £25 in silver currency of New England for his trouble, and naming 56 Proprietors as grantees, omitting the Allens, the Soules, and William Wood (as well as numerous others in Emery's list of 128 Proprietors). Bradford confirmed the conveyance both from the standpoint of his father's role as leader of the Plymouth Old Comers ("in performance of the true intent and meaning of the said William Bradford, my father, in and by the said grant") as well as for his father's share as one of the 36 original Proprietors ("and also that particular moiety in said township granted to my father, William Bradford, as appears upon record"). In other words, he released any interest the government of Plymouth might still have, because his father had been a government official, and he released any interest his father might still have as a private individual. However, he specifically excluded "one whole half share . . . now being in the possession of Increase Allen and also another parcel of land . . . seized for the Country use from Zachariah Allen for a fine due from said Allen."[47]

In the section of the Proprietors' records dealing with the derivation of claims from share rights can be found, "Mr. William Bradford's Share: Increase Allen claims one-half of said share of lands by deed from Alice Bradford to Ralph Allen dated October 15, 1663."[48] So the Allens held clear title to that one-half share.

The story surrounding the parcel of land seized to pay Zachariah Allen's fine is an amusing one. The *Judicial Acts* of Plymouth Colony Records reveal that in March 1679, Zachariah Allen, "late of Sandwich," was convicted before Governor Thomas Hinckley "by testimony of sundry Indians" for the offense of giving them liquor. Allen demanded and received a trial by jury, which found him guilty. The court sentenced him to pay £25 but agreed to reduce the fine to £12 10s., if paid "forthwith."[49] In March 1681/2, Allen was fined £20 for the same 1679 offense, "since he hath done it several times" and apparently had not taken up the court's offer for "forthwith" reduced payment.[50]

In September 1682, the governor issued an execution against Allen, "late of Sandwich, now of Dartmouth," convicted the previous March of violating the "wholesome law" which forbade selling liquor to Indians. Here the record disclosed that the fine of £20 represented four transgressions at £5 each.[51] The Chief Marshall's deputy, Stephen Skiffe, reported back to the court the next month that he had gone to Zachariah Allen's house in Dartmouth and demanded the fine. Allen offered him 2 1/2 acres of land in satisfaction and showed him the land "lying in the bottom of the neck of land called Panomesett Neck [Paskamansett, i.e., Barney's Joy] bounded by a river or bay eastward and by the sea southward and by a pond westward." Skiffe and Allen each chose an appraiser, and with Skiffe serving as the third, they valued the land at £21 5s., and therefore it was seized in payment.[52] In October 1684, Governor Hinckley entered into the Plymouth court records the following: "Zachariah Allen owned before the Court [admitted] that the land lying in Dartmouth shewed unto Stephen Skiffe, then Marshall's Deputy, to satisfy his fine, was no otherwise his than as he had a common right in the undivided lands at Dartmouth."[53] In other words, he did not have sole title to the land and therefore could not convey it. It was at this very time that the suits against the Proprietors were commenced by Allen and associates to force partition of all the Dartmouth lands. Surely he had reason for wanting his share, but one would assume that his standing with the court would have been less than reputable. The postscript to the story is this entry in the General Court records dated June 2, 1691: "At the request of Major William Bradford, the Court grants the colony's right to the land in Dartmouth, taken in execution for a fine due the colony from Zachariah Allen, to said Major Bradford, his heirs, etc. . . ."[54] This is the second piece Bradford excludes from his confirmatory deed three years later. By this reckoning, a piece of the Dartmouth Propriety ended up back in Bradford's pocket!

Litigation did not come to an end with the confirmatory deed. At a Proprietors' meeting in November 1709, the oldest minutes preserved by means of a copy, the Proprietors acknowledged that they needed the help of non-resident surveyors to exercise impartiality in the laying out of lands. The minutes stated that

> Joseph Allen, John Allen and William Allen have of late commenced an action against the Proprietors . . . so that they may hold their parts in severalty [sole ownership] from the rest . . . also pretending [with several others] that the surveyor with those that have assisted him in laying out the lands of late, being persons concerned with the lands, have made unreasonable allowance in proportioning the same to themselves and their friends more than the quality of the land hath required. . . .

Therefore, the Proprietors voted that anyone dissatisfied with the unnamed surveyor and his associates could appeal to the magistrates at the Bristol County Court of Quarter Sessions for appointment of three "unconcerned men" to lay out their lands.[55]

Six months later, the Proprietors met again, having sought the assistance of Nathaniel Byfield and Nathaniel Pain "to advise what might be for their peace and contentment."[56] By Proprietors' vote, a committee of disinterested persons, consisting of Capt. Thomas Grey, Lt. William Fobes and Lt. Samuel Crandall, was chosen to examine all deeds and claims to determine whether each had his fair share of the 800 of upland and 36 of meadow, and if not, to make adjustment.[57]

They either neglected to do the job or rejected the task as one of insurmountable difficulty, because later in 1710, the Proprietors hired Benjamin Crane of Berkley (then part of Taunton) to survey all the land in Dartmouth, both divided and undivided. Crane was an impartial outsider whose honesty and integrity the Propriety so desperately needed. He was also a fully qualified surveyor, whose accurate work has withstood the test of time.[58] Crane did surveys in Dartmouth from October 1710 until the end of July 1721 (shortly before his death), assisted by Benjamin Hammond of Rochester and William Manchester of Tiverton. Goodspeed, in his introduction to Crane's *Field Notes* rightly pointed out that Crane could not possibly have done the entire town by himself, and the initials "bh" and "wm" after some of the surveys undoubtedly identify fieldwork done by his assistants. Nevertheless, Crane was obviously in charge, and the work bears witness to his meticulous supervision. In August 1716, the Proprietors voted to pay Crane one penny an acre to complete a general survey of all the undivided land.[59] Apparently, up until that time he had been occupied with surveys of divided lands, for which work he was to have been paid by the reputed owners. Crane boarded with those for whom he was doing work or with those nearest to his fieldwork.[60]

In June 1723, two years after Crane's death, the Proprietors appointed Benjamin Hammond as his successor to finish the layouts.[61] Hammond served in the post until 1741. Samuel Smith was appointed the Proprietors' surveyor from 1767 to 1793.[62] The contents of 14 original journals of these three surveyors, eleven from Crane (1710-1721), two from Hammond (1723-1741), and one from Smith (1768-1793) were collected into the fully indexed volume, entitled *The Field Notes of Benjamin Crane, Benjamin Hammond, and Samuel Smith*, published by the New Bedford Free Public Library in 1910. There were other surveyors who worked in Dartmouth, of course, including the one accused of bias in 1709. However, Crane, Hammond and Smith were the most important, and Crane most particularly of the three, because his work was first, most voluminous, and took place before the Propriety records were burned.[63]

The enormous difficulties which beset the Propriety in 1725— the increasing number of shareholders with undetermined interests, the petulance of those who had not succeeded in partitioning all the Propriety lands, and the neglect of some Proprietors to get their returns of surveys made and recorded — were compounded tenfold when the Proprietors' books burned at the clerk's house in December of that year. The person most knowledgeable who might have rendered invaluable assistance, Benjamin Crane, was now dead, but fortunately his journals were in Rochester, saved from the flames.

At a meeting held July 19, 1726, the Proprietors had to start from scratch. They voted to confirm Thomas Hathaway as clerk and to buy new books "to enter and record all acts and returns of the division of lands" and related matters. They voted to confirm the act dated 1710 for the division of 800 acres of upland and 36 acres of meadow to a share and to confirm all subsequent acts "for the several divisions of lands, meadows, and cedar swamps." Benjamin Hammond, surveyor, and Richard Borden, John Akin, Nathaniel Delano and William Wood were chosen a committee to carry out these votes and to find attested copies of all the previous votes enacted by the Proprietors to enter them into the new book. This committee was empowered to examine all returns of survey brought in by owners and to validate and record all returns signed by Crane or his assistants in accordance with the various divisions voted. The committee was also empowered to issue new returns where owners had lost theirs or never had them in the first place, if the evidence drawn from Crane's journals or those of the other surveyors (Hammond and/or Manchester) appeared "intelligible" that the survey had been done. For those who might not have "taken up their lands, meadows, or cedar swamps" exactly where the acts specified, the committee was to allow them to remain where they were and further give relief to "all persons aggrieved . . . to make them equal in their lands, meadows or cedar swamp with the rest of their neighbors either in quantity or quality." The committee was to report its determinations at the next Proprietors' meeting for acceptance and recording, and thereafter to finish the laying out of all remaining undivided lands, meadows and cedar swamps in the Propriety. For all of the above, the surveyor and committee were to be paid "proportionably according to the service done" by whoever employed them.

At this meeting it was also voted that future Proprietors' meetings could be called by those holding at least five shares through notification signed by the clerk and posted at least 14 days in advance in each of the villages. Finally, a committee of James Tripp, John Kirby and Stephen West, Jr. was appointed to prosecute anyone trespassing on undivided lands by cutting timber or "boxing of pine trees" (tapping them for resin or pitch), which was a common occurrence.[64]

The article to confirm all acts before 1710 was voted down, being protested by Nathan, Nathaniel and Jacob Soule, who were against any act "for the establishing of thirty-five whole shares," in other words, the Mill Share voted in 1684, since "the Soules do challenge and claim the thirty-fourth part or share of all the lands belonging to said Propriety."[65]

The meeting was adjourned to November of 1726. Before the adjournment took place, it would appear that the Soule faction appealed to Thomas Church of Little Compton, Justice of the Peace, in order to get a warrant adding to the agenda the business of allowing them to be exempt from contributing to the Mill Share, thus retaining their 34th interest, and also putting "more suitable men" on the committee empowered with such great authority at the July meeting.[66] As mentioned earlier in this chapter, at the November meeting, the Mill Share was indeed confirmed with the Soule exception, and Jabez Delano, Jabez Barker, Isaac Smith and Nathaniel Soule were duly added to the July committee.[67]

Two years later, in April 1728, the Proprietors decided that a committee of nine "probably would create a needless charge" to the Proprietors, so they voted a new committee of John Akin, Richard Borden, Nathaniel Delano and Beriah Goddard to serve with Benjamin Hammond, the surveyor. Any three of them could "view returns" to determine if they were good, and any two, acting with Hammond, could make new returns "to whom is wanting." The committee was to be paid by the Propriety six shillings per day plus food and lodging "for the time they spend indoors in viewing and giving returns" and an extra two shillings per day "for the time they ride or journey or lay out lands."[68]

The work was to be completed in six months; it would remain unfinished one hundred years later. After the initial period expired, there was an eight-month extension granted in December 1728.[69] In 1730 an effort to reappoint the committee died without action, but in March 1731, the same persons were reconstituted a committee with the same powers, including "to rectify mistakes." At the same meeting, a time limit of eight months was placed on the right of Proprietors to "join their 300 acre division to their land already laid out" and "for taking up their 800 and 400 acre division."[70] This 1731 meeting marked the first time that money issues took hold. A tax of £1 10s. was levied on each share to underwrite the Propriety's expenses. Nathaniel Delano, Stephen West, Jr. and John Russell were chosen assessors and Samuel Pope, Thomas Smith, and Jonathan Wood were to collect the tax and pay it to the Proprietors' clerk. The themes raised at the 1731 meeting would reoccur with increasing intensity during the next three-quarters of a century.

The corporate form of ownership of land in Dartmouth, their requirements for holding Proprietors' meetings and conducting their business, and their method of recording land transactions were not unlike those of other New England colonies which had Proprietors, but the origin and development of the Dartmouth Propriety were different. There were none of the restrictions imposed by the General Court as conditions for receiving the grant, since the bargain made in 1627 between Plymouth Old Comers and New Comers called only for the surrender of the Warwick Patent in exchange for the three tracts, of which Dartmouth was one. After that, the Dartmouth Propriety had to answer only to its shareholders. The town and the Propriety shared no common origins and never achieved any later synthesis. The functions, records and officials of the two entities were always recognized as separate.[71]

With regard to the development of the Propriety, there is no indication in the surviving evidence that the Proprietors of Dartmouth did not strive for fairness in its land decisions, limited, of course, to shareholders rather than inhabitants. They allowed shareholders to "pitch their claims" in some instances and in other instances used lotteries. They brought in non-resident surveyors after 1710 to increase impartiality and encouraged dissatisfied claimants to present their grievances to the Proprietors' committee for resolution. Having chosen not to lay out all their lands in the early years, it became harder to do so as time went on, as shareholders became ever more numerous and shares were ever more fragmented. The paralyzing event was the 1725 fire which destroyed their records.

The issues of lost records, the refusal or inability of the Proprietors to deal with the situation, and mounting debts would lead to the demise of the Propriety, a tale to be told in a later chapter. In the meantime, an acquaintance with other dimensions of the town workings will put the Propriety in better perspective.

VI. HIGHWAYS, DRIFTWAYS, WATERING AND LANDING PLACES

Given the geographic makeup of the township, Dartmouth was never a bustling crossroads of commerce. Water transportation was preferred, and land transportation was difficult, at best. Regional land routes, for the most part, bypassed the township. The difficulties of travel to the county seat became a political issue as well. Locally, the issue was often one of whether ways would be laid through a landowner's good farmland or have to detour around owners' boundaries and to the edge of badlands.

For all the inhabitants of Plymouth Colony, interregional transportation was heavily by water wherever possible. However, the jutting peninsula of Cape Cod and its shoal waters were impediments which made even boat travel between Plymouth and Dartmouth long and difficult. On the other hand, the ease of sailing from Buzzards Bay southwest to Narragansett Bay facilitated contact with the Rhode Island communities of Newport, Portsmouth and Providence as well as points further south. Plymouth and Dartmouth went their separate ways economically, even though they remained tied politically. Plymouth looked to the north; Dartmouth looked to the south and west.

Dartmouth had three villages clustered around waterways. Coakset had two branches of the Acoakset River [Westport] and one harbor where the branches met, but it was a dangerous harbor to enter and leave. Ponaganset [Dartmouth] had two rivers, the Apponagansett and the Paskamansett, but Cushnet [New Bedford/Fairhaven] had the most commodious harbor and by the mid-18th century would develop as the industrial center of the region. However, in contrast to the substantial early development of trade along the Taunton River watershed, attributed to the size and navigability of the Taunton River, all three villages of Dartmouth remained relatively undeveloped and quite evenly matched in population until 1750.[1]

Where overland routes were necessary, the English did not have to trail blaze through the wilderness. The colonial road system simply adopted the Indian network, both regional and local, to save time, effort, and expense.[2] "Little brown paths," one to two feet wide, had been walked "Indian file" for centuries.[3] The Indians had intelligently established trails along the contours of the terrain, making gradual directional and minimal elevational changes, and skirting natural obstacles like steep hills and bogs.[4] The English widened these trails to accommodate horses and carts, added spurs leading to new settlements, and placed their ferries, and later their bridges, at native fording places. Had any of the Dartmouth communities originally been a planned settlement, a new category of roads, street grids, would have appeared.[5] Bedford Village, in the mid-18th century, was the first to lay out new streets in grids to plan for its future growth.

A Massachusetts Historical Commission map (Appendix 7, map A) for the "Plantation Period" shows regional trails from 1620 to 1675. The most important route (now Route 44), connecting Plymouth with Providence through Middleboro and Taunton, was the same route traveled by Winslow, Hopkins and Squanto in 1621 on the visit to Massasoit. In Dartmouth, there was one trail that led in from the north to the head of the Acushnet River and one east-west trail where Old Fall River Road now is, intersecting with the north trail at the head of the Acushnet River and then proceeding east toward the head of Buzzards Bay. By the "Colonial Period" (1675-1775) a few local routes and shipbuilding sites were added, but on the whole, the later map (Appendix 7, map B) shows little growth in this region.[6]

In order to participate in colonial government, representatives to the General Court had to make the arduous trip to Plymouth until 1691, after which they were forced to go all the way to Boston. Annual town meetings always voted the representative an extra stipend for having to make that journey.[7] In 1685, Bristol County was carved out of Plymouth County and the county seat was placed at Bristol (Rhode Island) until 1746, so Dartmouth residents no longer had to travel to Plymouth at all after 1691.

By 1732 the town began to consider the possibility of forming a different county to save the cost and difficulty of going to Bristol. In October 1738, the town petitioned the General Court to have the towns of Dartmouth, Little Compton, Tiverton and Freetown constituted a separate county. In area, these four towns "are thus situated so fair as they contain about 20 miles square and are in a regular and good form to accommodate a county." The inhabitants would benefit "in avoiding two very hazardous, expensive, and difficult ferries" and in not having to lodge overnight when Bristol County court business was so brisk it had to be held over to a second week. In particular, relief was sought for the "great expense, charge and hardship the poor widows . . . have been exposed to . . . especially in the winter season in passing over said ferries to accomplish their probate affairs."[8]

Apparently, nothing came of the petition because in February of the next year, the town voted to send a committee to consult with the committees of the other three towns to see about putting in another petition.[9] The unwillingness of the Massachusetts General Court to act favorably on this petition may have been an important factor in the town's vote of 1741 that it was "the town's mind to come under the government of Rhode Island." Stephen West, Jr. and Beriah Goddard were chosen agents to convey the town's sentiments to the commissioners who were re-setting the boundary between Massachusetts and Rhode Island.[10] In August 1741, the town warrant asked for deliberation on "whether to join Rhode Island in an appeal from the judgment of the Court of Commissioners" who had retained Dartmouth in Massachusetts, but no vote was entered into the record.[11] With the re-setting of the line in 1746, Bristol, Tiverton and Little Compton were joined to Rhode Island, and the Bristol county seat was moved to Taunton.

Dartmouth's inhabitants were no more willing to travel to Taunton than they had been to travel to Bristol. The December 1746 warrant asked for a petition to have "a county taken off or made on this side of the Assonet River; otherwise we must unavoidably be expected to go and our children after us" to Taunton, a 35-mile journey "extreme tedious and expensive," because of the necessity to go the day before to be on time for the convening and to stay over during adjournments. Again, poor widows were painted as the hapless victims because they were "oft times obliged to go several times before an estate can be settled."[12] The vote passed, but again the petition did not succeed. In the spring of 1747, the town abandoned the request for a new county and concentrated on trying to get the county seat moved to the middle of the county, either to Freetown or Dighton, and in the alternative, to hold sessions under a circuit system in Dartmouth at least twice a year.[13] The county seat was never moved from Taunton, but after 1800, New Bedford became a half-shire town, and the grandchildren of the petitioners finally had less distance to travel.

Regional highways had long been called "country roads" or "the king's road" ("the queen's road" during the reign of Queen Anne) by the English. In 1683, when town meeting appointed three men to survey "the road that lies through the town so that it may be brought to record" and in September 1684

sent Seth Pope to Plymouth to "acquaint the court concerning the manner of laying out the roadway," the

town was undoubtedly referring to the king's road from Plymouth to Newport.[14] At the December 1684

town meeting, twelve jurymen were impaneled to lay out the roadway, for which they were each to be

paid 2s. 6d. per day.[15] The road came from Plymouth into Cushnet Village by Main Road at the head of

the river, followed Tarkiln Hill Road and the stretch still called King's Highway, to Hathaway Road into

Ponaganset at Smith Mills, then on Old Westport Road into Coakset at the Head of Westport, and

continued west to the ferry at Tiverton.

Another important country road ran by the head of the Apponaganset Harbor to the head of Clark's

Cove and up the western ridge of the Acushnet River to its head— the current route of Russells Mills

Road, Cove Road, and County Street. This was the "Forest Path" along which the Indian prisoners,

including King Philip's wife and small son, were allegedly marched from the Russell Garrison to

Plymouth to be sold into slavery in King Philip's War.[16] This is also the only road depicted on the British

naval map (Appendix 9) used during the American Revolutionary War when they burned Bedford

Village. Although the northern section of County Street does not appear on the map, it was utilized by

the British, who marched around the head of the Acushnet and down the Fairhaven side to Fort Phoenix.[17]

Within the town, the Propriety, which initially controlled all the land in Dartmouth, never disputed

the need for a good network of roads. In fact, the laying out of roads was actively encouraged. They

desired to visit each other, go to the meetinghouse, take their business to the gristmill or sawmill, use

watering places for their animals, fish and take seaweed for their fields at the seashore, get hay from their

meadows, reach their common lands, and travel to the fording places. Because of longtime Indian

occupation of the area, the Propriety had a good grasp of where they would be needing roads laid out.

There were undoubtedly trails along the ridges of all the necks and along the upland parallel to the rivers.

Others led down to the springs, ponds, coastal fishing places and inland fording places. Where a parcel of

land was to be laid out to a shareholder in an area where a way existed or was likely to be needed, the

Proprietors' surveyor and committee included an ample allowance in calculating the qualified acreage to

provide for the later formal layout of the way. In other cases, they would leave allowance for a way between two parcels of land. The actual layout of the ways was usually done by the selectmen of the town and the layout was presented to town meeting for acceptance. Afterward, it was owned by the town and maintained at town expense. This was the one area in which the Propriety shared resources with the town.

As early as 1685, town meeting voted that the inhabitants in each village would be responsible for repairing the roads in their section of the township. Coakset was to take charge of the area from the town's western boundary to Peleg Slocum's (Paskamansett River) and to the east side of the Noquochoke River. Ponaganset was to take care of roads from those bounds east "to Hezekiah Smith's" (Smith Neck?) and "to the east of the swamp one-half the way between the mill and Acushnet" (the Great Cedar Swamp, now the New Bedford Airport). Cushnet took charge of the roads in the rest of the territory to the eastern boundary.[18]

Every year the town meeting selected highway surveyors. In the early years before 1700, there were usually three chosen, very likely one resident from each village. It is doubtful that these surveyors were more than maintenance supervisors, since there were no ways accepted at town meetings during those years. Probably most of the major ways in the town were laid out between 1705 and 1722 when town meeting voted "that all highways in the Town of Dartmouth shall be surrendered up to the town."[19] A 1717 vote by the Proprietors appointed a committee to see if all Proprietors had been given allowance for ways running through their land, and if not, to make allowance out of the undivided land. The town was to pay the committee to do the work, and all such ways for which allowance had been made would henceforth belong to the town.[20] By 1725 there were 12 highway surveyors elected, but laying out ways was under the jurisdiction of the selectmen, often assisted by a specially appointed committee.

By the turn of the 18th century, many ways had been in use for over 20 years, and the town had grown to the point where the issue of roads was an important one. No Proprietors' records survived this period, but it appears that in March 1704/5 the selectmen, Joseph Tripp, Nathaniel Howland and Thomas Taber, Jr., decided to take an inventory of all the ways in the town and officially lay them out. All of the major roads were laid out as open ways four rods wide. In Ponaganset Village, for example, these included Russells Mills Road, Tucker Road (only 40 feet wide through the Tucker lands and the full width at the ends), Smith Neck Road, Rock O'Dundee Road, Bakerville Road, and Horseneck Road, among others. In addition to open ways, the selectmen laid out a number of "driftways," which were lanes "through gates and bars" to springs, creeks, brooks and other watering places.[21] One of the driftways was to "the bar at the mouth of Ponaganset Harbor" (now the Padanaram Bridge causeway) and two others were on Namquid Neck (Smith Neck), one "unto the great meadow" and the other to Mishaum. A fourth through Soule and Slocum land "to the landing place" might have been on the west side of the Paskamansett River, which at its mouth was called Paskamansett Harbor.[22]

Apparently, the selectmen had no specific authority to lay out new ways without a petition from residents, a town meeting vote, or an order of the Proprietors. On April 1, 1706, town meeting voted that the layouts of ways by the selectmen in 1704 and 1705 were to be null and void because of "said ways not being done as they ought to be done" and because the selectmen "did lay out several ways which were concluded by the town to be greatly prejudicial to several persons. . . ."[23] The next year (1705/6), two new selectmen, Thomas Gatchell and Joseph Hix were chosen, "being under oath according to law as well to lay out convenient ways as to make rates."[24]

In 1708, inhabitants living on the west side of the Paskamansett River petitioned town meeting for more convenient ways. Town meeting voted a committee of Thomas Taber, George Cadman and John Akin to go with the selectmen to view the area, and if they saw justification, they were empowered to make alterations, which they did.[25] Also in 1708, Peleg Slocum complained that the open way through his homestead on the west side of Paskamansett Harbor was "pregudishall" and asked to have it changed, which was also done.[26] In 1714, a number of inhabitants of Ponaganset Village requested that selectmen lay out Russells Mills Road west from the head of the harbor to Bakerville.[27] Although there was already a way there, it is likely that it was not straight enough nor wide enough to please the inhabitants, especially since the way led to Apponeganset Meeting House. When selectmen laid out a way across the Noquochoke River, the Proprietors ordered them to put it where it already was, "there being no other place that we could find so good and convenient for the Proprietors in general as . . . where now laid."[28] That sentiment notwithstanding, since this layout was done in 1705, it was a casualty with the others voided in April 1706.

On another occasion, the Proprietors complained that they needed access for themselves and their cattle to Horseneck, where they had undivided lands and "marsh meadows." Three open ways were laid out "at the going on to the Horse Neck near the sea at a place called Notoquanset" (East Beach). One went west along Horseneck Beach, another east along East Beach and a third north on Horseneck Road to the queen's highway.[29] An intriguing explanation was recorded by selectmen Gatchell and Hix with the layouts. They stated that one of the ways (Horseneck Road) was originally laid out to Horseneck before any land was laid out to any persons. Consequently, "all rational men will conclude the way was to be the most convenient and straight way that could be." The first (unidentified) surveyor died and the bounds lost, which was the reason it was re-surveyed in 1705 or 1706, when it was done "the most convenient, straightest and best for the Proprietors" as had been done in the first place. After the second layout, persons holding land on both sides of the way complained that they owned where the new way was laid out. The selectmen dismissed that complaint with the comment: "Reason tells that no person would lay a way out for themselves crooked and inconvenient except they were bribed. . . ."[30]

As usual, the controversy was not over. Several Proprietors (William Earl, William Wood, Zachariah Allen and others) complained to the rest of the Proprietors of the actions taken by selectmen Gatchell and Hix. In 1707, new selectmen, Joseph Tripp and Thomas Taber, Jr., saw fit to remedy the matter by routing the way between the lands of different owners from a place called Puakachuck up to the queen's road "which by reason of its [formerly] running over several men's lands was greatly prejudicial to them."[31] This controversy may have added to the reasons Benjamin Crane was hired three years later.

Open ways, whether they were regional country roads or merely local routes, were uniformly laid out to be four rods wide except where bad ground caused them to be widened to five to eight rods. At watering places by springs, ponds or swamps, ways were widened to four to eight rods so that cattle would have plenty of room to drink.

The locations of early layouts were identified in relation to local landmarks, the names of landowners, and existing ways. Homesteads, corners of tilled fields, pasture, fresh meadow, cedar swamp, streams and ponds, "new fenced land," and gates served as landmarks. The bounds of the way were marked by trees, most often white, black, red or gray oaks but also pine trees, into which one or

more letters had been carved. Usually the letters were the initials of the abutting landowner's but often the letter "W" appeared and occasionally there was a sequence of the alphabet, "VWXY," for example. Stakes surrounded by a pile of stones, flat rocks, or great rocks occurring naturally were other markers used.

In April 1717, the town ordered the selectmen to lay out all ways by point of compass and number of rods. The locations of ways laid out after this date are more difficult for the layperson to pinpoint since the identifiable landmarks are missing. During the 1740's and 1750's, many of the roads laid out in the first two decades of the 18th century were resurveyed in a more technical manner to correct errors. There were always new ways being laid out by the town and proposed for acceptance by town meeting, just as there are today.[32] In addition, old ways have been straightened from time to time.

Dartmouth adopted and expanded upon the transportation imprint left by the Indians, and with the assistance of Benjamin Crane and his successors in later years, the current outline of the town's major road network took shape before the middle of the 18th century. There was always agreement that roads—country roads, open ways and driftways— were necessary, but there was not always agreement about where to put them. It was a cooperative arrangement between the Propriety and the town that had to be worked out over a period of time. A brief explanation of the structure of town meetings in Dartmouth follows, to round out the picture of the township, before we return to the institution of the Propriety.

VII. TOWN AFFAIRS

An exposition of the intricate workings of town government is beyond the scope of this present work. However, in order to bring the Propriety into better focus, it is worthwhile to touch upon how the township functioned in areas outside of land ownership, especially since Dartmouth was never a typical New England town.

In the first place, Dartmouth never received a land grant from the General Court from which to give land to its inhabitants.[1] As has been already established, Dartmouth derived title to its land through unique circumstances which were duplicated only for the other two reserved tracts claimed by Bradford and the Plymouth Old Comers; and thereafter the character of Dartmouth was further modified by the actions taken by the township's own Proprietors.

Secondly, Dartmouth never experienced the growth pattern of other New England towns. Many of them began with one compact settlement, and as the pressure of population increased, the original settlement sent out offshoots which later broke away and claimed a greater allegiance to their new communities. Dartmouth was one town in name only; the township was really three communities--the villages of Cushnet (east village), Ponaganset (middle village), and Coakset (west village) (see Appendix 5). The population of each village was further fragmented around its shoreline or clustered around its many mill sites. In Cushnet, the greatest density was at the head of the Acushnet River, at Oxford and Long Plain on the east side of the river, at Belleville on the west side and later (further south) at Bedford Village. In Ponaganset, the greatest density was at the head of the Apponagansett Harbor, at Russells Mills and Smith Mills. In Coakset, the population density was greatest at the heads of both branches of the Westport River, at Westport Mills and at Westport Point.

The split-up in 1787 was a mere formality. The Federal Census of 1790, taken only three years later, tallied 454 houses in New Bedford (Cushnet), which included Fairhaven and Acushnet at that time, 392 in Dartmouth (Ponaganset), and 365 in Westport (Coakset). There were 582 families in New Bedford, 448 in Dartmouth and 452 in Westport. These households are listed in Appendix 11.[2] In area today, New Bedford, Fairhaven and Acushnet together contain 49.17 square miles, Dartmouth contains

61.82 square miles, and Westport contains 55 square miles.[3] The three communities were evenly matched

in population and land area.

The separateness of the villages was accepted from the earliest days of settlement. Road

responsibility was apportioned one-third to each. Notices for town meetings were posted one in each

village. In 1681, the places were William Spooner's house in Cushnet, the mill in Ponaganset, and

Richard Sisson's house in Coakset; by 1695, the posting places were each of three mills. After 1707

notice was posted by a constable at the mill at Cushnet, the meetinghouse at Ponaganset, and the ferry at

Coakset. Constables were chosen for each village, as were fence viewers, assessors, tax collectors, and

numerous other officers. There is the strongest evidence that every March one of the three selectmen was

elected from each village, whenever possible. Schools were always a cantankerous issue since no village

wanted to support a schoolmaster in any other village. Cushnet and Coakset always complained that

when the township hired only one schoolmaster, they never got equal time for their children proportionate

to the rate they had to pay.

Dartmouth was predominantly Quaker and Baptist. The early inhabitants who had come from

Duxbury and Sandwich, whose relatives had been forced to leave Plymouth, had suffered greatly at the

hands of the Puritans. Those who had come from Portsmouth and other Rhode Island settlements came

less to escape from religious persecution than to escape overcrowding and diminished land opportunities

in Rhode Island.

The history of Dartmouth's early refusal to support a minister is well known. In 1685 the town

chose agents to appear at Plymouth to answer to the charge that they had not raised funds "for the

encouragement of a minister to preach the word of God amongst them."[4] In 1694, assessors refused to set

a rate to include the support of a pastor and were indemnified by the town.[5] In the town meeting records

for 1705, a response directed to the Court stated:

> We understand that our town is presented for want of a minister according to
> the law, to which we answer that we have one qualified as the law directs, an
> honest man fearing God and hating covetousness and a learned orthodox
> minister able to dispense the Word and Gospel to us.[6]

But having one and paying for one were apparently not the same. In 1722, Selectmen were imprisoned for refusal to pay the province tax which included moneys to support the Puritan ministries of the Commonwealth. The town voted to indemnify them and pay them while in jail, while a minority (very likely non-Quakers) protested.[7] The next year, Nathaniel Howland was chosen minister for the town with 55 votes to 12 votes for Samuel Hunt.[8] In 1730, at the request of "a gathered people in the name of Christ," Nicholas Davis and Philip Taber were appointed ministers for their churches.[9]

The Presbyterians in Cushnet Village petitioned the general Court in 1747 to have their village set off from the rest of Dartmouth so that they could have a "settled minister." The town voted down the idea overwhelmingly and sent a committee, probably made up of Quaker residents of Cushnet, to contest the petition successfully in Boston.[10]

Towns in the 17th century set their own criteria for admitting inhabitants. These criteria generally fell into three categories: (1) sufficient means to be self-supporting; (2) upright moral behavior; and (3) religious compatibility. A particular religious persuasion was never a condition for admittance into Dartmouth, and little was said in the public records disparaging particular behavior. On many occasions, town meeting voted payment to those who "warned persons out of town" and this is most likely related to their abhorrence of having to support those without means or those idle and spendthrift persons who refused to help themselves.

The town routinely appropriated money to support poor persons who were residents of the town and made an effort to look after the legal interests of those persons who had become town charges. On the other hand, the town was under no inclination to accept any additional burdens arriving from other communities. In addition to prosecuting those arriving "illegally," the town sought to prosecute its own "delinquent" residents who had "received non-residents into this town and have not kept to the rules of law in such case made."[11]

There were no "Town Fathers" in Dartmouth. No leader emerged in the first century to guide the town's development with insight and resourcefulness. Certain officials served a number of terms in office, but this was probably because they viewed it as a duty rather than a privilege in offering their services. No maneuvering for political power by one or a small group of individuals can be discerned from the town meeting records. If there were dissatisfaction with action taken at town meeting, the vote was often later rescinded or modified. If the discontent arose because persons exceeded their specific authority, they were simply replaced. If the problem involved the issue of fairness, it was submitted to arbitration.

The overriding impression elicited from the town meeting minutes is government operating on a subsistence level. The town meeting votes were less formal than those of Proprietors' meetings. While the customary procedure for calling a meeting was for the constables to notify all freeholders and inhabitants by order of the selectmen, the warrants and details of notification were not generally recorded in the minutes unless the matter was one of unusual importance. There were perhaps two town meetings annually in the early years, but the town met much more frequently by 1720. This was not indicative of an eagerness by the townspeople to participate in democracy; the frequent meetings were necessitated by the need to fill countless vacancies in offices where those chosen refused to serve and chose rather to pay a fine. Refusal to accept a position to which one's fellow residents had chosen one was the most reoccurring theme throughout the town's first century of existence. In 1751, residents of the middle village grumbled that those of the other two villages had avoided their duty to take a share of "troublesome offices" on the excuse that the townhouse in Ponaganset was too far away.[12] It is not clear whether the more frequent refusals in later years resulted from an increase in the number of town jobs which had to be filled or from preoccupation by the inhabitants with non-political matters, such as farming and commerce.

If the matters which kept townspeople from political involvement were not economic, they may have been religious. No town meetings were ever held at a Quaker meetinghouse. They were held first at private houses, then at the mill (1686), in the 1690's at the house of Widow Russell, and after 1700 at the townhouse. In 1783, a letter to the Dartmouth selectmen from the Quakers objected even to the posting of town meeting business at their meetinghouses, especially those relating to military matters and marriage notices, citing the posting as a disruption to their religious practices. The Quakers added that, should their request give rise to the "suspicion that we mean to be independent of the government we live under," they reminded the town that their Society's leaders had long ago published statements that all Quakers would be "peaceable subjects, either active or passive," to which principles they still adhered.[13]

The town's coffers received a good deal of revenue from the payment of fines by those refusing to serve. Perhaps understandably, the office of constable was particularly hated. Repeated refusals were the source of unending concern of town officials, who feared possible intervention by the General Court, if they were unable to find one to serve in each village. In 1702, town meeting agreed that no one should have to serve twice as constable until "every other suitable person in the township" had served once.[14] The only effective solution was to pay anyone who volunteered to do it for their village. Fines were excused for reasonable cause, and the most common excuse given by those chosen was that they had not been "warned" of their election.[15] One reason for an inhabitant to attend a town meeting was to insure that he was _not_ picked for an office he did not want. Then he would not have to go to the trouble of paying or contesting the fine. Moreover, there was a "forfeit" to pay if he did not attend the annual meeting.[16]

The normal agenda for an annual town meeting included choosing town officers, deciding on the number of schoolmasters for the year, setting the rate to pay the schoolmaster and town charges, and receiving and approving layouts of ways made by selectmen. The purpose of the meeting was also to allow or disallow accounts presented by those who had performed services for the town or advanced money in its behalf and to choose a committee to meet with the town treasurer to examine the town's own accounts and to examine the accounts of selectmen, who were overseers of the poor. Other routine issues were actions concerning the poor and regulations concerning animals running loose.[17] Issues from the larger world outside the town were unlikely to be discussed unless they affected the inhabitants directly. Of course, the town had its share of controversies requiring attention from time to time. However, there was no reference to land issues from the earliest recorded town meeting in 1674; such matters were the separate province of the Propriety from the beginning.

Any freeholder, who was a resident of the town and had taken the oath of fidelity, was entitled to vote at town meeting if he had a suitable estate. In 1724, a voter needed to have "an estate of freehold in lands within this Province or Territory of 40 shillings per annum at the best or other estate to the value of

£50 sterling."[18] He did not have to own land in the town. A partial list of taxable residents and how they held their assets appears as Appendix 10, and the federal census of 1790 (Appendix 11) gives some information on the names of potential voters in each community and their household makeup.[19]

At the annual March meeting, the following offices were generally filled (with approximate year for new offices): 3 selectmen, constables, highway surveyors, fence viewers, raters to assess for both town and county charges, clerk, treasurer, pound keepers, commissioner for Bristol County (1685), tithingmen (1708), field drivers (1710), moderator (1716), hog reeves (1716), surveyors of timbers and cutters of staves (1720), sealer of leather (1720/1). The representative to the General Court was chosen in May. Grand jurymen and petty jurymen were chosen in advance of any court session where they would be required. Agents were chosen to answer any charge brought against the town by the General Court or by any individual plaintiff. Rates (tax budgets) were set in March, but additional sums were voted as needed, such as to employ attorneys to defend the town in suits.

It was the town's responsibility to perambulate the town bounds and settle boundary disputes with its neighbors, which was done on many occasions. The line between Dartmouth and Freetown was fixed in the 17th century and was the least controversial boundary. Dartmouth settled the township's eastern boundary with Rochester in 1701. The Dartmouth-Tiverton line was changed innumerable times because it was the focus of the boundary dispute between Massachusetts and Rhode Island. In 1746, Dartmouth was forced to call a special town meeting to replace one of three assessors, Philip Taber, Jr., "who was taken into Rhode Island government" when Adamsville was severed from the rest of Coakset Village. The other two assessors were unable to function without him. After New Bedford and Westport separated from Dartmouth, there were many times that those bounds were moved until final resolution by statute in the latter part of the 19th century.[20]

In one of the rare instances where the town records mentioned the Propriety, relations became strained. In 1739, the town voted to help out the Propriety by lending Captain Samuel Cornell £25 out of the town treasury in exchange for his promise not to levy an execution against the Proprietors to satisfy a judgment he had procured in Bristol Inferior Court that year.[21] The next year, the warrant asked town meeting to "call in the money" which the selectmen had allowed to be paid on an "illegal vote," but the matter rested without action for one more year.[22] In 1741, the warrant called the 1739 vote "an

oppression upon the poor . . . and falls entirely upon them, the rich having paid . . . their just debts

thereby, . . . said poor, being deprived by law to vote in town affairs, could not vote said money out nor

vote it in again."

This time the town voted to call in the loan.[23] The suggestion that the Proprietors were rich and

should pay the Propriety's own debts while the "poor" inhabitants all contributed to the town's charges,

even if they did not have sufficient estate to qualify as voters, is one of the few examples of tension

between the two "classes" to be found in the records. The cost of running the town, of course, had

nothing to do with the cost of running the Propriety.

There was another example of such friction. A new townhouse had been built in 1739 on

Proprietors' land, but the land was never given to the town. The location was on the north side of

Hathaway Road, west of the intersection with Slocum Road. In 1751, the townhouse, which was the

property of the town, was in danger of being taken by execution along with the land to pay Proprietors'

debts, so a group of inhabitants raised funds and moved it without cost to the town to a quarter-acre lot

donated to the town by William Sanford at the corner of his homestead farm.[24]

For the first one hundred years after the founding of the township of Dartmouth, there was one

town government recruited from the three separate and relatively equal villages of Cushnet, Ponaganset,

and Coakset. If there was any emphasis of Ponaganset, this was merely the inevitable by-product of its

central location and not necessarily appreciated by the "middle villagers." Both geographic isolation and

Quaker religious principles were likely to have contributed to the rather grudging manner in which the

villages fulfilled their community obligations. The Quaker predominance was certainly a significant

factor affecting rocky relations with the Puritans of Massachusetts Colony. Nevertheless, town govern-

ment in Dartmouth township would endure, while the Propriety, as a viable institution, after 1730 entered

into a period of accelerating decline.

VIII. THE DECLINE OF THE PROPRIETY

The meeting which the Proprietors had held in July 1726 to establish a program for recovering their records destroyed by fire was a sound one, but it could not be implemented. The Proprietors committee was unable to find attested copies of all the previous votes authorizing divisions before the fire. Many owners did not bring in their returns to be validated and recorded. It was a number of years before the Proprietors retrieved Benjamin Crane's journals and those of his assistants in order to transcribe "intelligible" evidence into new returns where owners had lost them or never had them. Finally, since the committee was not able to satisfy outstanding claims from the past, which needed to be completed in one way or another, they were hardly in a position to finish laying out all the remaining undivided lands, meadows and cedar swamps in the Propriety. As a result, the themes for the next fifty years would be increasing preoccupation with court suits brought against the Propriety and mounting debts associated with them.

There were two types of suits which dogged the Proprietors. In what might be called "equity actions," from an early date shareholders used the court system to complain that they had not received lands which were equal in quality and quantity with others. They also sued to get private title to their share of the rest of the common lands which had not yet been divided into private ownership, as the Allens, Soules and Woods had done on multiple occasions in the 17th century.

There were also suits on purely monetary matters, which were derivative of the equity suits. The land produced no income, since it was never leased or mortgaged, but it was increasingly necessary to raise funds for defense. The Propriety had no operating budget. Therefore, individual Proprietors advanced their own funds to the corporate Propriety on the understanding that they would be reimbursed with interest after all the other Proprietors had contributed their fair share. Also, individual Proprietors "hired" money under their own names, which usually came due and had to be repaid to the lender before the Propriety was able to provide reimbursement. Eventually, individual Proprietors had to resort to suing the Propriety themselves to demand repayment for loans.

The Propriety's debts mounted because defense of any suit was costly, as well as inconvenient for those who had to travel to the county seat to testify. Attorneys had to be employed. The loans made by individuals had to be repaid with interest. In contrast to the 17th century suits, it appears that the Proprietors lost or were forced to settle all the suits in the 18th century and had to pay damages, either in cash or in land. The problem with paying settlements in land was the Proprietors' inability to know what land the Propriety still owned that had not already been claimed by a shareholder. There was a decided reluctance to act in any way which might compromise the rights of other shareholders who had not yet filled up their claims with lands laid out in all the divisions.

There were so many suits in the 18th century that the Proprietors chose a "standing committee" to defend them after January 1735/6.[1] The need to respond to suits on short notice caused them to supplement the procedure for calling meetings after 1755 by having the clerk post notice of the meeting without requiring application by shareholders.[2]

To raise funds for defense and to augment the loans made by individual Proprietors, the Propriety from time to time after 1733 chose assessors and collectors and charged each whole share its proportionate amount of a particular expense. Before 1753, the assessors had no legal authority to tax because they had never been formally granted that power by the General Court, so these early assessments were purely voluntary. Even if the legal power to tax had been granted at that time, the Proprietors had gotten themselves into unsolvable difficulties, for they did not know who owned the shares. Tragically, they most needed funds to defend suits by those wanting their land rights, but they were unable to raise the funds because they did not know who should be assessed and how much. If they were willing to meet the crisis— and the evidence is still too fragmented to judge conclusively on that point— they clearly were not able.

In 1733, Christopher Gifford challenged the Proprietors to answer the following questions. How could a man demand a layout of some of the undivided land without proving his chain of title from one of the original shareholders? Into which division did necks and islands fall? How was Benjamin Crane's work verified? If an acre were bought with a "metes and bounds" description, might he put it in more than one place? If 100 acres were bought from a shareholder, how much right to vote in the Propriety did he have?[3]

At the Proprietors meeting which followed, none of his queries, which were quite valid, were directly addressed. The Proprietors did not have the answers to how to determine the validity of any claim submitted to the Propriety by a shareholder demanding more common land. Therefore, they evaded the issue and simply confirmed again all former acts and orders of the Proprietors without re-examining their basis. At the same time, the importance of the work which had been done by Benjamin Crane from 1710 to 1721 was recognized, as well as the need to have this documentation locally available for inspection. Therefore, the Proprietors appointed Henry Tucker and Thomas Smith to get Crane's plots and journals which were still in Rochester at Benjamin Hammond's house. They also voted to pay Christopher Gifford "for all his copies and papers."[4] A most meticulous man, Gifford had apparently procured some attested copies of the acts of the Proprietors voting the various divisions at the time that they were made. In the post-fire years, the Propriety often voted to pay him for lending his copies, which they borrowed on repeated occasions. Unfortunately, even Christopher Gifford was missing the crucial one for the consolidated 800 acre division.

As early as 1730, Gifford had complained that his lands were not equal in quality and quantity with other Proprietors. When he requested a different surveyor to requalify his lands, the Proprietors declined to act, but Gifford was not one to be cast easily aside.[5] In August 1735, he filed suit against the Proprietors, and they were forced to send Philip Taber and Jabez Barker to the Bristol Inferior Court to defend the action and hire attorneys, if necessary.[6] Other entries in the Proprietors' records appear to confirm that Gifford's suit claimed that he had not had all his lands properly laid out, some on which he had built and made improvements. This was an equity action. On September 8, 1735, the Proprietors voted to re-survey or otherwise cause his claim "to be filled up if it be wanting" from the remaining undivided land.[7]

The *Field Notes* disclose that Gifford's homestead had been laid out in 1712 (142 acres qualified for 99) along with "a great island" in the Acoakset River and another parcel at Paquachock Point (East Beach or Westport Point?). His meadows were laid out in 1713.[8] There are no later layouts in the *Field*

Notes after 1713 indexed to him, yet in 1743, the Propriety voted to pay the committee for its work and nothing more was heard from Gifford. In this suit, the record does not support the conclusion that Gifford received any additional land. His main concern was probably to re-confirm his title to his lands, which he may have feared was in jeopardy as a result of the fire. Also, he may have been involved in the Horse-neck Road controversy. Some of his lands may have been in dispute because they interfered with the layout of ways. He probably received new returns of survey, perhaps with an enlargement of the old lines, but until those records are properly indexed, it is difficult to confirm that he did. On the other hand, Christopher Gifford had such an ornery reputation, he may have been silenced only by death!

The equity suit which dealt the crushing blow to the Propriety was filed by John and Abigail Butts of Portsmouth in 1753. They claimed 1/4 of a share or 1/140 part of the Propriety (35 X 4 = 140), less 19 acres. Thomas Butts of Little Compton had owned some part of a share in Dartmouth at the time of his death, which occurred sometime before 1712. By his will, he distributed his share to children and various grandchildren, one of whom appears to have been the same John Butts, later plaintiff. In 1714/5, John Butts conveyed to Benjamin Chase of Tiverton his 1/7 of 1/32 of a purchase right in Dartmouth "which was given me by my grandfather, Thomas Butt [sic] of Little Compton, deceased."[9] Another grandchild, Mary Butts sold her identical fractional share to the same Benjamin Chase,[10] and a third grandchild, Sarah Airl, sold hers to Jacob Chase.[11] John's father, also named John Butts, sold his inherited portion to William Manchester.[12] Consequently, John Butts did not derive his claim from his grandfather, Thomas Butts. Instead, he and Abigail derived their claim through her father, Enoch Briggs of Portsmouth, who "in consideration of the natural love which I have and bear to my well-beloved son-in-law, John Butts, and my daughter Abigail, his wife . . . as also for their more comfortable maintenance and support" deeded to them "all my land, both divided and undivided, situate . . . in the township of Dartmouth." No further description is given. The deed was dated September 17, 1731 and recorded on December 4, 1750 in Taunton, where all deeds were then recorded for Bristol County.[13] The 19 acres excluded from the Butts claim must have been sold by Enoch Briggs prior to his gift to John and Abigail.

The Butts suit dragged on for years, and costs of defense for the Propriety mounted. In the same year the suit was initiated (1753), the Massachusetts General Court came to the aid of all Proprietors in the Commonwealth by giving them the statutory power to levy taxes "for completing the settlement of such common lands," for prosecution and defense of lawsuits, and for "carrying on and managing any other affairs for the common good of such proprieties." At this time, the offices of treasurer, assessor and collector were legalized.[14]

However, the Proprietors did not immediately invoke this power, preferring instead to rely on loans and voluntary assessment. In 1753, the Propriety voted to authorize Benjamin Akin to "hire" £25 and guaranteed repayment with interest. Over the next three years, similar arrangements were made with other individual Proprietors for other sums totaling more than £28.[15] In 1757, the Proprietors again resorted to voluntary assessment and appointed assessors and collectors. By 1762, they had increased the assessments to a total of £160.[16] However, there is no evidence to suggest that they were ever able to raise money of any substantial amount by this type of voluntary assessment.

Another five years went by. In June 1767 the Proprietors decided that "if the [voluntary assessment] method heretofore gone into should prove ineffective" to defray the Butts debt during the four-month period after the meeting, a committee would petition the General Court "to be put into some legal method to lay a tax on the said Proprietors and Purchasers to raise money" to defray current and future charges. In December 1770, they acknowledged that the "means. . . proves ineffectual."[17] By 1771, they had little choice but to invoke their statutory power, although they were still beset with the difficulty of determining <u>who</u> should be taxed. They voted "that there be a tax on all the land contained in the original Propriety" sufficient to pay existing debts, which in 1771 amounted to 187 pounds, 15 shillings, three pence, and one farthing. They chose David Smith as treasurer, for which office he gave a £200 surety bond, and new assessors and collectors were chosen. The Proprietors also voted to have the town's representative, Elisha Tobey, petition the General Court on the Proprietors' behalf for a formal dissolution of the Propriety to stop mounting debts.[18]

This action was occasioned most directly by the Butts suit. With regard to the outcome of the litigation, there is no record in the *Field Notes* of any land ever laid out to John or Abigail Butts, either before or after the date of the suit. Nor is there a public record of any deeds from the Propriety to them, voluntary or involuntarily by execution. Consequently, in the absence of any records to the contrary, the assumption is that the Butts were paid a settlement in cash, and, indeed, in the Proprietors' minutes, the matter was sometimes referred to as "the Butts debt." Certainly, by the 1760's the best lands were gone, and there is no reason to believe that the Butts family wanted to move to Dartmouth. Moreover, if they had taken land, they would have been subject to the tax! So, to use the vernacular, paying them off in cash must have cost a bundle.

By 1773, Benjamin Akin had lost patience with the Proprietors, for whom he had done so much service on the Butts suit and for which he had received no reimbursement. He filed suit himself against the Propriety for £25 1s. 1d. and obtained an execution, the Propriety reported, "for near 80 pounds, part of the abovesaid debt now in the hands of the sheriff." The Proprietors did not dispute the debt. In fact, they wanted to "vote said Akin something that shall be adequate for his extraordinary trouble and expense on account of his being obliged to sue for the money hired . . . so that he be not a loser by hiring said money."[19] In September 1774, the Proprietors allowed the execution to be levied on eight parcels of undivided land totaling more than 172 acres and valued at £89 17s. and the sheriff delivered title to Akin.[20]

This was not the first taking of Proprietors' undivided lands by execution. Jabez Barker had sued in 1740, perhaps to be paid for his services in doing the research on the Gifford suit, and he obtained 12 acres 117 rods in Ponaganset Village in payment.[21] The publicity of such suits may have been what prompted the citizens of the town to move their townhouse off Proprietors' land in 1751. In 1773, along with Akin, Ebenezer Willis got satisfaction by enforcing his execution by receiving 67 acres, valued at £20.[22] In none of these actions did the debtors choose to send a representative to attend the selection of the lands.

Several times the Propriety proposed to set a time limit for Proprietors to fill up all their claims, so that they could proceed with the distribution of the remaining lands. A suggestion to that effect in 1733 was not voted; in 1735 it was voted down. In 1757, the Proprietors complained that "whereas it hath been found by experience that the neglect of many people having land laid out. . . and not putting the returns of survey thereof in said Proprietors Book of Records" was causing "ill configuration to the Proprietors in general," they voted that any shareholder holding a return of survey not on record had 12 months from the date of the meeting (August 1, 1757) to put it on record with the clerk of the Propriety, or the survey would "be deemed void and the land so surveyed to be free for any other Proprietor or Purchaser to take up" if they had "a good right in the undivided lands." The same one-year deadline was to apply for future surveys.

They also voted on August 1, 1757 that Crane's journals were to be lodged with the Proprietors clerk and "esteemed equal with our Proprietors Book of Record, except that part which shall appear to said committee [appointed for the purpose] to be corrupted or folly by any other handwriting and so by them cancelled or written upon disallowed." The authenticated parts were to be the basis for issuance or re-issuance of surveys where the layout had occurred before that date.[23]

In 1762, the Propriety noted that there were "some rights still to be filled up in the several divisions," and setting a time limit would allow them to sell any "surplusage" or (God forbid!) grant another division after the time expired, but no vote was taken at the meeting.[24] Five years later, they did vote

> that there be one year allowed from the 23rd day of June 1767 to all those persons that have any right or claim in the Propriety in upland, salt meadow or cedar swamp within the township of Dartmouth to bring in their right or claim and have their rights laid out to them in the former grants or divisions, and if they don't appear within said time, they shall be forever after debarred from having any right in the former grants or divisions of Propriety laid out to him or them.[25]

In 1770, the Proprietors acknowledged that the time had long expired, but "lest it should so happen that there are some that hath not yet got all their rights," they voted a four-month extension from December 18, 1770.[26] The meeting in April 1771 "met and dissolved," but by the end of that year, they had instituted the formal tax and voted to petition the General Court to close the Propriety.[27] Subsequent minutes did not report on the status of the petition.

In December 1773, the Proprietors finally took the situation firmly in hand and resorted to sale of undivided lands by public auction or to private individuals, usually abutters. A committee of William Wood, cordwainer, William White, yeoman, and Samuel Smith, yeoman, were empowered to give deeds for the Proprietors.[28] During the 1780's and early 1790's, they gave about 30 deeds, and in 1795 reported to the Propriety that, pursuant to their appointment, they had "paid, settled and discharged all the Proprietors and Purchasers debts."[29]

Still, the Propriety remained open. They held an annual meeting by adjournment on December 25 of every year until 1800. In 1799, they actually reported a balance on hand in the treasury of $12.48.[30] Samuel Smith, son of the former surveyor of the same name, served as surveyor for a while and with a committee continued to issue returns of survey and lay out more undivided land. The last return of survey was entered in 1835, but there were no Proprietors meetings recorded after 1800, except for one in 1821, when five Proprietors (John Wing, Ephraim Tripp, Wilbur Gifford, Richard Lawton, and George Allen) requested a meeting at Adam Gifford's house in Westport.

There were four votes cast in the elections, the only time numbers were ever reported in Proprietors' votes. Abner B. Gifford was chosen moderator, clerk and surveyor and was sworn in to the last two offices. Ephraim Tripp was chosen treasurer. John Howland, John Wing, William White, Adam Gifford and Ephraim Macomber were constituted the committee to serve "until another committee shall be chosen," any two members of which were empowered to "view and qualify and make returns of all such undivided lands as they shall . . . find to be regularly entered a pitch upon by any person having a legal right to lay out undivided lands." The meeting was adjourned to the following November, and there the records end.[31] How the Propriety ever was closed is a tale remaining to be told; probably, the General Court intervened later in the 19th century and acted on the request for formal dissolution made in 1771.

IX. CONCLUSION

By the year 1800, the character of the township had taken shape. The Propriety was by then but a shell of its former self, but its work had been completed as well as it ever would be. The three villages of Cushnet, Ponaganset, and Coakset had achieved their inevitable severance. Two of these towns remained rural and relatively unchanged for the next century and a half before accelerating in growth. The third had already begun to successfully promote its maritime and mercantile advantages.

The Propriety of Dartmouth left its indelible stamp on the structure of the township because its rights were territorial, while those of the freehold inhabitants were only political. If many individuals possessed both rights, that duality does not diminish the need to understand the territorial rights in order to put the political rights into proper context.

With regard to the aspects of land ownership, one of the difficulties experienced by laymen is being confronted with a confusion of unintelligible written legal instruments. Legal instruments are especially intimidating if there is no frame of reference into which to fit them. By outlining the basic legal framework of the land-owning dimensions of the township, namely the Proprietors' records, I have endeavored to provide at least a point of beginning.

The process of English settlement in the region, the establishment of title to the lands in Dartmouth under the English form of land tenure known as "East Greenwich," and how the Dartmouth Propriety originated in exchange for the surrender of the Warwick Patent by Plymouth Old Comers have been briefly discussed. When the English actually settled on the former Indian lands of Dartmouth, their methods of agriculture and animal husbandry wrought an irreversible transformation of the landscape. They formed a town, laid out roads, and carried on all the necessary functions of government.

The legal focus of landholding was the Propriety, which voted divisions of land and controlled how those divisions would be carried out. The development of the Dartmouth Propriety was unique because it operated free of the restrictions generally imposed by General Courts when making grants. However, although it controlled how the land was given out, the Dartmouth Propriety did not control who was entitled to get it. Shareholder rights were bought, sold, given away, and inherited independently. So were innumerable small parcels of land owned privately to which rights in the commons were still attached. Under the best of recordkeeping, it would have been a difficult task to keep track of all landholding rights over a century and a half, but the destruction of the Proprietors records in 1725 and the missing surveyors' plot plans midway through that period complicated the course of the Propriety's history enormously. Crane and his assistants, Hammond and Manchester, later Hammond alone, and finally Smith did yeoman service for the Propriety, and the journals of these surveyors were accepted into the permanent records of the Dartmouth Propriety and reconfirmed repeatedly.

In 1807, the Massachusetts Superior Court ruled:

> All the titles, which have been derived from the proprietors of townships, have nothing better to depend upon than a vote recorded in the proprietors' books, and when a possession was taken in confirmity to the vote, and transmitted by the grantee to his heirs or assigns, titles so acquired have been respected and maintained in our courts of law.[1]

In 1813 and again two years later, the court ruled that proprietors' records "constitute chief evidence in land transactions" and in 1851, that a "proprietors' vote granting common land was 'prima facie' evidence of title."[2]

In the case of Dartmouth, the Proprietors' records may not have been complete, but they were relied on, and with the incorporation of Crane's journals and those of his successors into the Proprietors' records, there is little likelihood that those holding returns of surveys drawn from those sources had any doubt cast upon their titles. The unanswered questions remains: What happened to the rest of the undivided and common land that was never laid out? There can be only speculation. Judging from the fact that the later returns of surveys were mostly in northern swamps, it is fair to guess that much of it is the watershed protecting our public water supplies.

The complete history of Dartmouth is a book waiting to be written. The political, economic, religious and social aspects of Westport and Dartmouth, in particular, have never been explored. New Bedford has had some attention focused on it, both with the formation of the Old Dartmouth Historical

Society at the turn of the century and in recent years with the increasing interest in the sociological developments in the region.

Much work remains to be done to investigate and reconstruct the impact on the 17th century landscape as a result of English settlement in Dartmouth. The question must also be addressed as to whether their uses of the land were the implementation of concepts imported from England or whether the new settlers formulated them here in response to an unfamiliar environment. The Massachusetts Historical Commission, for example, lists a number of suggested topics for further research, both along these lines and along others, in *Historic and Archaeological Resources of Southeastern Massachusetts.*

With regard to the Proprietors' records, there are many areas into which further research should be directed. Such research is made possible today with the use of computer technology. An analysis of the old land instruments should begin with the preparation of a computerized index of all the old returns of surveys to include the following information: the name to whom the return was given, the acreage, the category of land (upland, meadow or cedar swamp) and in which division, the locations of parcels to the extent identified, the date of the return, and to whose share it was charged. Then the results of a tabulation of the claims to original shares made by subsequent owners could be added and compared. The comparison might continue with computerized indexing of names (grantor and grantee) of all deeds given before the split-up of the township in 1787, with acreage and location or fractional shareright, consideration (price paid), dates and unusual provisions. Through integration of town meeting records, vital records (place of birth, marriage, death, residence, and occupation), and tax lists, it might be possible to identify the land-holding residents and non-residents of the township. Women's legal rights in the land could also be explored. Probate records would also be a necessary component, and in this area, the work of Elisha B. Leonard (*Family Histories*) provides some groundwork. In addition, the information supplied by this process would be valuable to historians examining the non-legal aspects of the make-up of the early communities.

There are some in the community besides this author who still entertain the hope that the plot plans made by Benjamin Crane and his assistants will be found or that they can be reconstructed with modern technology. The possibility is intriguing, and it would have a further practical application for surveyors currently doing work in the area.

The landscape does not remain static, but perhaps through the old legal records we can rediscover some semblance of what life was like in the "ancient Propriety of Dartmouth" and preserve it for posterity through the written word.

X. NOTES

I. INTRODUCTION (pages 1 - 4)

1. The *Old Dartmouth Historical Sketches* (New Bedford: Old Dartmouth Historical Society, Nos. 1-74) are the best source for this type of Dartmouth history. The "standard" works are all histories of New Bedford: Daniel Ricketson, *History of New Bedford* (New Bedford: By Author, 1858); Zephamiah W. Pease, ed., *History of New Bedford* (New York: The Lewis Historical Publishing Co., 1918); and Leonard Bolles Ellis, *History of New Bedford and Its Vicinity: 1602-1892* (n.d.).

2. Daniel Ricketson, *History of New Bedford*, p. 405.

3. Nathaniel B. Shurtleff and David Pulsifer, eds., *Records of the Colony of New Plymouth in New England* (Boston: 12 vols., 1855-1861), hereinafter cited "Plymouth Colony Records," Court Orders, 10/4/1675, V., p.177. John Stetson Barry's three-volume *The History of Massachusetts* (Boston: Phillips, Sampson & Co., 1855) mentions Gosnold's visit (I., p.11) and the destruction of King Philip's War (I., p.416), but there is no other reference to Dartmouth. The five-volume *Commonwealth History of Massachusetts* (A.B. Hart, ed., New York: Russell & Russell, 1966) gives the date of the town's founding, a few comments under "Indian Troubles," mention of privateering in the American Revolution and distribution of taxes in 1781, all in Volume III (1775-1820). Volume I (1605-1689) deals with Massachusetts Bay, a common occurrence in Mass. history texts. In Roy Akagi's 38 pages of bibliography of works on proprietors in the New England colonies, including his own doctoral thesis, no works on Dartmouth are listed nor is the town mentioned in his text: *The Town Proprietors of the New England Colonies: A Study of their Development, Organization, Activities and Controversies, 1620-1770* (Gloucester, MA: Peter Smith, 1924, 1963 reprint). His work is very helpful, however, as a yardstick against which to measure the development of the Dartmouth Propriety. Finally, in *New England Community Studies Since 1960: A Bibliography*, a reference work (1984) by Robert Dale Karr, there are no entries for Dartmouth or Westport. New Bedford has one entry, a study of industrial and social change from 1865 to 1900 by Thomas A. McMullin.

4. John Cooke is the only *Mayflower* passenger to settle within the bounds of the town. He became a resident of Oxford Village (Fairhaven).

5.. Town Meeting vote passed 3/30/1741, Town of Dartmouth, *Records of Town Meetings: 1674-1779*, (1888) pp.179-180.

6. Ricketson, Pease and Ellis fit this definition of "aristocratic" historians.

II. FIRST INHABITANTS (pages 5 - 9)

1. Howard S. Russell, *Indian New England Before the Mayflower* (Hanover, NH: University Press of New England, 1980), p.200.

2. To what extent, see Francis Jennings, *The Invasion of America: Indians, Colonialism, and the Cant of Conquest* (New York: W.W. Norton & Company, Inc., 1976), p.15ff. He cites Jamestown, Plymouth, Salem, Boston, Providence, New Amsterdam, Philadelphia, Quebec, Montreal, Detroit, and Chicago as examples of sites where Indian communities preceded white settlement, p.30.

3. Russell, *Indian New England Before the Mayflower*, p.3; Massachusetts Historical Commission, *Historic and Archaeological Resources of Southeastern Massachusetts* (Boston: By Author, June 1982), p.23; William Cronon, *Changes in the Land: Indians, Colonists, and the Ecology of New England* (New York: Hill and Wang, 1983), p.33.

4. Russell, *Indian New England Before the Mayflower*, p.7.

5. Russell, *Indian New England Before the Mayflower*, pp. 27-28; Cronon, *Changes in the Land*, p.42; Henry F. Howe, *Salt Rivers of the Massachusetts Shore* (New York: Rinehart & Co., Inc., 1951), p.18; Mooney's estimates of only 25,000 are discounted in Jennings, *The Invasion of America*, p.17 and p.29.

6. Cronon, *Changes in the Land*, p.42.

7. Russell, *Indian New England Before the Mayflower*, p.3.

8. Russell, *Indian New England Before the Mayflower*, p.22.

9. Lincoln A. Dexter, ed., *Maps of Early Massachusetts: Pre-History Through the Seventeenth Century* (Brookfield, MA: By Author, Rev. Ed. 1984), pp.22-23.

10. Russell, *Indian New England Before the Mayflower*, p.19.

11. Russell, *Indian New England Before the Mayflower*, p.19.

12. Massachusetts Historical Commission, *Historic and Archaeological Resources of Southeastern Massachusetts*, p.39; can be seen at Plimoth Plantation.

13. Russell, *Indian New England Before the Mayflower*, p.19, p.22.

14. Marshall Harris, *Origin of the Land Tenure System in the United States* (Westport, CT: Greenwood Press Publishers, 1953, 1970 reprint), pp.66-68.

15. Russell, *Indian New England Before the Mayflower*, p.51.

16. Russell, *Indian New England Before the Mayflower*, p.29.

17. Russell, *Indian New England Before the Mayflower*, p.140.

18. Howe, *Salt Rivers of the Massachusetts Shore*, p.23; Cronon, *Changes in the Land*, p.48.

19. Russell, *Indian New England Before the Mayflower*, pp.165-166.

20. Russell, *Indian New England Before the Mayflower*, p.168; an estimated 80,000 ancient Indian cornhills on 30 acres were still visible in Assonet in the 1930's. They were located on hillsides near Mt. Hope Bay and had been planted by Indians driven out of the area during King Philip's War.

21. Russell, *Indian New England Before the Mayflower*, p.160.

22. For description, see Russell, *Indian New England Before the Mayflower*, pp.76-80; Howe, *Salt Rivers of the Massachusetts Shore*, p.19.

23. Russell, *Indian New England Before the Mayflower*, p.35.

24. Russell, *Indian New England Before the Mayflower*, p.176; grain made up approximately one-half of their diet according to Cronon, *Changes in the Land*, p.42.

25. John Brereton's version in Gabriel Archer and John Brereton, *The Gosnold Discoveries . . . in the North Part of Virginia, 1602*, Lincoln A. Dexter, ed. (Brookfield, MA: Lincoln A. Dexter, 1982), June 8?, 1602, p.39.

26. John Brereton's version in Gabriel Archer and John Brereton, *The Gosnold Discoveries*, p.41.

27. Russell, *Indian New England Before the Mayflower*, p.112; Lincoln A. Dexter, *Maps of Early Massachusetts*, p.27; Howe, *Salt Rivers of the Massachusetts Shore*, p.18, p.44; Cronon, *Changes in the Land*, p.87.

28. Cronon, *Changes in the Land*, p.86; for statistical methods, Jennings, *The Invasion of America*, p.22.

29. Howe, *Salt Rivers of the Massachusetts Shore*, p.44; Cronon, *Changes in the Land*, p.87.

30. Howe, *Salt Rivers of the Massachusetts Shore*, p.44.

31. Russell, *Indian New England Before the Mayflower*, p.12.

32. Heath, Dwight B., ed. *Mourt's Relation: A Journal of the Pilgrims at Plymouth*, p.41.

33. Its value is in its emphasis on description rather than religion. The identity of G. Mourt remains a mystery; he was not listed as a *Mayflower* passenger. The book was likely a collaborative effort, with Edward Winslow the primary author and William Bradford also a contributor. The account may have been disguised for publication because Separatists were not in favor in England at the time.

34. *Mourt's Relation*, p.55.

35. *Mourt's Relation*, p.55; Howe, *Salt Rivers of the Massachusetts Shore*, pp.44-45.

36. *Mourt's Relation*, p.60.

37. *Mourt's Relation*, pp.61-62.

38. *Mourt's Relation*, p.63.

39. Jennings, *The Invasion of America*, p.30.

40. Gabriel Archer, *The Gosnold Discoveries*, p.32.

41. *Mourt's Relation*, p.63.

42. *Mourt's Relation*, p.64.

43. *Mourt's Relation*, p.84. The letter is signed "E.W." *Mourt's Relation* contained such "sales hype" that it omitted mention that over one-half of the *Mayflower* passengers had died.

44. We call them "Pilgrims," but "Saints" was the name the Separatists gave to themselves and "Strangers" was the name the Separatists gave to their fellow passengers, most of whom were Anglicans.

III. CHARTER RIGHTS (pages 10 - 20)

1. Howe, pp.46-47.

2. Harris, *Origin of the Land Tenure System in the United States*, p.62. Jennings, *The Invasion of America*, p.132.

3. Jennings, *The Invasion of America*, pp. 132-134. He cited the Dutch in New Amsterdam in 1625 and later in the Delaware and Connecticut Valley using Indian deeds as a defense against the Swedes and the English. Although the Dutch lost their territories, their technique impressed "their equally legalistic English adversaries," who promptly adopted the idea to support their own claims.

4. Jennings, *The Invasion of America*, p.105.

5. Harris, *Origin of the Land Tenure System in the United States*, p.83; for example, the Cabots, Gilbert, Raleigh. For discussion, see Harris, p.73.

6. For commentary, Harris, *Origin of the Land Tenure System in the United States*, pp.82-85 with sketch on p.84. For text of the charter, see MacDonald, *Select Charters and Other Documents Illustrative of American History, 1606-1775* (New York: The MacMillan Company, 1899), pp.1-11.

7. MacDonald, *Select Charters*, p.2. For orientation purposes, the present names of geographical areas appear in parentheses.

8. This overlap of grants naturally caused many future disputes.

9. Harris, *Origin of the Land Tenure System in the United States*, p.83. MacDonald, *Select Charters*, p.4.

10. Harris, *Origin of the Land Tenure System in the United States*, pp.84-85. MacDonald, *Select Charters*, p.5.

11. Harris, *Origin of the Land Tenure System in the United States*, p.85.

12. Harris, *Origin of the Land Tenure System in the United States*, p.85.

13. The full title of the corporation was "The Treasurer and Company of Adventurers and Planters of the City of London for the first Colony in Virginia."

14. Harris, *Origin of the Land Tenure System in the United States*, pp.86-87. For text of Second Charter, MacDonald, *Select Charters*, pp.11-16; for text of Third Charter, MacDonald, pp.17-23.

15. Harris, *Origin of the Land Tenure System in the United States*, p.88.

16. Harris, *Origin of the Land Tenure System in the United States*, p.99.

17. William Bradford, *Of Plymouth Plantation, 1620-1647*, Samuel Eliot Morison, ed. (New York: Alfred A. Knopf, 1952), p.23.

18. Bradford, *Of Plymouth Plantation*, p.25.

19. Bradford, *Of Plymouth Plantation*, p.17. Morison pointed out in footnote 8 on page 26 that in the Netherlands the Pilgrims had good access to published accounts of exploration in America.

20. For Guiana, Bradford, *Of Plymouth Plantation*, pp.28-29; for Dutch, Bradford, p.37.

21. The Peirce Patent was the second one the Separatists received. The first was procured in June 1619 in the name of John Wincop, who served as a "front man" for the group. Bradford, *Of Plymouth Plantation*, p.34.

22. Bradford, *Of Plymouth Plantation*, p.29. Successful colonies included Martin's Hundred, Southampton Hundred, Berkeley's Hundred and Fleur de Hundred. Archaeological excavations at Wolstenholme Towne, the administrative center for the Society of Martin's Hundred, can be seen today at Carter's Grove, Williamsburg, VA. By 1622, 30 to 40 settlers inhabited a 21,500-acre tract along the James River, but about one-half perished in the Indian uprising that year.

23. See Bradford, *Of Plymouth Plantation*, pp.60-61. The Dutch did not establish a colony on Manhattan until 1626.

24. Bradford, *Of Plymouth Plantation*, pp.40-41 for terms.

25. Whether they had planned to land in New York or New England is also a point in contention between scholars, based on the ambiguity of Bradford's text, Bradford, *Of Plymouth Plantation*, p.39.

26. "The Council established at Plymouth in the County of Devon for the planting, ruling, ordering and governing of New-England in America" was commonly shortened to "Council for New England," Bradford, *Of Plymouth Plantation*, p.38. See also Harris, *Origin of the Land Tenure System in the United States*, p.99. For text of the charter, see MacDonald, *Select Charters*, pp.23-33.

27. Harris, *Origin of the Land Tenure System in the United States*, p.104.

28. Harris, *Origin of the Land Tenure System in the United States*, pp.99-100. The Council was dissolved in 1635.

29. Harris, *Origin of the Land Tenure System in the United States*, p.104.

30. For Bradford's comments on the "conclusion of a long tedious business," *Of Plymouth Plantation*, see especially p.322.

31. Bradford, *Of Plymouth Plantation*, pp.185-186. Note: Plimoth Plantation is reconstructed in the year 1627 because it is the last year before the common ownership began to be dissolved, and the settlers dispersed into the surrounding countryside. A contemporary visitor can engage "residents" [actors playing the roles of Pilgrims] on the subject of their discontent with the Adventurers.

32. Bradford, *Of Plymouth Plantation*, p.187.

33. For partial text, MacDonald, *Select Charters*, pp. 51-53. In the "old style" or Julian calendar, January was still part of the old year, which did not begin until March 25; thus, when writing dates before 1752, both old and new years are given.

34. Harris, *Origin of the Land Tenure System in the United States*, p.105.

35. Plymouth Colony Records, *Laws*, p.23.

36. For full discussion, see Harris, *Origin of the Land Tenure System in the United States*, pp.21-61. See also, James Sullivan, *The History of Land Titles in Massachusetts* (Boston: I. Thomas and E.T. Andrews, 1801).

37. Harris, *Origin of the Land Tenure System in the United States*, pp.29-30 and pp.37-38. Actually, the law of descent and distribution in the colony at this time, in the absence of a will, provided for the oldest son to get a double share, Sullivan, *The History of Land Titles in Massachusetts*, pp.372-373.

38. Harris, *Origin of the Land Tenure System in the United States*, p.73.

39. Harris, *Origin of the Land Tenure System in the United States* and Akagi, *The Town Proprietors of the New England Colonies*. Land tenure is the subject of Harris' entire treatise, but he summarizes colonial grants at p.75. Akagi's book deals primarily with the third type, corporate propriety grants but also gives some attention to "Lord Proprietors." After the restoration in 1660, the character of old feudalism was changed by statute. Military tenures and their incidents were abolished, Aaron M. Sakolski, *Land Tenure and Land Taxation in America*, p.15.

40. Plymouth Colony Records, *Laws*, p.23 for patent and p.24 for sample deed to be given. The only time there was any attempt to collect quitrents was under the Andros regime.

41. Plymouth Colony Records, *Laws*, p.21. Full declaration of authority given the Governor of the colony to grant deeds creating private ownership appears in Plymouth Colony Records, *Laws*, pp.74-78. These pages also recite the whole legal history up to the Wawick Patent.

42. For text, MacDonald, *Select Charters*, pp.205-212. For full discussion, see Akagi, *The Town Proprietors of the New England Colonies*, pp.115-123. Also, Harris, *Origin of the Land Tenure System in the United States*, p.80.

43. By a document entitled, "A form to be placed before the Records of the several inheritances granted to all and every the King's subject inhabiting within the Government of new Plymouth," Plymouth Colony Records, *Laws*, p.20, also appears at Plymouth Colony Records, *Laws*, pp.74-78.

44. Plymouth Colony Records, *Laws*, p.20.

45. *Mourt's Relation*, pp.56-57.

46. *Mourt's Relation*, p.88.

47. *Mourt's Relation*, p.92.

48. *Mourt's Relation*, pp.92-93.

49. Plymouth Colony Records, *Laws*, pp.34-35.

50. Bradford, *Of Plymouth Plantation*, pp.428-429. (Plymouth Colony Records, II, p.10 and XI - Morison ref.) Emery, writing in 1930, stated that the original document was in the possession of the Bradford Family until this century and is now in the Plymouth County Registry of Deeds, p.10.

51. For description, Bradford, *Of Plymouth Plantation*, p.429. For map, Bradford, pp.306-307.

52. From "Official Documents, No. 4: Surrender of the Patent to the Body of Freemen, March 1641," Bradford, *Of Plymouth Plantation*, p.429.

53. Plymouth Colony Records, *Laws*, p.60. It was not stated who granted which part to whom, but Plymouth was to have endless border disputes with Rhode Island and Massachusetts Bay. The Council of New England had been dissolved by 1635, but that did not affect the validity of the Warwick Patent. Title to lands not under patent reverted to the Crown. The Crown had also established a "Royal Commission for Regulating Plantations in 1634, giving it power to recall Governors and revoke charters for just cause. Bradford had copied this document onto the back of the sheets containing his narrative, Bradford, *Of Plymouth Plantation*, pp.422-425.

54. Plymouth Colony Records, *Laws*, p.60.

55. Spellings of Indian names were phonetic, since there was no written language. Wasomequin was also spelled Osemequin, Ousamequin and Woosemequin and meant "Yellow Feather." Dexter, p.26. "Massasoit," his English name, actually meant "chief" or "sachem." Wamsutta was called Alexander and his brother, Metacom or Metacomet, was called Philip by the English, who named them after the Macedonians, Ricketson, p.21.

56. In ancient times, the forerunner of the deed was a ceremony in which a clump of sod was handed over in symbolic gesture before witnesses.

57. For first recording procedure, Plymouth Colony Records, *Laws*, p.63. Cronon stated that there was decided sloppiness in early recording systems, pp.74-75. For the county recording orders, Sullivan, *The History of Land Titles in Massachusetts*, p.369, and for recording procedure, p.374. The original Dartmouth deed may still be in the custody of the Plymouth Country Registry of Deeds or it may have been removed to the new State Archives Building. The copy in Appendix 3 is recorded in Bristol County (S.D.) Registry of Deeds in Dartmouth Proprietors, *Land Records*, Vol. 1, page 1. An earlier copy can be found in Dartmouth Proprietors *Book of Records*, No. 4, page 1. There is a printed copy in Milton A. Travers, *The Wampanoag Indian Federation of the Algonquin Nation* (Boston: The Christopher Publishing House, rev. ed. 1961), p.220.

IV. CHANGING USE (pages 21 - 30)

1. *Our County and Its People*, p.7.

2. *Our County and Its People*, p.8.

3. *Our County and Its People*, p.8.

4. *Our County and Its People*, p.9.

5. The Indians suspected he had been poisoned by the English.

6. The English forced him to do the same for the other purchases, *Our County and Its People*, p.10.

7. The details of the course of King Philip's War has filled volumes and cannot be explored here.

8. As spoken by King Philip to his friend, John Borden of Rhode Island. Milton A. Travers, *The Wampanoag Indian Federation of the Algonquin Nation*, p.138.

9. Wampum belts were kept as a permanent record of proceedings and were later used to educate younger leaders on tribal policy. Jennings, *The Invasion of America*, p.121.

10. Russell, *Indian New England*, pp.185-186. The Narragansett and Block Island Indians had the best supplies and consequently were "richer" than other Indians. Tobacco pipes also served as another medium of exchange among Indians. Copper, on the other hand, was exceedingly scarce since it had to come from the Great Lakes area.

11. The Plymouth government forbade selling liquor to the Indians and had stiff fines for doing so.

12. Cronon, *Changes in the Land*, pp.161-162.

13. See Russell, *Indian New England*, Chapter 8, pp.58-71 for description of household and personal possessions.

14. Jennings, *The Invasion of America*, p.124.

15. Cronon, *Changes in the Land*, pp.166-167.

16. Quoted in Cronon, *Changes in the Land*, p.170.

17. Cronon, *Changes in the Land*, p.168.

18. *Our County and Its People*, p.11.

19. Cronon, *Changes in the Land*, pp.50-51.

20. Cronon, *Changes in the Land*, p.118.

21. Cronon, *Changes in the Land*, p.120.

22. Cronon, *Changes in the Land*, p.49.

23. Cronon, *Changes in the Land*, pp.120-121.

24. Cronon, *Changes in the Land*, p.119.

25. Southeastern Massachusetts was known as the oak-chestnut region by ecologists until the 20th century when a blight destroyed many chestnut trees, Cronon, *Changes in the Land*, p.26.

26. Cronon, *Changes in the Land*, p.28.

27. Cronon, *Changes in the Land*, p.112.

28. Cronon, *Changes in the Land*, p.30

29. Cronon, *Changes in the Land*, p.26.

30. Cronon, *Changes in the Land*, p.114.

31. Cronon, *Changes in the Land*, p.116.

32. A fungus "blast" attacked and destroyed wheat crops.

33. Cronon, *Changes in the Land*, p.150.

34. Cronon, *Changes in the Land*, p.128.

35. Cronon, *Changes in the Land*, p.147.

36. Cronon, *Changes in the Land*, p.24 and p.153.

37. Cronon, *Changes in the Land*, p.141. The need for more grazing land meant the end of compact settlement, as William Bradford lamented as early as 1631.

38. Cronon, *Changes in the Land*, p.135.

39. Cronon, *Changes in the Land*, p.130.

40. Cronon, *Changes in the Land*, p.130.

41. Cronon, *Changes in the Land*, p.128. Wolves found cattle easier prey than fleeting deer so there were special hunts organized. Bounties offered created a "court-ordered market" for them and encouraged fraud. There was no way to determine where the wolves had been killed. Often the same head was presented twice for payment! Wolves were gone from Southern New England by the end of the colonial period. Ibid., pp.133-134. In 1713, Dartmouth town meeting agreed to give a tax credit of 20 shillings for each wolf killed, *Records of Town Meetings*, March 30, 1713, p.33.

42. Cronon, *Changes in the Land*, p.142.

43. Cronon, *Changes in the Land*, pp.159-160. Forests have now reclaimed much of the land, as is evident from the many stone walls now found in woods.

V. THE PROPRIETY (pages 31 - 47)

1. The calendar changing the beginning of the new year from March 25 to January 1 was adopted by England in 1752. In the "new style" ten days were also added to all dates before 1700, and eleven days were added for dates after 1700 before the change. When the change took place, September 2, 1752 became September 14, 1752. Dates before March 25 for years before 1752 are shown with both years, but the difference in days has been omitted.

2. Emery stated that there were 58 Old Comers in 1640 who were entitled to the three tracts, *Lands of Old Dartmouth*, p.8.

3. Ricketson, *History of New Bedford*, pp.26-29.

4. See James Sullivan, *The History of Land Titles in Massachusetts*, for background on resolves of the Massachusetts General Court after 1691 to standardize proceedings relative to earlier land grants, pp.122-123.

5. The Proprietors' records stated at the first post-fire meeting in 1726 that "by accident the former books of records of lands...is burnt." Dartmouth Proprietors' *Records of Meetings*, p.2. This statement is repeated in numerous subsequent warrants. The June 7, 1733 warrant specifically mentioned that the consolidated act for 800 acres upland plus 36 acres meadow "was burned with and in the house of the clerk," p.32. Thomas Hathaway was clerk in April 1725 and re-elected in March 1725/6, so it is presumed he was the clerk in December 1725. In an article entitled "Arthur Hathaway and His Immediate Descendants" by Caroline Hathaway (*Old Dartmouth Historical Sketches*, No. 31), there is a picture of Thomas Hathaway's (new) house "built about 1725" and a description that it was "next north of the Capt. Franklyn Howland place," pp.6-14. That location is most likely in Acushnet on the King's Road not far from the head of the river. Other family members lived nearer to Tarkiln Hill Road and Hathaway Road (named for the family).

6. The Parker deed is dated May 3, 1786 and is recorded in Bristol County (S.D.) Registry of Deeds, Old Book 13, Page 364. The grantees were Ebenezer Willis, Esq., Henry Smith, and William Almy, yeoman, Selectmen of the Town of Dartmouth, or their successors. The deed conveyed "18 acres of land to be laid out or set off in the Proprietors' land in the 300 acre division, it being the right I bought of Isaac Tobey which he purchased of Isaac Wood which was in lieu of land formerly laid out to Peleg Slocum." In the Crane *Field Notes* for the same year is the note that the acreage was laid out "at Quonpogue" near the Freetown line, p.719. A way laid out in 1773 in the vicinity mentioned that Parker's house was on the Freetown Road near the town line, *Field Notes*, p.667.

7. Dartmouth Proprietors' *Records of Meetings*, p.9.

8. The number of shares and shareholders reported in Dartmouth histories ranges from 34 to 37; in actuality, there were 34 original shares, 35 with the Mill Share, 36 original Proprietors, and 37 Proprietors, adding the Mill Share as a Proprietary interest.

9. Dartmouth Proprietors' *Records of Meetings*, p.9.

10. Dartmouth Proprietors' *Records of Meetings*, p.52.

11. Dartmouth Proprietors' *Records of Meetings*, p.48.

12. From 1793 to 1800 the Proprietors met at the dwelling house of John Smith, Esq. Their final meeting in 1821 was held at Adam Gifford's in Westport.

13. The General Court passed an act regulating Proprietors' meetings in the Commonwealth in 1712, Sullivan, *The History of Land Titles in Massachusetts*, p.122.

14. Dartmouth Proprietors' *Records of Meetings*, pp.6-7.

15. After New Bedford and Westport separated from Dartmouth in 1787, notice was still posted in all three towns: see for example, return of warrant for 1792, Dartmouth Proprietors' *Records of Meetings*, p.95; for 1794, p.99; and for 1821, in which Fairhaven was included, p.117.

16. Akagi explains the history of the Proprietors' form of organization. It was a voluntary and flexible association in the 17th century but became legalized and rigid in the 18th century through regulatory legislation passed by the General Courts in 1713 and clarified in 1753, *The Town Proprietors of the New England Colonies*, pp.55-56.

17. This was the fifth item in the warrant issued for the July 19, 1726 meeting, Dartmouth Proprietors' *Records of Meetings*, pp.2-5; the vote passed and Benjamin Hammond, surveyor, together with Richard Borden, John Akin, Nathaniel Delano, and William Wood were chosen a committee to effectuate the vote, Dartmouth Proprietors' *Records of Meetings*, pp.6-7. There were copies of 15 meetings between 1709 and 1723 located and gathered into the records between 1726 and 1728, recorded in Dartmouth Proprietors' *Records of Meetings*, pp.10-20.

18. This writer transcribed the 118 faded and disintegrating pages of this book into 70 typewritten pages (single-spaced) for legibility. The original is in the Bristol County (Southern District) Registry of Deeds.. This writer found no substantiation for Akagi's claim that Proprietors' meetings were elaborate social events with liquor, entertainment and travel expense paid for by the Propriety or that the initial meeting was strictly social, with the real business pushed over to adjournment. Akagi, *The Town Proprietors of the New England Colonies*, p.64.

19. Emery cited the date 1682 for the 400 acre division and 1694 for the second 200 acre division, *The Lands of Old Dartmouth*, p.25. There is a 1691 deed from Return Badcock to Thomas Taber for 50 acres, "being a part of the 400 division agreed upon at a meeting of the Proprietors of Dartmouth, March 30, 1682," Bristol County (S.D.) Registry of Deeds, Old Book 1, Page 68.

20. Dartmouth Proprietors' *Records of Meetings*, pp.2-5; the original act may have been passed in November 1709, but because of objections that the vote was passed by "a bare major part of them present," it was ratified and confirmed at a "full meeting" in March 1710. Dartmouth Proprietors' *Records of Meetings*, p.11. Later references to this special act state "bearing date 1710", e.g. Dartmouth Proprietors' *Records of Meetings*, pp.6-7; see also pp.33-34.

21. Dartmouth Proprietors' *Records of Meetings*, p.13 for the 400 acre division. There is no identifiable surviving copy of the act voting the 300 acre division re-entered in the minutes. There is a reference to "this division" in a fragment of a copy of the minutes of the meeting on August 14, 1716, Dartmouth Proprietors' *Records of Meetings*, p.17, and a reference to "this last division" in an undated fragment of a meeting which constituted the last copy re-entered in 1728, after which date meetings are recorded as they occurred.

22. Dartmouth Proprietors' *Records of Meetings*, p.14.

23. The approximately acreage of the area in the township was 106,000 acres.

24. Dartmouth Proprietors' *Records of Meetings*, May 12, 1713, p.15.

25. Dartmouth Proprietors' *Records of Meetings*, May 12, 1713, pp.12-13.

26. Dartmouth Proprietors' *Records of Meetings*, March 14, 1714, p.16.

27. The reasons why rest on speculation, but the result clearly was confusion.

28. Dartmouth Proprietors' *Records of Meetings*, p.13.

29. Dartmouth Proprietors' *Records of Meetings*, p.14.

30. Dartmouth Proprietors' *Records of Meetings*, vote passed Jan. 5, 1713/4, p.14.

31. In the Proprietors' *Books of Records*, there are 552 pages of returns of survey in *Book No. 1*, 180 returns in *Book No. 2*, and 146 returns in *Book No. 3*. Averaging at least one per page, the total number undoubtedly exceeds 875.

32. The return of survey for Abraham Tucker's homestead is recorded in Proprietors' *Books of Records No. 2* at page 71.

33. Samuel Hix's meadow was surveyed in June 1713 and appears in Crane's *Field Notes* on page 7 "... contain by measure 13 acres 15 rods and lies for so much — bh." The "bh" most probably stood for Benjamin Hammond, who was assisting Crane with the surveys. Hix's homestead was near land owned by Samuel Hammond, Hunt and Ward but is otherwise not identified as to location. Other meadow was laid out to Hix on "Mirry Necke" (*Field Notes*, p.507 and p.523) and with John and William Spooner (p.259).

34. Philip Taber's farm was surveyed June 1712 (*Field Notes*, pp.174-175).

35. This other land of Taber was surveyed August 1718 (*Field Notes*, p.575) and qualified for 162 acres 50 rods. Lawton's homestead was surveyed October 1711 (*Field Notes*, p.72).

36. For examples of layouts in the 800, see pages in Proprietors' *Books of Records No. 1*: 1-7, 9, 10, 15, 296, 517; *No. 2*: 1, 73, 78; and *No. 3*: 81. For the meadows, Proprietors' *Books of Records No. 1*: 8, 9, 11, 12, 13, 286, 337, 515, 552. For the 400, Proprietors' *Books of Records No. 1*: 14, 16, 17, 336, 417; and *No. 2*: 168; No. 3: 83, 88. For the 300, Proprietors' *Books of Records No. 1*: 14, 17, 276, 277, 376; and *No. 2*: 74, 163; No. 3: 80, 87. For the cedar swamp, Proprietors' *Books of Records No. 1*: 13, 297; and *No. 2*: 70, 73, 162.

37. See Introduction to Crane's *Field Notes*, p.xiii-xvi. Elisha Leonard made some plot plans based on the field notes. These are in the possession of the New Bedford Free Public Library.

38. The Proprietors' *Books of Records, No. 1*, pp.1-16. The returns of survey are dated 1710 to 1715. There were about five men named Peleg Slocum who lived in the town, but these returns were laid out within a five-year period and all brought in for recording in January 1728, so this is undoubtedly the same man who gave the six acres for the Apponegansett Meeting House in 1699, out of a 40-acre tract bought from Hugh Mosher in 1698, part of the original Stephen Tracy (Treasee or Trasear) share. Outside Dartmouth, Peleg Slocum owned Cuttyhunk Island and at one time maintained a sheep ranch there.

39. Deed dated Jan. 30, 1693, recorded in Bristol County (S.D.) Registry of Deeds, Old Book 1, Page 8. In another example, in 1681 George Sisson of Dartmouth sold all of his 1/8 share to James Tripp of Portsmouth, by deed recorded in said Registry, Old Book 1, Pages 204-205. These were common transactions.

40. Deed recorded in said Registry, Old Book 1, Pages 10-12.

41. Deed dated September 22, 1688, recorded in said Registry, Old Book 1, Page 3.

42. Dartmouth Proprietors' *Records of Meetings*, warrant December 22, 1733, pp.33-34.

43. There are over a dozen volumes between 1687 and 1800 with approximately 500 pages in each, averaging about one legal instrument per page. The great majority are deeds for Dartmouth land transactions. These volumes also contain the land records for Tiverton, but there are relatively few because Tiverton was much smaller.

44. *Our County and Its People*, p.9. None of the original purchasers settled on their lots.

45. Plymouth Colony Records, *Judicial Acts*, pp.283-284 for the first suit, pp.292-293 for the second, pp.295-296 for the third. These are all mentioned in Emery, *The Lands of Old Dartmouth*, pp.25-28. For the fourth suit, Emery also reported that in 1930 there were 30 court papers in existence (Supreme Court, Old Files, Boston, No. 3334) of which 26 were subpoenas to Proprietor defendants, p. 28. These papers may now be in the new Mass. State Archives Building.

46. Emery, *The Lands of Old Dartmouth*, pp.29-30.

47. Deed dated November 13, 1694, recorded in Bristol County (S.D.) Registry of Deeds, Old Book 1, Pages 16-19, a typed copy of which appears as Appendix 6. Although not included in the confirmation, the titles of the Allens, Soules, and Wood were apparently unimpaired.

48. Dartmouth *Land Records*, Vol. 1, p.4; claims are listed pp.2-37; copies from Proprietors' *Books of Records, No. 4*, pp.2-29; Zachariah Allen apparently ended up with part of this share because William Earl, Jr., Ralph Allen and Edward Wing later claim part of the William Bradford share, each of them by deed from Zachariah Allen dated 1711/2, Dartmouth *Land Records*, Vol. 1, pp.13-14.

49. Plymouth Colony Records, *Judicial Acts*, pp.242-243.

50. Plymouth Colony Records, *Judicial Acts*, pp.247-248.

51. Plymouth Colony Records, *Court Orders*, pp.95-96.

52. Plymouth Colony Records, *Court Orders*, pp.96-97.

53. Plymouth Colony Records, *Court Orders*, p.147.

54. Plymouth Colony Records, *Court Orders*, p.267. There is no record under Bradford of transfer out from 1691 to 1775. It must have passed by his Will to someone with another name who later sold to Slocum.

55. Dartmouth Proprietors' *Records of Meetings*, November 4, 1709, p.10.

56. Byfield was a strange choice because as a Proprietor in Bristol, Rhode Island, he had a reputation for being an indiscriminate litigator.

57. Dartmouth Proprietors' *Records of Meetings*, meeting held last Friday in March 1710 and by adjournment to third Tuesday in June, p.11.

58. See Alexander McL. Goodspeed, "Benjamin Crane and Old Dartmouth Surveys," an address given before the Old Dartmouth Historical Society on December 15, 1904, which serves as the introduction to Crane's *Field Notes*, especially page x and pages xiii-xv.

59. Dartmouth Proprietors' *Records of Meetings*, p.17.

60. Goodspeed, Introduction, *Field Notes*, p.xi.

61. Dartmouth Proprietors' *Records of Meetings*, p.19.

62. Dartmouth Proprietors' *Records*. The appointment was made at the meeting held June 23, 1767, p.77. Smith apparently did not start work until 1768.

63. Goodspeed stated that there were at least nine surveyors, of whom the earliest known by name was John Mumford. Introduction, *Field Notes*, p.viii and p.xiii.

64. Dartmouth Proprietors' *Records of Meetings*, warrant, pp.2-5 and minutes of meeting held July 19, 1726, pp.6-7.

65. The protest was entered at the end of the minutes of the July 19, 1726 meeting, Dartmouth Proprietors' *Records of Meetings*, p.7.

66. Dartmouth Proprietors' *Records of Meetings*, warrant October 14, 1726, pp.8-9.

67. Dartmouth Proprietors' *Records of Meetings*, meeting held first Tuesday in November 1726, p.9.

68. Dartmouth Proprietors' *Records of Meetings*, April 23, 1728, p.23.

69. Dartmouth Proprietors' *Records of Meetings*, December 3, 1728, p.25.

70. Dartmouth Proprietors' *Records of Meetings*, March 30, 1731, p.31.

71. While the Proprietors' records before 1725 have not survived, we have the town records, which support this conclusion by their omission of land matters.

VI. HIGHWAYS, BY-WAYS AND WATERING PLACES (pages 48 - 55)

1. For Taunton River development in the colonial period, see Massachusetts Historical Commission, *Historic and Archaeological Resources of Southeastern Massachusetts*, p.65.

2.   Massachusetts Historical Commission, *Historic and Archaeological Resources of Southeastern Massachusetts*, p.51.

3. Russell, *Indian New England*, pp.199-201. See map at the beginning of Chapter II.

4. Massachusetts Historical Commission, *Historic and Archaeological Resources of Southeastern Massachusetts*, p.36.

5. Massachusetts Historical Commission, *Historic and Archaeological Resources of Southeastern Massachusetts*, p.51.

6. Massachusetts Historical Commission, *Historic and Archaeological Resources of Southeastern Massachusetts*, Map 5 (1620-1675), following p.51; Map 8 (1675-1775), following p.67.

7. Town of Dartmouth, *Records of Town Meetings*; the usual vote was for an additional two shillings per day over the stipend allowed by law.

8. *Records of Town Meetings*, October 20, 1738, pp.146-147.

9. *Records of Town Meetings*, February 28, 1738/9, pp.153-155.

10. *Records of Town Meetings*, March 30, 1741, pp.179-180.

11. *Records of Town Meetings*, August 11, 1741, p.184.

12. *Records of Town Meetings*, December 12, 1746, pp.250-252.

13. *Records of Town Meetings*, February 4, 1746/7, p.254; April 10, 1747, p.261; June 2, 1747, p.264.

14. *Records of Town Meetings*, June 1, 1683 and September 24, 1684, p.4.

15. *Records of Town Meetings*, December 10, 1684, p.5.

16. Ellis, p.27-28. The reconstructed foundation of the Russell Garrison can be seen at the foot of Lucy Street in South Dartmouth. The other two garrisons used during King Philip's War were the Cooke garrison in Fairhaven and Palmer's Island in New Bedford Harbor. While the legend lives that King Philip's wife and son were marched through Dartmouth on their way to slavery in the Barbados, Travers presents evidence that leads to the conclusion that they were taken from their capture on the Taunton River through Bridgewater to Plymouth, *The Wampanoag Indian Federation*, p.134.

17. This British naval map first appeared in "The Atlantic Nepture." It was reprinted by permission in The Standard Times Bicentennial Issue (New Bedford, MA), July 4, 1976.

18. *Records of Town Meetings*, May 29, 1685, pp.5-6.

19. *Records of Town Meetings*, November 26, 1722, p.47. Jabez Barker protested.

20. Dartmouth Proprietors' Records, March 28, 1717, p.18.

21. *Records of the Town of Dartmouth: Highways, etc.*, pp.5-14.

22. *Records of the Town of Dartmouth: Highways, etc.*, p.14.

23. *Records of Town Meetings*, April 1, 1706, pp.25-26.

24. *Records of the Town of Dartmouth: Highways, etc.*, p.18.

25. *Records of Town Meetings*, March 30, 1708, p.27; layout recorded in *Records of the Town of Dartmouth: Highways, etc.*, p.29.

26. *Records of the Town of Dartmouth: Highways, etc.*, November 8, 1708, pp.30-32.

27. *Records of the Town of Dartmouth: Highways, etc.*, p.33.

28. *Records of the Town of Dartmouth: Highways, etc.*, March 9, 1705/6, pp.15-16.

29. *Records of the Town of Dartmouth: Highways, etc.*, 1705/6, p.20.

30. *Records of the Town of Dartmouth: Highways, etc.*, pp.21-22. Christopher Gifford was a likely candidate for one of the complainers.

31. *Records of the Town of Dartmouth: Highways, etc.*, pp.22-24.

32. By statute, the town has the eminent domain right to take private land for public ways.

VII. TOWN AFFAIRS (pages 56 - 62)

1. In a warrant for the town meeting dated March 18, 1734/5, there was an item to petition the General Court "for a grant of a tract of the unappropriated lands for this town." There is no vote in the meeting held March 29, 1735, for which the warrant was issued. *Records of Town Meetings*, p.114. There is also no record of any such transfer in the Registry of Deeds indices.

2. U.S. Government Dept. of Commerce and Labor, Bureau of the Census, *Heads of Families of the First Census of the United States Taken in the Year 1790: Massachusetts*, (Washington, DC: Government Printing Office, 1908). For Dartmouth, pp.42-42; for New Bedford, pp.47-49; and for Westport, pp.58-59.

3. Figures supplied by town and city officials in 1987. The endless border shifts have been ignored because they were not significant enough to challenge these conclusions. Fairhaven separated from New Bedford in 1812, and Acushnet from Fairhaven in 1860.

4. *Records of Town Meetings*, February 4, 1685, p.6.

5. *Records of Town Meetings*, December 21, 1694, pp.11-12.

6. *Records of Town Meetings*, January 4, 1705/6, p.24.

7. *Records of Town Meetings*, November 26, 1722, pp.46-47.

8. *Records of Town Meetings*, March 28, 1723, p.48.

9. *Records of Town Meetings*, September 22, 1730, p.84.

10. *Records of Town Meetings*, September 22, 1747, pp.265-267.

11. *Records of Town Meetings*, p.177.

12. *Records of Town Meetings*, warrant September 10, 1751, vote September 26, 1751, pp.309-310.

13. *Records of Town Meetings*, June 4, 1783, pp.574-575.

14. *Records of Town Meetings*, April 17, 1702, p.19.

15. *Records of Town Meetings*, p.216.

16. *Records of Town Meetings*, p.607. At the first meeting in 1674, this fine was set at one shilling, six pence, p.1.

17. *Records of Town Meetings*, for a specimen warrant, see March 7, 1748/9. pp.278-279.

18. *Records of Town Meetings*, warrant May 1724 for meeting to elect a representative to the General Court, p.49.

19. Bettye Hobbs Pruitt, ed. *The Massachusetts Tax Valuation List of 1771*, (Boston: G.K. Hall & Co., 1978) for Appendix 10 and U.S. Government, *First Census of the U.S.* for Appendix 11.

20. For the history and placement of the boundary markers, see Emery Woodward, Charles C. Doten, and George E. Smith, Commissioners, *Atlas of the Boundary Lines of the Cities of Fall River and New Bedford and the Towns of Acushnet, Berkley, Dartmouth, Dighton, Fairhaven, Freetown, Somerset, Swansea, and Westport* (Mass. Harbor and Land Commission, 1904). Rough split granite monuments marked "D" for Dartmouth on the appropriate side now mark most of the boundary lines of the current town. The Dartmouth-Rochester agreement is recorded in Bristol County (S.D.) Registry of Deeds, Old Book 1, Page 67. A report of a 1736 perambulation of the Dartmouth-Little Compton line is included in *Records of Town Meetings*, pp.143-144.

21. *Records of Town Meetings*, August 13, 1739, p.157.

22. *Records of Town Meetings*, April 18, 1740, p.167. The selectmen accused of the "illegal vote" were Capt. Nathaniel Soule, Holder Slocum and Benjamin Allen.

23. *Records of Town Meetings*, February 25, 1741, pp.191-192.

24. *Records of Town Meetings*, September 26, 1751, pp.309-310.

VIII. THE DECLINE OF THE PROPRIETY (pages 63 - 70)

1. Dartmouth Proprietors' *Records of Meetings*, p.39.

2. Dartmouth Proprietors' *Records of Meetings*, p.61.

3. Dartmouth Proprietors' *Records of Meetings*, pp.33-34.

4. Dartmouth Proprietors' *Records of Meetings*, January 8, 1733/4, p.35. The plots were never brought back. They remain lost to this day.

5. Dartmouth Proprietors' *Records of Meetings*, p.28, p.30.

6. Dartmouth Proprietors' *Records of Meetings*, p.37, p.47.

7. Dartmouth Proprietors' *Records of Meetings*, warrant pp.40-44, vote September 8, 1735, p.45.

8. *Field Notes*, pages 162, 163, 164, 165, 218, 226, 238, 246, 487.

9. Deed recorded in 1734, Bristol County (S.D.) Registry of Deeds, Old Book 23, Page 181.

10. Deed recorded in said Registry, Old Book 4, Page 35.

11. Deed recorded in said Registry, Old Book 9, Page 313.

12. Deed recorded in said Registry, Old Book 2, Page 116.

13. True copies of the Taunton Records are recorded for the convenience of the public in the "Old Books" (the books in 1838 start again with Book 1) at the New Bedford Registry, being the Southern District of Bristol County (cited "Bristol County (S.D.) Registry of Deeds"), formed in the 1830's. Therefore, the deed is recorded in said Registry in Old Book 5, Page 359.

14. Akagi, *The Town Proprietors of the New England Colonies*, p.63 and p.77.

15. Dartmouth Proprietors' *Records of Meetings*, pp.57-58.

16. Dartmouth Proprietors' *Records of Meetings*, p.66, p.70 and p.73.

17. Dartmouth Proprietors' *Records of Meetings*, pp.75-77.

18. Dartmouth Proprietors' *Records of Meetings*, pp.82-83.

19. Dartmouth Proprietors' *Records of Meetings*, p.88.

20. Instruments recorded in said Registry in Old Book 9, pp.484-486.

21. Instruments recorded in said Registry in Old Book 4, pp.349-350.

22. Instruments recorded in said Registry in Old Book 9, pp.397-399.

23. Dartmouth Proprietors' *Records of Meetings*, p.64, p.67.

24. Dartmouth Proprietors' *Records of Meetings*, p.71.

25. Dartmouth Proprietors' *Records of Meetings*, p.76.

26. Dartmouth Proprietors' *Records of Meetings*, p.78, p.80.

27. Dartmouth Proprietors' *Records of Meetings*, p.83.

28. Dartmouth Proprietors' *Records of Meetings*, p.90.

29. Dartmouth Proprietors' *Records of Meetings*, p.103.

30. Dartmouth Proprietors' *Records of Meetings*, p.111.

31. Dartmouth Proprietors' *Records of Meetings*, p.117.

IX. CONCLUSION (pages 71 - 74)

1. Adams v. Frothingham, 3 Mass., 360 (1807) quoted in Akagi, *The Town Proprietors of the New England Colonies*, p.82.

2. Akagi, *The Town Proprietors of the New England Colonies*, p.82.

XI. BIBLIOGRAPHY

Manuscripts, Non-printed Sources and Special Collections

Bristol County (Southern District) Registry of Deeds, New Bedford, Mass. Grantor and Grantee indices. Copies of Recorded deeds and other land records.

Carey, Ann. T. and Frederick V. Gifun. *Land Use in Dartmouth: Historical Trends and Present Options.* Dartmouth, MA: S.M.U., 1976.

Dartmouth Proprietors. *Books of Records and Records of Meeting.* 5 vols., n.p., n.d.

Dartmouth Proprietors. *Land Records.* New Bedford, MA: City of New Bedford, 2 vols., n.p., 1867.

Dartmouth, Town of. *Records of Town Meetings: 1674-1779.* New Bedford, MA: City of New Bedford, 1888.

Dartmouth, Town of. *Record of the Layout of Highways, Driftways, & Town Landings in the Township of Dartmouth, 1705-1786.* New Bedford, MA: City of New Bedford, 1888.

Emery, William M. *The Lands of Old Dartmouth.* n.p., 1930.

Leonard, Elisha B. *Family Histories.* 3 vols. [red set], n.p., 1903.

Leonard, Elisha B. Layouts of Crane Surveys [several loose sheets], n.p., n.d.

Worth, Henry B. Papers.

Worth, Henry B. *Some Old Burial Grounds in New Bedford and Vicinity.* n.p., 1917.

Printed Sources

Archer, Gabriel and Brereton, John. *The Gosnold Discoveries . . . in the North Part of Virginia, 1602.* Lincoln A. Dexter, ed. Brookfield, MA: Lincoln A. Dexter, 1982.

Barber, John Warner. *Historical Collections: Being a General Collection of Interesting Facts, Traditions, Biographical Sketches, Anecdotes, Etc. Relating to the History and Antiquities of Every Town in Massachusetts with Geographical Descriptions.* Worcester, MA: Dorr, Howland & Co., 1839.

Bradford, William. *Of Plymouth Plantation, 1620-1647.* Samuel Eliot Morison, ed. New York: Alfred A. Knopf, 1952.

Comiskey, Kathleen Ryan. *Secrets of Old Dartmouth.* New Bedford, MA: By Author, 1976.

Crane, Benjamin, Benjamin Hammond and Samuel Smith. *The Field Notes of Benjamin Crane, Benjamin Hammond and Samuel Smith.* New Bedford, MA: New Bedford Free Public Library, 1910.

Ellis, Leonard Bolles. *History of New Bedford and Its Vicinity:1602-1892*, n.d.

Heath, Dwight B., ed. *Mourt's Relation: A Journal of the Pilgrims at Plymouth.* Cambridge, MA: Applewood Books, 1986.

Howe, Henry F. *Salt Rivers of the Massachusetts Shore.* New York: Rinehart & Co., Inc., 1951.

Howland, Franklyn, *Souvenir of the Bi-Centennial of the Dartmouth Monthly Meeting of the Society of Friends.* Massachusetts: By Author, 1899.

Hurd, Duane Hamilton, ed. *History of Bristol County, Massachusetts, with Biographical Sketches of Its Prominent Men.* Philadelphia: J.W. Lewis and Co., 1883.

Hutt, Frank Walcott. *A History of Bristol County, Massachusetts.* New York: Lewis Historical Publishing Co., Inc., 2 vols., 1924.

MacDonald, William. *Select Charters and Other Documents Illustrative of American History, 1606-1775.* New York: The MacMillan Company, 1899.

Massachusetts Historical Commission. *Historic and Archaeological Resources of Southeastern Massachusetts.* Boston: By Author, June 1982.

"The Mayflower Descendant." Boston: Society of Mayflower Descendants.

Old Dartmouth Historical Society. *New Bedford and Old Dartmouth.* New Bedford, MA: Old Dartmouth Historical Society, 1975.

Old Dartmouth Historical Society. *The Old Dartmouth Historical Sketches.* New Bedford, MA: Old Dartmouth Historical Society, Nos. 1-74.

Our County and Its People: A Descriptive and Biographical Record of Bristol County, Massachusetts. Prepared and Published under the Auspices of The Fall River News and The Taunton Gazette with the Assistance of Hon. Alanson Borden of New Bedford. Boston: The Boston History Company, 1899.

Pease, Zephamiah W., ed. *History of New Bedford.* New York: The Lewis Historical Publishing Co., 1918.

Pruitt, Bettye Hobbs, ed. *The Massachusetts Tax Valuation List of 1771.* Boston: G.K. Hall & Co., 1978.

Ricketson, Daniel. *History of New Bedford.* New Bedford: By Author, 1858.

Ricketson, Daniel. *New Bedford of the Past.* Anna and Walton Ricketson, eds. Boston: Houghton, Mifflin and Company, 1903.

Sherman, Ruth Ann Wilder, ed. *Plymouth Colony Probate Guide.* Warwick, RI: Plymouth Colony Research Group, Publication No. 2, 1983.

Shurtleff, Nathaniel B., and Pulsifer, David, eds. *Records of the Colony of New Plymouth in New England.* 12 Vols. Boston, 1855-1861.

Travers, Milton A. *The Wampanoag Indian Federation of the Algonquin Nation.* Boston: The Christopher Publishing House, rev. ed., 1961.

U.S. Government Dept. of Commerce and Labor, Bureau of the Census. S.N.D. North, Director. *Heads of Families at the First Census of the United States Taken in the Year 1790: Massachusetts.* Washington, DC: Government Printing Office, 1908.

Vital Records of Dartmouth, Massachusetts, to the Year 1850. Boston: New England Historic Genealogical Society. 3 Vols. 1929.

Treatises

Akagi, Roy Hidemichi. *The Town Proprietors of the New England Colonies: A Study of their Development, Organization, Activities and Controversies, 1620-1770.* Gloucester, MA: Peter Smith, 1924. 1963 reprint.

Cronon, William. *Changes in the Land: Indians, Colonists, and the Ecology of New England.* New York: Hill and Wang, 1983.

Deetz, James. *In Small Things Forgotten: The Archeology of Early American Life.* Garden City, NY: Anchor Books, 1977.

Geldart, W.M. *Elements of English Law.* New York: Henry Holt and Company, n.d.

Harris, Marshall. *Origin of the Land Tenure System in the United States.* Westport, CT: Greenwood Press Publishers, 1953. 1970 reprint.

Jennings, Francis. *The Invasion of America: Indians, Colonialism, and the Cant of Conquest.* New York: W.W. Norton & Company, Inc., 1976.

Moynihan, Cornelius J. *Introduction to the Law of Real Property: An Historical Background of the Common Law of Real Property and its Modern Application.* St. Paul, MN: West Publishing Co., 1962.

New England Yearly Meeting of Friends. *Faith and Practice.* Worcester, MA: New England Yearly Meeting of Friends, 1985 [Book of Discipline].

Russell, Howard S. *Indian New England Before the Mayflower.* Hanover, NH: University Press of New England, 1980.

Russell, Howard S. *A Long Deep Furrow: Three Centuries of Farming in New England.* Hanover, NH: University Press of New England, 1982.

Sakolski, Aaron M. *Land Tenure and Land Taxation in America.* New York: Robert Scholkenbach Foundation, Inc., 1957.

Stilgoe, John R. *Common Landscape of America, 1580 to 1845.* New Haven, CT: Yale University Press, 1982.

Sullivan, James. *The History of Land Titles in Massachusetts.* Boston: I. Thomas and E.T. Andrews, 1801.

Tracey, John Clayton. *Surveying: Theory and Practice.* New York: John Wiley & Sons, Inc. 1947.

Newspapers

The Standard-Times Bicentennial Issue. New Bedford, MA, July 4, 1976.

Atlases and Maps

Beers, Frederick W. *Atlas of Bristol County, Massachusetts*. New York: F.W. Beers & Co., 1871.

Dexter, Lincoln A., ed. *Maps of Early Massachusetts: Pre-History Through the Seventeenth Century*. Brookfield, MA: By Author, Rev. Ed. 1984.

Woodward, Emery; Doten, Charles C.; and Smith, George E., Bristol County Commissioners. *Atlas of the Boundary Lines of the Cities of Fall River and New Bedford and the Towns of Acushnet, Berkley, Dartmouth, Dighton, Fairhaven, Freetown, Somerset, Swansea, and Westport*. Mass. Harbor and Land Commission, 1904.

APPENDIX

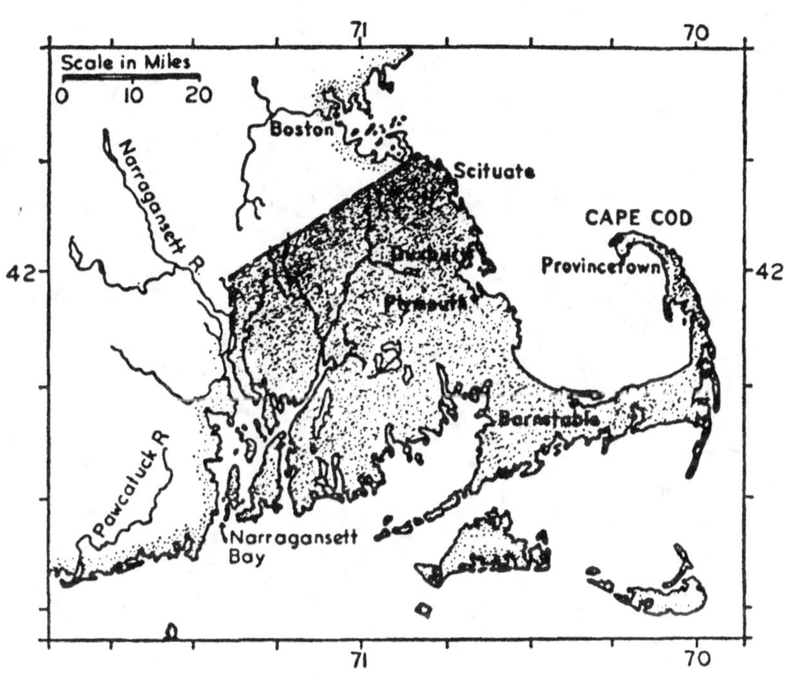

THE WARWICK PATENT *

January 1629/30

*Marshall Harris, Origin of the Land Tenure System in the United
States (Westport, CT: Greenwood Press Publishers, 1970 reprint,
1953), p.105.

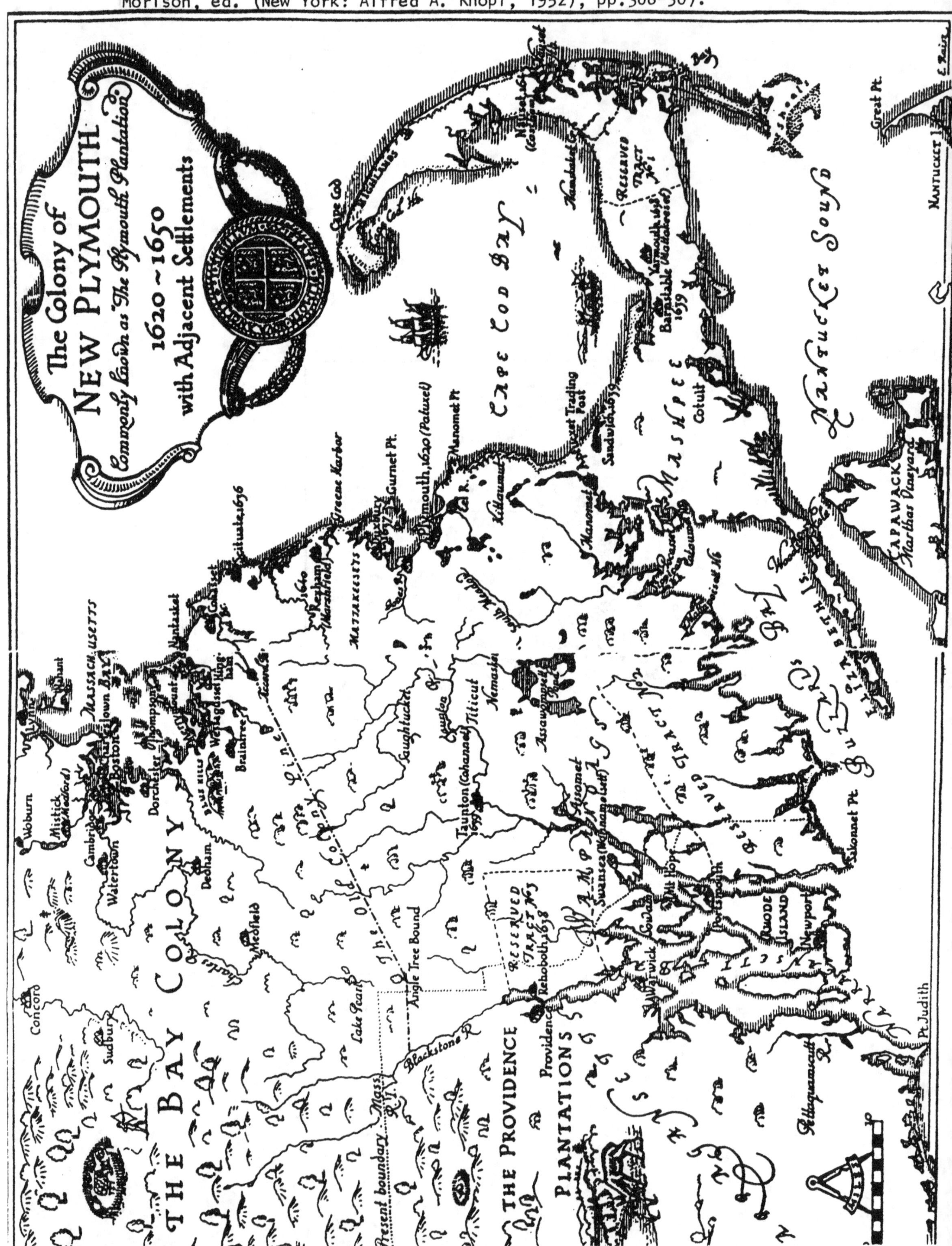
The Colony of
NEW PLYMOUTH
Commonly known as The Plymouth Plantation
1620 ~ 1650
with Adjacent Settlements
Cape Cod Bay
NANTUCKET SOUND
CAPE COD
MASSACHUSETTS BAY
THE BAY COLONY
THE PROVIDENCE PLANTATIONS
MASSACHUSETTS
MATTAKEESE
MASHPEE
BUZZARDS BAY
RHODE ISLAND
CAPAWACK
Martha's Vineyard
Nantucket I.
Great Pt.
Plymouth, 1620 (Patuxet)
Manomet Pt.
Gurnet Pt.
Green Harbor
Scituake 1636
Barnstable (Mattakeese) 1639
Sandwich 1639
Cotuit
Aptucxet Trading Post
Woburn
Mistick (Medford)
Cambridge
Watertown
Boston
Dorchester
Dedham
Braintree
Weymouth
Wesymouth
Concord
Sudbury
Providence
Warwick
Newport
Pt. Judith
Taunton (Cohannet) Titicut
Saughtucket
Angle Tree Bound
Lake Pearl
Blackstone R.
Rehoboth 1638
Present boundary Mass. R.I.
Swansea (Wannamoiset)
Mt. Hope
Sakonnet Pt.
RESERVE TRACT
RESERVED TRACT N°3
RESERVED TRACT N°5
The Old Colony Line
N

A Deed appointed to be Recorded.

1654
Bradford:
Governor.

New Plymouth November 29th 1652

Know all men by these Presents that I Wasamequin
and Wamsutta my son have sold unto Mr William Bradford, Capt: Standish Thomas Southworth John Winslow
John Cooke and their Associates the Purchasers or old Comers
all the tracts or tract of Land Lying three miles Eastward
from a River called Cushnett, to a Certain harbor called
Acoaksett to a flat Rock on the westward side of the sd
Harbor; and whereas the said Harbor devideth itself into
several branches, the Westermost arm to be the bounds.
and all the tract or tracts of Land from the said Westermost
arm to the said River of Cirishnett three miles Eastward of the same, with all the Profits and Benefits
within the said tract, with the River, Creeks, meadows,
Necks, and Island, that Ly in or before the same, and
from the sea upwards, to Go so high that the English
may not be annoyed by the hunting of the Indians in
any sort of their Cattle, and I Whsamequin and Wamsutta
do Promise to Remove all the Indians within a year
from the date hereof that do Live in the said tract, And
we the sd Wasamequin and Wamsutta have fully Bar-
gained, sold unto the aforesd Mr William Bradford,
Capt Standish Thomas Southworth John Winslow John
Cooke and the Rest of their Associates the Purchasers
or old Comers
To have and to hold for them their Heirs and assigns
forever   And in Consideration hereof we the
above mentioned are to pay to the said Wasamequin and
Wamsutta as followeth;-   thirty yards of Cloth, eight
moose skins, fifteen axes, fifteen hose, fifteen Pair
of breaches, Eight blankets two Kittles, one Cloak,
2 £ in wampum, Eight pair of Stocking Eight pair
of shoes one Iron Pott, and Ten Shillings in another
Commodity; and in Witness whereof we have Inter-
changeably set our hands, the day and year above
written-
In Presence of,   John Winslow,
Jonathan Shaw   John Cooke,
Samuel Eddy

                              Wamsutta xxxx his mark.

The above taken of a copy of a copy from Plymouth
Records by Josiah Coffin Regr

<u>LIST OF PROPRIETORS OF DARTMOUTH IN 1652</u>
Each With One Full Share Except As Noted

ALDEN, John
BARTLETT, Robert
BASSETT, William**
BRADFORD, William
BREWSTER, Sarah* (widow of William)
BROWNE, Peter
BUMPAS, Edward
COLLIER, William*
COOKE, Francis
COOKE, John
CUTBERT, Samuel
DELANO, Philip
DOTEY, Edward
DUNHAM, John Sr.
EATON, Samuel
FAUNCE, John
HICKS, Samuel
HOLMAN, Edward
HOWLAND, John**
HURST, James
JENNEY, Sarah (widow of John)
KEMPTON, Manasses
MORTON, George
MORTON, Thomas
PALMER, William
PRATT, Joshua
SAMPSON, Henry
SHAW, John Sr.
SIMONS, Moses
SOULE, George
SOUTHWORTH, Constant
SOUTHWORTH, Thomas
SPRAGUE, Francis
STANDISH, (Capt.) Myles
TRACY, Stephen
WARREN, Elizabeth(?) (widow of Richard)

 * shared one full share
** shared one full share

This list is a composite prepared from a number of sources
listed in the bibliography.

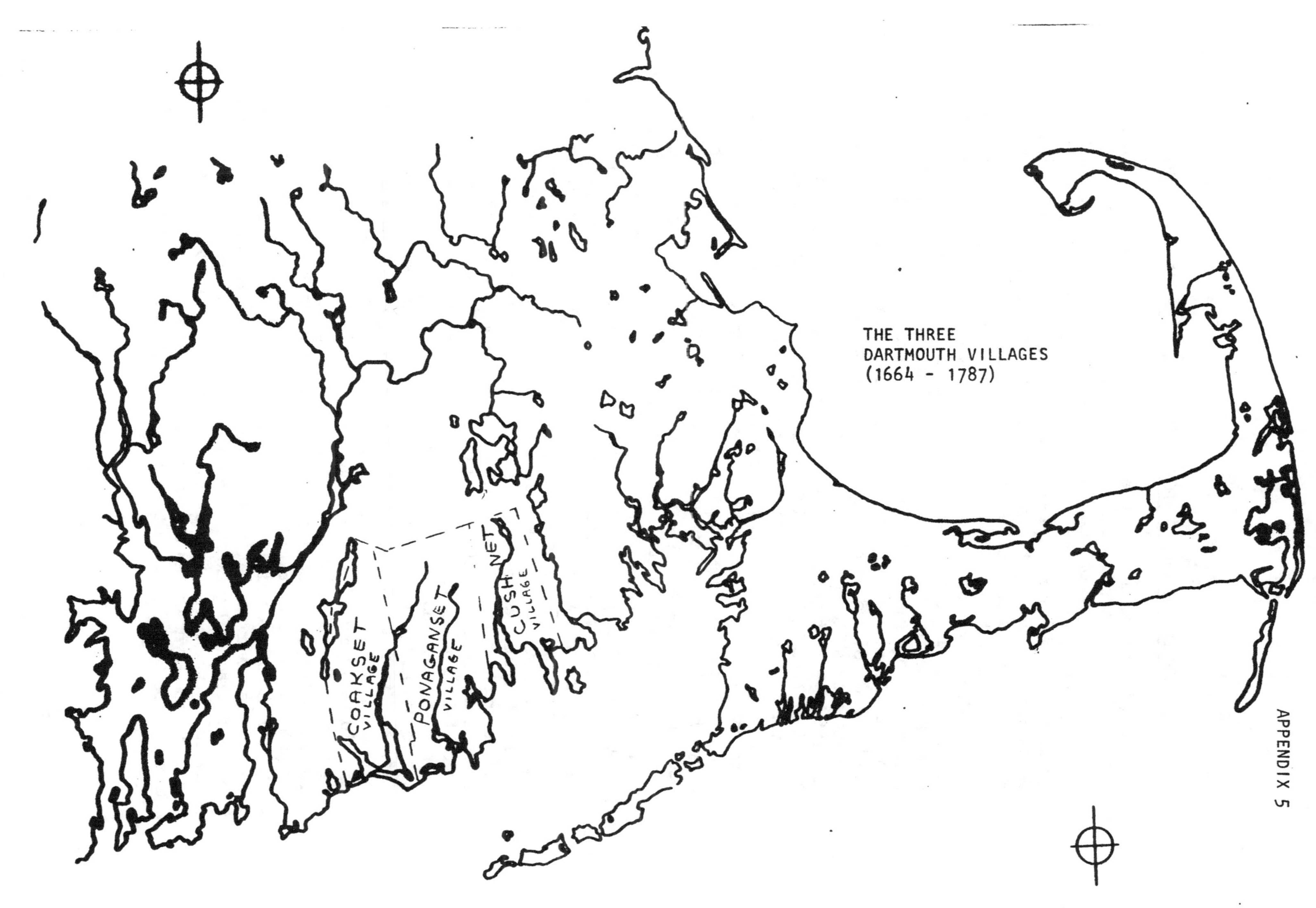

THE THREE
DARTMOUTH VILLAGES
(1664 - 1787)
COAKSET VILLAGE
PONAGANSET VILLAGE
CUSH NET VILLAGE
APPENDIX 5

CONFIRMATORY DEED FROM MAJOR WILLIAM BRADFORD IN 1694

To all unto whom these presents shall Come Greeting, &c. whereas
the Hono^bl ye Councill established at Plimouth in ye County of Devon for
the planting Ruleing ordering and Govering of New England in america By
vertue & authority of letters Patents under the Great Seale of England
from or late Sovereign lord King James the first Bearing Dat[e] at
westminster in the Eighteenth year of his said majesties Reign of
England &c. for & in Consideratio that William Bradford Esq^e & his
asosiats Had at their owne prop^e Cost & Charges planted and Inhabited a
towne caled by the Name of New plimoth in New England afores^d and for
their better Subsistance and encoragment to proceed in so pious a work
espetially tending to the propagation of Religion and the great
encoragment of Trade to his Maj^tie Relmes and Advancement of the
Publique plantation. The Councill by their Patent or Grant under their
Common Seale Signed by the Right Honble Robert Earle of warwicke
President of s^d Councill Bearing Date the Thirteenth Day of January in
the fifth year of the Reigne of our late Sovereigne Lord King Charles
the First Anno Dom^d 1629 Did Give Grant enfeoff assigne and Confirme
unto the same william Bradford his heires associats & assignes forever
All that part of New England in America afforesd and Tract or Tracts of
land that lye within or Between a Certaine Rivolett or Runnlett there
Commonly Called Cohasset alias Conihasset towds the North and the River
Commonly Called Naragansett River toward the South and ye Greate
westerne Ocean toward ye East and between & within a streight line
Directly exstending up into the Main land toward the west from the Mouth
of the said River called Naraganset River to the uttmost bounds or
limmits of a Coutry or place in New England Commonly Called Pocanoket
alias Sawamsett westward And another like Strait line extending it selfe
Directly from the Mouth of the said River Called Cohassett alias
Conihassett toward the west so far up into the Maine land westward as
the uttmost limmitts of the said place or Country Commonly Called
pocanoket alias Sawamsett Doth extend &c: All all lands Rivers waters
Havens Brooks ports fishings and all Heridittaments profitts &
Comodities Sittuate Lyeing being or ariseing wth in or between any of the
said limitts or Bounds Together with all Rights Royalltyes priviledges
Franchisses &c. and thereof was put into quiet & peaceable possession
and Seizen as by the said patent or grant and endorsment thereon
Reference thereunto being had may more fully appeare. And whereas the
said william Bradford his Grants Surrenders or Conveyances of any part
of said Lands and other the premisses to his Declared associats or
assignnees. and also his & their grants to perticular persons and
Townships And amonst others to Severall of the Purchassors and
Propriettors of a certain Tract or Tracts of land formerly Known by the
Names of Accushenah alias Aguset entering in at the wester end of Nakata
and to the River Cookset alias Ackeess and places adjacent -- The Bounds
of which Tract fully extend three Miles to the eastward of the most
easterly part of the River or Bay Accushenah afores^d & so along ye Sea
side to the River Called Cooksett Lyeing on the west side of point
Pirrill and to the most westermost side of any Branch of the afores^d

2

River and Extending eight mile into the woods with all Marshes Meadows
Rivers waters woods & appurtenances thereto belonging Now called & known
by the Name of Dartmouth which Now Seems by some to be Questioned as to
the legall Conveyance For the Better Confirmation whereof Now Know yee
that I william Bradford of New plimouth in ye County of New plimouth Son
& heire to the above Named william Bradford esq^e Dec^d as well in
performance of the true Intent & Meaning of the s^d william Bradford my
father, in & by the said grant And also in Consideration of Twenty five
pounds Silver money Currant in New England to me in hand paid before the
sealeing and Delivery of these presents as also for Divers other good
Causses & Considerations me at this time ESPETIALLY Moveing Have Granted
Remised Released and forever quite Claimed And by these presents for me
& my heires Doe grant Remise Release and forever quite Claime unto
Manasseth Camton Seth Pope John Russell Aurthur hathaway Pelege Slocum
Stephen west James Sisson John Russell Jun^e Abraham Tucker John Tucker
Jonathan Russell Thomas Briggs John Hathaway George Cadman Jacob Mott
Thomas Taber Jonathan Delano Joseph Russell Stephen Pueckham Isace Pope
Eliaser Slocom John Lappam Joseph Ripley Daniel Shearman Mary Davis
Thomas Taber Jun^e Lettice Jenny Samuel Allen Valentine Hudlestone Edmund
Shearman Eliazer Smith Return Badcock Benjamin Howland william Shearman
Ralph Earle Jun^e william Earle son of Ralph Earle John Shearman Saml
Spooner william Spooner Samuel Jenny Mark Jenny John Spooner John
Spooner Jun^e Thomas michell John Tinkam Aron Davis Giles Slocum Joseph
Tripp James Tripp william Macumber Samuel Cornwell Samuel Shearman
Gershom Smith Sam^{ll} Hickes Elizabeth Ricketson Joseph Taber being all
purchassers & Propriettors of the lands above Named and to their heires
& assignes forever to their proper use & behooffe all such Right Estate
Title Interest Posession & Demand whatsoever which I the said william
Bradford ever had Now have or ought to have of in or to all & Singular
the Messuages lands Tenements Grounds Soiles waters Rivers Havens Creeks
Ports ffishings Heradittaments Royallties Mineralls Profitts Priviledges
Commodities whatsoever Scittuat Lyeing & being ariseing hapening or
accrueing or which shall arise hapen or accrue in or within the limmits
& Bounds of said Township of Dartmouth aforesaid Including likewise the
Iland of Nakata before mentioned And also that perticular Moyety in s^d
township granted to my father william Bradford as appeares upon Record
(Excepting & allwayes Reserved out of this my present grant one whole
halfe Share of land in s^d Township & Now being in the Possession of
Increase Allen and also another p^{e}cell of land in said Township Seized
for the Country use from Zachariah Allen for a fine Due from s^d Allen as
appeares upon Record, So that is to say That I the said william Bradford
Nor My heires from henceforth Shall or May have or Claime any Right
title Estat Interest or Demand of in or to the said Premises Nor any of
them but thereof Shall forever hereafter be Barred & Excluded by these
Presents. Know yee farther also that I the s^d william Bradford for the
Considerations & ends afores^d have approved and by these presents Doe
for me My heires Ratify & Confirme unto the said Manasseth Camton Seth
Pope John Russell Arthur hathaway Pelegg Slocum Stephen West and all &
Singuler the propriettors above Named and to their Heires & assignes
forever In their and every of their peaceable & ffull Possesion and
Seizen and to their and every of their heires and assignes forever all &
Singular my Right in the aforesd lands (excepting what is above

excepted) and other Premisses and their & every of their appurtenances
within the said Bounds & limitts or any part or Percell thereof To have
and to hold to the said Manasseth Camton Seth Pope John Russell Arthur
Hathaway Pelege Slocum Stephen west and all & Singuler the propriettors
above Named and to their heires and assignes forever. All that My Right
title estate or Claime to all & every part of the land above said
(except what is above excepted) to be holden off his Matie according to
the Costom of his mann^e of East greenwich in Kent in the Realme of
England in free & Common Soccage and not in Capetie nor by Kn^{ts} Service
free & Cleare of all former Grants titles Sales rents Mortgages Dowries
and all & Singuler encumbrances had made or Done By me william Bradford
my heirs or assignes or any of them heretofore. Moreover I the said
william Bradford for my Self my heires executors & administ^{es} Doe
Covenant and promise to & with the said Manasseth Camton Seth Pope John
Russell Aurthur Hathaway Pelege Slocum Stephen west and the Propriettors
above Named their heires x^t to warrant and Defend the premisses against
all Persons Lawfully Claimeing any title or Interest therein or in any
percell thereof by from or under me or them or any of them Provided the
said Manasseth Camton Seth Pope John Russell Aurthur Hathaway Pelege
Slocum Stephen West and the Propriettors above Mentioned their heires x^t
yeild and paye to our Sovereign Lord the King his heirs and Successors
forever one-fifth part of the Oare of the Gold and Silver and one other
fifth part thereof to the said President and Councill, which shall be
had Possessed & obtained within the limits aforesaid for all Services &
Demands whatsoever as is expressed in said Lett^{es} patents of Grants of
the said Councill. In witness whereof I the said william Bradford have
hereunto sett my hand and Seale this Thirteenth Day of November in the
year of our Lord god 1694 Annoge Regis Gulielme & Maria Anglia Scotice
Galid & Hibernie R & R 6 to.

Signed sealed & Delivered   William Bradford   seale
in the presence of us witnesses

        John wadsworth
        Ichabod wisswalls

william Bradford Comeing Personly before me the Thirteenth Day of
November Did freely acknowledge the above written Deed as his owne Act:
before me
                John wadsworth Justice of Peace 1694

Thus entered and Recorded ffebruary 28th Anno Dom 1695/6 By John Cary
Record^e.

A true copy from Book 1, Pages 365-6-7, of Bristol Co. No. Dist. Land
Records.-
                Attest:-Emma E. Gray, Examiner

Recorded in Bristol County (S.D.) Registry of Deeds, Old Book 1, Pages 16-19.

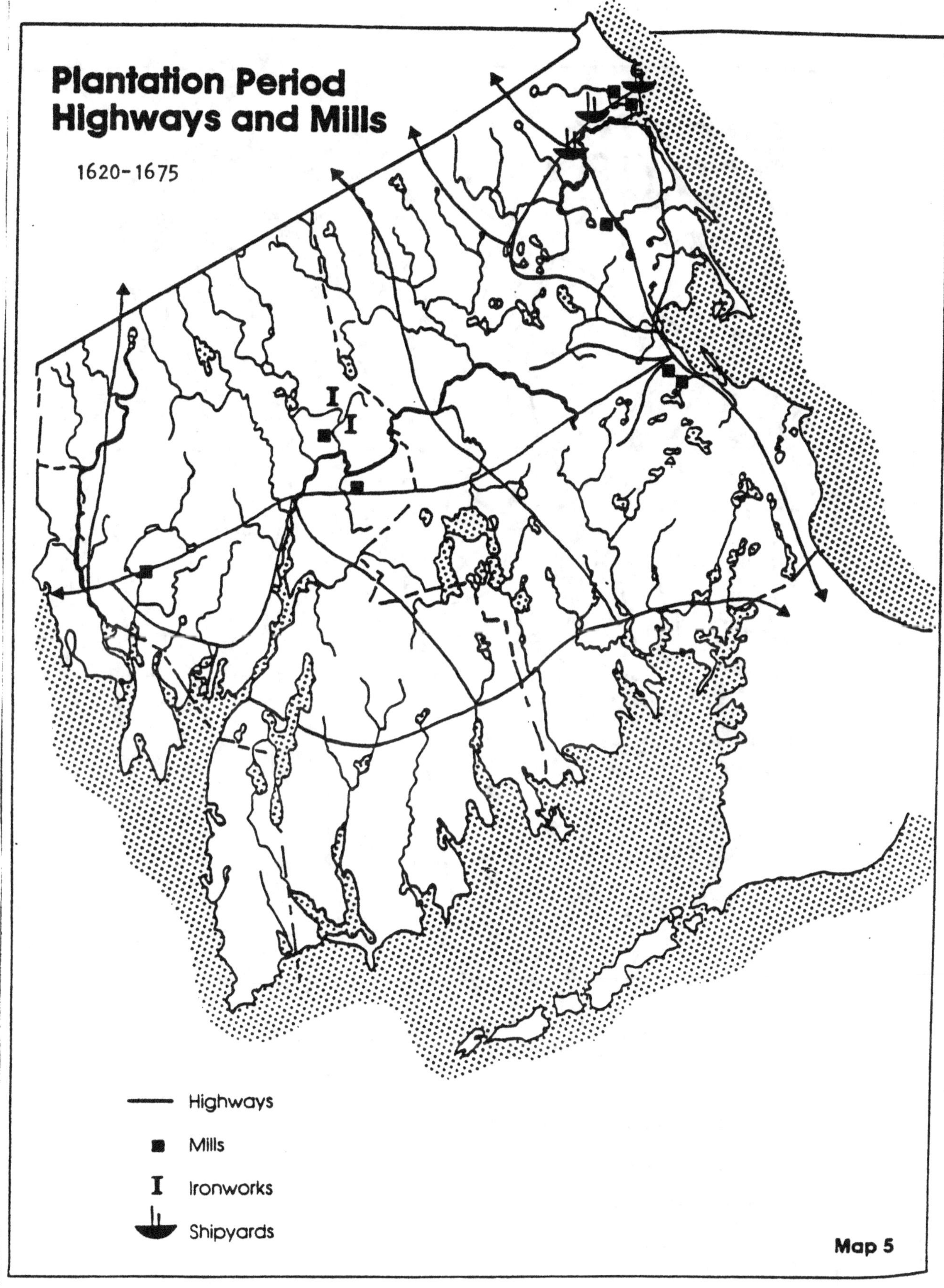

*Massachusetts Historical Commission, Historic and Archaeological Resources of Southeastern Massachusetts, (Boston: By Author, June 1982), following p.51.

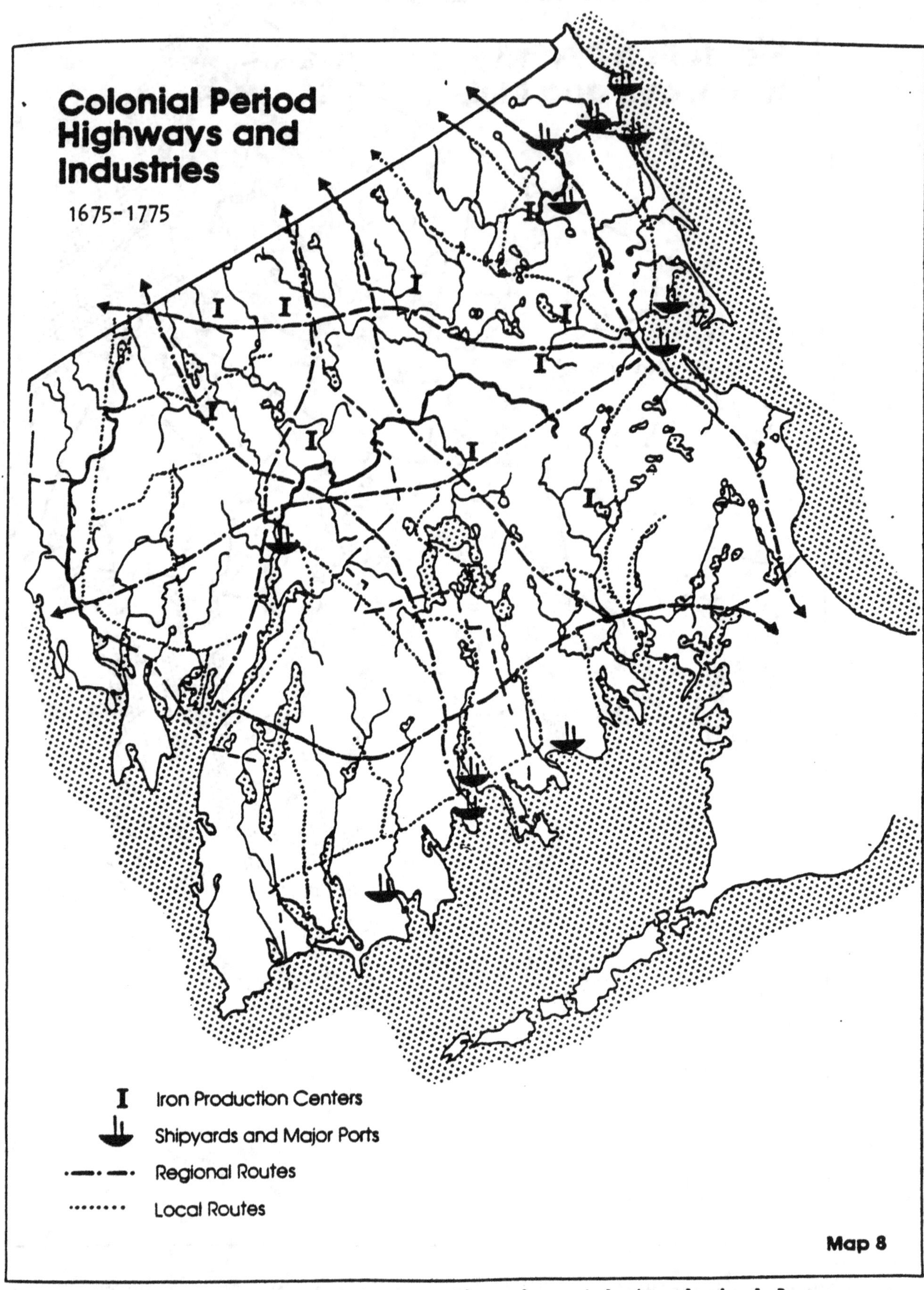

*Massachusetts Historical Commission, <u>Historic and Archaeological Resources of Southeastern Massachusetts</u>, (Boston: By Author, June 1982), following p.67.

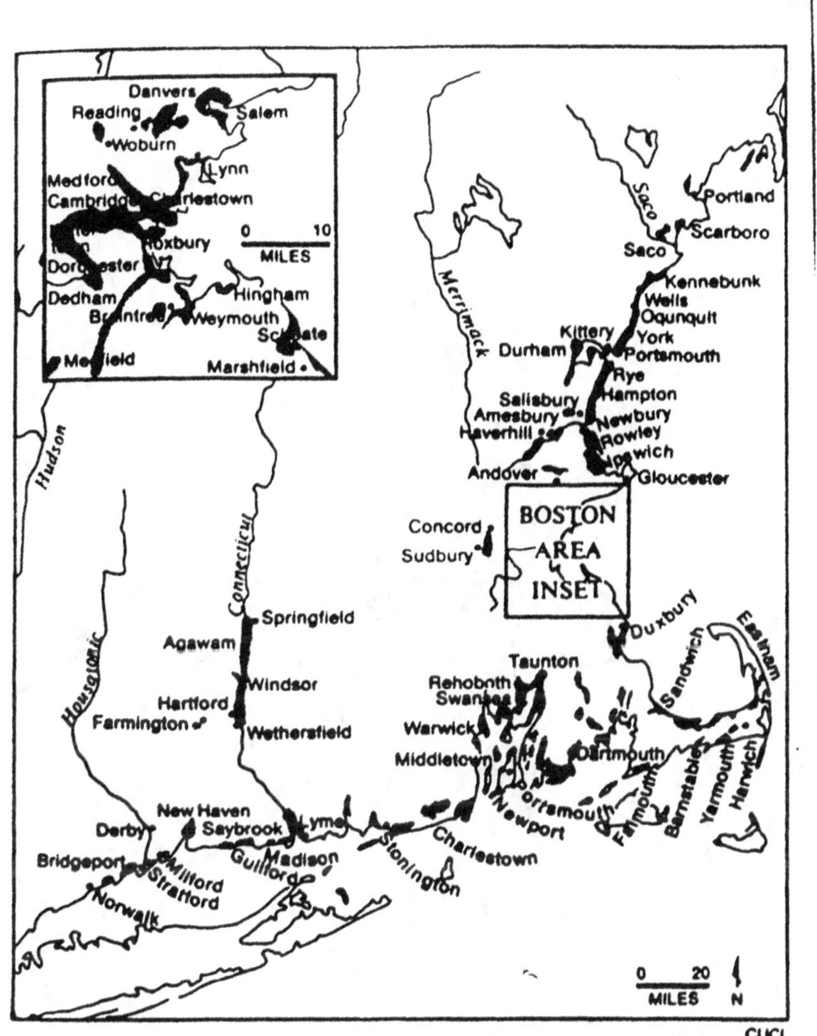

6. This map (based on U.S. Geodetic surveys) illustrates the importance to the English colonists of available feed for their cattle. The site of every town named (all settled by 1650) adjoined natural salt or fresh hay marsh. The marsh offered the prospect that by breeding livestock the village could live and prosper (as all did). *Cartography Laboratory, Clark University.* *

*Howard S. Russell, <u>A Long, Deep Furrow</u>, p.31.

1. British landing in Clark's Cove
2. Sconticut Neck debarkation of portion of British troops
3. Bedford Village where warehouses and docked ships were burned
4. Head-of-the-River where American artillery officer was fatally wounded
5. Fort Phoenix, Fairhaven, evacuated by patriots and burned by the British
6. Padanaram Village, also attacked by British troops
7. Approximate site of Fairhaven naval battle in which Yankee sloop Success recaptured first of two ships retaken from British prize crews

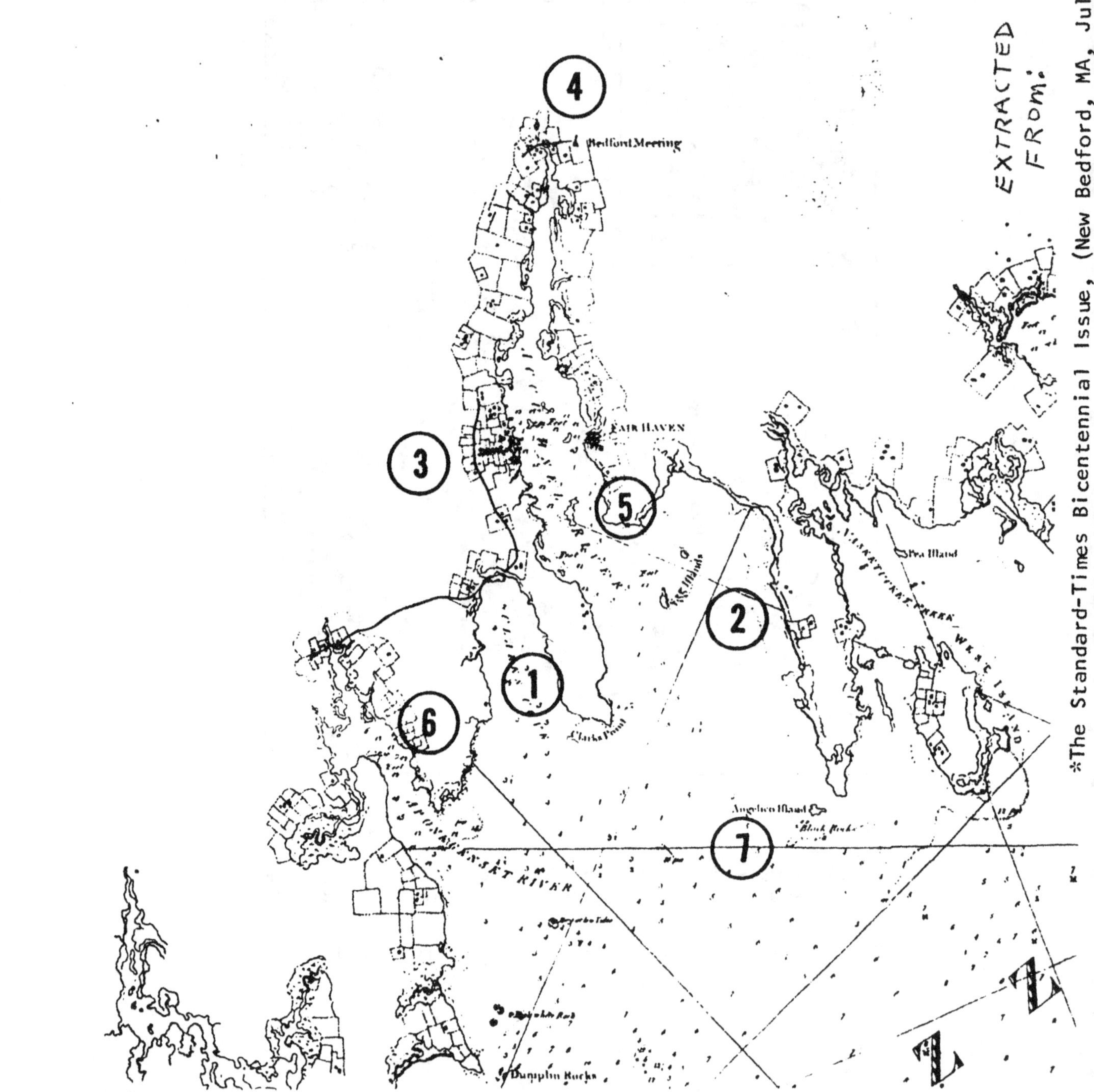

*The Standard-Times Bicentennial Issue, (New Bedford, MA, July 4, 1976), p.23.

EXTRACTED FROM:

ACTION IN THIS AREA — Pictured here is portion of Royal Navy nautical chart of this area made in Revolutionary War era and used by British Navy officers on patrol in area waters. First published in book form in 1781; as "The Atlantic Neptune," this chart and others were republished in 1966 by Barre Publishers of Barre, and is reproduced here by permission.

*Bettye Hobbs Pruitt, ed., The Massachusetts Tax Valuation List of 1771 (Boston: G.K. Hall & Co., 1978)

TOWN ID	INDIVIDUAL ID	NAME	TITLE	STATUS	POLLS RATEABLE	POLLS NOT RATEABLE	HOUSES AND SHOPS ADJOINING	SHOPS ADJOINING	TWN MKS DISTINCTION	TANHOUSES, ETC.	TANHOUSES: TYPE	STILLHOUSES	WAREHOUSES	SUPERFICIAL FEET OF WHARF	MILLS	MILLS: TYPE	IRONWORKS, ETC.	IRONWORKS: TYPE	ANNUAL WORTH £	s	d	SERVANTS FOR LIFE	TONS OF VESSELS	VALUE OF MERCHANDISE £	s	d	VALUE OF FACTORAGE £	s	d
1003	0321	MACUMBER, NATHANIEL																	1	10									
1003	0322	MACUMBER, JOHN																		12									
1003	0323	MIRICK, EBENEZER			2		1.00												10	4									
1003	0324	MIRICK, NATHAN			1		1.00												1										
1003	0325	MIRICK, EBER			1																								
1003	0326	MIRICK, SAMUEL			1																								
1003	0327	NICHOLS, JOHN			1		1.00												1										
1003	0328	NEWHALL, NEHEMIAH			2		1.00												2	10			16						
1003	0329	NEWHALL, NATHAN			1						1.00	3								6									
1003	0330	PAULL, BENJAMIN																		12									
1003	0331	PAULL, JOHN			1		2.00												29			2							
1003	0332	PAULL, EBENEZER			2		1.00												10	18									
1003	0333	PAULL, JOHN II			3		1.00												11	12	6								
1003	0334	PAULL, EBENEZER II			1		1.00												12	3									
1003	0335	PAULL, JOHN III			1		1.00													2									
1003	0336	PHILLIPS, NATHANIEL			1		1.00												8	10									
1003	0337	PHILLIPS, NATHANIEL JR			1		1.00													14									
1003	0338	PHILLIPS, RALPH			2		1.00												2										
1003	0339	PHILLIPS, STEPHEN																											
1003	0340	PHILLIPS, SAMUEL			1																								
1003	0361	POTTER, BENJAMIN			1		1.00													2			2						

TOWN ID	INDIVIDUAL ID	NAME	TITLE	STATUS	POLLS RATEABLE	POLLS NOT RATEABLE	HOUSES AND SHOPS ADJOINING	SHOPS ADJOINING	TWN MKS DISTINCTION	TANHOUSES, ETC.	TANHOUSES: TYPE	STILLHOUSES	WAREHOUSES	SUPERFICIAL FEET OF WHARF	MILLS	MILLS: TYPE	IRONWORKS, ETC.	IRONWORKS: TYPE	ANNUAL WORTH £	s	d	SERVANTS FOR LIFE	TONS OF VESSELS	VALUE OF MERCHANDISE £	s	d	VALUE OF FACTORAGE £	s	d
1004		**DARTMOUTH**																											
1004	0101	ALLEN, NOAH			2		2.00								460					15	10			17						
1004	0102	ALLEN, BENJAMIN			4		3.00				1.00	8			900					31										
1004	0103	ALLEN, FRANCIS			3		4.00													17										
1004	0104	ALLEN, GEORGE + RUFUS			2		1.00													13	10									
1004	0105	ALLEN, WILLIAM			2		1.00													7										
1004	0106	ALLEN, SAMUEL + PHILIP			1	1					1.00	6								7	10									
1004	0107	ALLEN, SILVANUS			4		2.00				1.00									23										
1004	0108	AULDEN, JOHN			1		1.00													3	5			35						
1004	0109	AKIN, JOHN			1															7				7						
1004	0110	ADAMS, WALLEY			1		1.00				1.00									7	10									
1004	0111	ANDREWS, WILLIAM			1		1.00													3										
1004	0112	ASHLEY, ABRAHAM		1																										
1004	0113	ANTHONY, JOB		1			1.00													2										
1004	0114	AYERS, THOMAS			1		1.00													1	10									
1004	0115	AUSTEN, JOSHUA			1		1.00													1	10									
1004	0116	BENNITT, JEREMIAH			1		1.00													20	10									
1004	0117	BENNITT, GIDEON			1		1.00													2	5									
1004	0118	BENNITT, WILLIAM			2		1.00													11	14									
1004	0119	BENNITT, WILLIAM JR			1		1.00													6	10									
1004	0120	BENNITT, JEREMIAH II			1		1.00													2	15									
1004	0121	BENNITT, JOHN		2																										
1004	0122	BENNITT, JOHN II			1																									
1004	0123	BLOSSOM, BENJAMIN			3		1.00				1.00				.25					11				10						
1004	0124	BROWNET, GEORGE			1		2.00													7	8	4								
1004	0125	BALL, DAVID		1			1.00													1	13	4								
1004	0126	BENNITT, ROBERT JR			2															1	8									
1004	0127	BENNITT, EDWARD			1															1										
1004	0128	BENNITT, ROBERT I			1		1.00																							
1004	0129	BENNITT, JEREMIAH JR			1		1.00													5										
1004	0130	BADCOCK, GEORGE			2		1.00								.50					4	15									
1004	0131	BLACKWELL, JOHN			1		1.00				1.00									3	13	4								
1004	0132	BURGG, LUTHER		1			1.00													1	6	8								
1004	0133	BALY, JOSEPH		1			1.00													2	6									
1004	0134	BRIANT, GAMALIEL			2		1.00													2	10									
1004	0135	BATES, JAMES			4		1.00													13	10									
1004	0136	COOK, JOSEPH			1		1.00													7										
1004	0137	CRANDON, THOMAS			1		1.00													2	8			40						
1004	0138	CROSSMAN, JESSE			2		1.00													1	13	4		30						
1004	0139	CUSHMAN, JAMES JR		1			1.00													2	10									
1004	0140	CUSHMAN, JAMES SR			1		1.00													5										
1004	0141	CHAFFE, JOHN			1		1.00				1.00									2										
1004	0142	CHANDLER, JAMES			2		3.00													14										
1004	0143	CORNISH, SAMUEL			2		1.00				1.00									4										
1004	0144	CHURCH, CHARLS			2																									
1004	0145	CLARK, DAVID			1															13	10			11						
1004	0146	CLARK, JAMES			1		1.00													6										
1004	0147	CRANDON, JOHN		1			1.00																							
1004	0148	CUSHMAN, SETH		1																										
1004	0149	CUSHMAN, ELISHAI			2		.40								460					6				50						
1004	0190	CHURCH, GAMALIEL			2		.40								230					16				16						
1004	0151	CHURCH, BENJAMIN			1		1.00				1.00				230					5	18			10						
1004	0152	CHURCH, MERCY					1.00													3										
1004	0153	CLAGHORN, WILLIAM			1		1.00													3										
1004	0154	CLAGHORN, JOSEPH		3			1.00													3										
1004	0155	BRIGHTON, SAVINSWITH			1		1.00													18	12			8						
1004	0201	DELANO, JETHRO			2	1	1.00													9				30						
1004	0202	DELANO, NATHAN			3		1.00													4				99						
1004	0203	DELANO, RICHARD			2		1.00				1.00	3			900	.25		1.00		4				34	24					
1004	0204	DELANO, CALVIN			1		1.00													4	13	4			8					
1004	0205	DELANO, EPHRAIM			1		2.00													4										
1004	0206	DELANO, PELEG			1		1.00													4										
1004	0207	DELANO, NATHANIEL			1		1.00													3	9									
1004	0208	DELANO, JONATHAN			2	1	1.00													21	15									
1004	0209	DAVIS, NATHAN			3		1.00								.50					14										
1004	0210	DAVIS, ABRAHAM			1		1.00				1.00				1.00					13	10				24					
1004	0211	DAVIS, NICHOLAS			1		2.00								.50					6	10									
1004	0212	DILLINGHAM, JOHN			2		1.00				1.00									6	10									
1004	0213	DILLINGHAM, IGNATIUS			1	1	2.00				1.00																			
1004	0214	DAVIS, JAMES			1		.66				2.00									2	10									
1004	0215	ASTENS, JOSEPH			1		.33				1.00									2	5									
1004	0216	DEMMONS, JOSEPH					2.00				1.00									13	5	8								
1004	0217	DELANO, ABISHAI					2.00								100	.12				3	5			67						
1004	0218	DEXTER, WILLIAM			2		1.00													1	15			24						
1004	0219	DRUE, ISAAC			1		1.00														15			24	14					
1004	0220	DRUE, EPHRAIM		1																1										

VALUE OF MONEY LENT AT INTEREST £	s	d	HORSES	OXEN	CATTLE	GOATS AND SHEEP	SWINE	ACRES OF PASTURE	NUMBER OF COWS PASTURE WILL KEEP	ACRES OF TILLAGE	BUSHELS OF GRAIN PRODUCED PER YEAR	BARRELS OF CIDER PRODUCED PER YEAR	ACRES OF SALT MARSH	TONS OF SALT MARSH HAY PRODUCED PER YR.	ACRES OF ENGLISH AND UPLAND MOWING LAND	TONS OF ENGLISH AND UPLAND HAY PER YEAR	ACRES OF FRESH MEADOW	TONS OF FRESH MEADOW HAY PER YEAR	NOTES	TOWN ID	INDIVIDUAL ID
										3.00	30				2.0	1.0				1003	0321
								4.0	1.0											1003	0322
			1	2	3.0	10.0	1	18.0	6.0	4.00	70	6			3.0	3.0	7.0	3.0		1003	0323
					1.0		1	4.0	1.0	2.00	12				1.0	1.0				1003	0324
																				1003	0325
20																				1003	0326
					1.0	8.0	1			2.00	20									1003	0327
					2.0		2	6.0	1.0	3.00	30		1.0	1.0						1003	0328
15																				1003	0329
								7.0	1.0											1003	0330
			3	2	8.0	20.0	5	42.0	12.0	12.00	200	10			12.0	8.0	11.0	11.0		1003	0331
12			1	2	4.0	15.0	3	21.0	6.0	5.00	90	6			12.0	8.0				1003	0332
				4	4.0	16.0	3	22.0	6.0	6.00	100	15			14.0	7.0	4.0	3.0		1003	0333
			2	2	5.0	21.0	4	33.0	8.0	6.00	80	10			12.0	7.0	3.0	2.0		1003	0334
					2.0	7.0	3													1003	0335
			1	2	2.0	8.0	3	18.0	4.0	4.00	50	4			5.0	3.0	4.0	5.0		1003	0336
					1.0		1			5.00	20									1003	0337
					2.0	9.0	1	6.0	1.0	3.00	20						2.0	1.0		1003	0338
																				1003	0339
																				1003	0340
					1.0															1003	0341
			2	2	4.0	20.0	3	17.0	4.0	4.00	40	10	7.0	3.0	15.0	7.5				1004	0101
			3	6	8.0	120.0	4	60.0	13.0	10.00	120	4	12.0	11.0	40.0	20.0				1004	0102
			2	4	4.0	30.0	3	15.0	6.0	7.00	100		6.0	6.0	25.0	10.0				1004	0103
			1	2	5.0	28.0	3	30.0	7.0	6.00	60		1.0	.5	12.0	18.0	6.0	4.0		1004	0104
				2	1.0	17.0	1	8.0	3.0	4.50	50	2	4.5	1.2	15.0	4.5				1004	0105
					3.0	15.0	1	11.0	3.0	6.00	42		3.0	2.0	8.0	4.0				1004	0106
			2	4	9.0	60.0	5	65.0	10.0	6.00	80	3	18.0	10.0	20.0	10.0	5.0	4.0	00	1004	0107
					1.0		1													1004	0108
					1.0		1													1004	0109
			1		2.0		1	11.0	2.0	1.00	15		2.5	2.0	3.0	3.0				1004	0110
			1		2.0	9.0	3	5.0	1.0	3.00	24				8.0	3.0				1004	0111
					1.0	7.0														1004	0112
																				1004	0113
																				1004	0114
																				1004	0115
15			1	2	3.0	30.0	2	35.0	7.0	12.00	150		1.0	1.0	18.0	12.0	6.0	6.0		1004	0116
			1		1.0			6.0	1.0						4.0	2.0				1004	0117
			1	2	5.0	7.0	1	23.0	6.0	4.00	50	4			14.0	10.0				1004	0118
					1.0		1			2.00	40				8.0	6.0				1004	0119
					2.0	4.0	1			2.00	30				4.0	3.0				1004	0120
					1.0															1004	0121
					1.0															1004	0122
60			1	2	5.0	30.0	2	15.0	4.0	4.00	50	1	8.0	3.5	15.0	7.5				1004	0123
			2		2.0			7.0	2.0	4.00	40				7.0	2.0				1004	0124
					1.0			7.0	1.0						1.0	.2				1004	0125
57					1.0			3.0	1.0						2.5	1.5				1004	0126
33			1	2	3.0	7.0	2													1004	0127
					1.0		1			2.00	20									1004	0128
					5.0	14.0	2	10.0	3.0	3.00	39				3.0	3.0				1004	0129
			1		2.0	4.0	1	3.0	1.0	2.00	15	1	7.0	2.0	3.0	1.0				1004	0130
								5.0		1.00	10									1004	0131
										1.00	15								00	1004	0132
																				1004	0133
							1		1.0						2.0	1.0				1004	0134
																				1004	0135
			1	2	3.0	15.0	3	16.0	6.0	7.00	80	5			20.0	10.0				1004	0136
			1				2													1004	0137
							1													1004	0138
					1.0	7.0	1													1004	0139
					2.0	9.0		6.0	1.0	1.00	10	2			1.0	.8				1004	0140
							2													1004	0141
																				1004	0142
			1	6	8.0	27.0	4	30.0	7.0	7.00	65	4	5.0	3.0	26.0	12.0	2.0	1.0		1004	0143
																				1004	0144
																				1004	0145
			3	4	3.0	25.0	3	15.0	5.0	6.00	72	5	8.0	6.0	22.0	10.0				1004	0146
			1		2.0		2	8.0	2.0	1.00	15				7.0	3.0				1004	0147
					1.0	10.0														1004	0148
					1.0															1004	0149
			1	1	1.0								1.0	.8	1.5	.8				1004	0150
					1.0															1004	0151
			1	1	2.0		2	4.0	1.0	2.00	25		3.0	2.0	3.5	1.2				1004	0152
																				1004	0153
																				1004	0154
					2.0	14.0	1	3.0	1.0	2.00	20				5.0	3.0				1004	0155
			2	2	6.0	100.0	4	45.0	10.0	7.00	120		8.0	4.0	35.0	20.0				1004	0201
			2	6	4.0	20.0	2	14.0	4.0	4.00	80		3.0	2.0	16.0	8.0				1004	0202
			1	2	2.0			6.0	2.0			4	2.0	1.5	4.0	3.0				1004	0203
					1.0															1004	0204
			1	2	3.0	11.0		6.0	2.0	3.00	30	1	3.0	2.0	8.0	4.0				1004	0205
			1	2	2.0	6.0	1	3.0	1.0				2.0	2.0	10.0	5.0				1004	0206
				2	3.0	13.0	3	15.0	3.0	5.00	60		2.0	1.5	9.0	5.0				1004	0207
			1		3.0	18.0		4.0	2.0	2.50	25				12.0	6.0				1004	0208
			2		5.0	16.0	1	25.0	10.0	8.00	100	6			25.0	16.0				1004	0209
			1		3.0		1	15.0	3.0	2.00	30				13.0	5.0				1004	0210
			1	3	4.0		2	15.0	4.0	4.00	55	1			12.0	6.0				1004	0211
			1		3.0		3	9.0	3.0	1.50	15	3			7.5	4.5				1004	0212
			2	2	4.0		4	8.0	3.0	3.00	30				9.5	7.0				1004	0213
					1.0															1004	0214
																				1004	0215
			1	2	1.0		1			1.00	10									1004	0216
			2	2	2.0	10.0	1	16.0	4.0	8.00	***		2.0	2.0	14.0	7.0	2.0	1.0		1004	0217
					2.0	8.0	1			4.00	***		2.5	2.5	4.0	2.0				1004	0218
					1.0															1004	0219
							1													1004	0220

TOWN ID	INDIVIDUAL ID	NAME	TITLE	STATUS	POLLS RATEABLE	POLLS NOT RATEABLE	HOUSES AND SHOPS ADJOINING	SHOPS ADJOINING	TWN MKS DISTINCTION	TANHOUSES, ETC.	TANHOUSES: TYPE	STILLHOUSES	WAREHOUSES	SUPERFICIAL FEET OF WHARF	MILLS	MILLS: TYPE	IRONWORKS, ETC.	IRONWORKS: TYPE	ANNUAL WORTH £	s	d	SERVANTS FOR LIFE	TONS OF VESSELS	MERCHANDISE £	s	d	FACTORAGE £	s	d
1004	0221	DRUE, JOSIAH				1	1.00														10									
1004	0222	ELLIS, BENJAMIN			1		1.00			1.00									9	12			5						
1004	0223	EGGREL, DANIEL			2		1.00							900					8				40	50					
1004	0224	ELDREDGE, SALATHIEL			1		1.00							250					3	10			9						
1004	0225	EAST, GEORGE			2		1.00												2	10									
1004	0226	ELLIS, JOSEPH				2	1.00												2										
1004	0227	ELLIS, SETH			1														1	5									
1004	0228	EATON, SETH			1		1.00												6	10									
1004	0229	ELDRIDGE, EDWARD			1		1.00												4										
1004	0230	ELDRIDGE, ISAIAH			1		1.00							600	.25				5	10			28						
1004	0231	ELDRIDGE, ELNATHAN				1	1.00												7	5									
1004	0232	FULLAR, THOMAS			1		1.00												2	13	4								
1004	0233	FULLAR, SIMEON				1	1.00													12									
1004	0234	FOSTER, CHILLINGSWORTH			2		1.00			1.00									13	10									
1004	0235	FULLAR, EBENEZAR				1	.33												2	15									
1004	0236	GARRESH, JOHN			1		1.00			1.00									4										
1004	0237	GIFFORD, ELIHU			2		1.00			1.00									6										
1004	0238	DILLINGHAM, BENJAMIN			1		1.00												2	6									
1004	0239	DURPHY, DAVID			3		1.00												6										
1004	0240	BARNEY, GRIFFITH			1		1.00												9										
1004	0241	HATHAWAY, THOMAS			1		1.00			1.00									17	10									
1004	0242	HATHAWAY, JETHRO			3		1.00			2.00			.25	500					12				37						
1004	0243	HATHAWAY, STEPHEN			1		1.00			1.00									17	5			37						
1004	0244	HATHAWAY, GAMALEL			2	1	1.00												10	10									
1004	0245	HATHAWAY, ELEAZAR			1		1.00												[illegible]	10			10						
1004	0246	HATHAWAY, JONATHAN			3		1.00								.25				8	19									
1004	0247	HATHAWAY, ELNATHAN			4		3.00												18										
1004	0248	HATHAWAY, SETH			2		1.00												10										
1004	0249	HATHAWAY, MONEWELL			5		1.66			1.00									19	15			44						
1004	0250	HATHAWAY, JONATHAN JR			1		.50			1.00									4	6	8								
1004	0251	HOWLAND, ISAAC			1		2.00			.50	21	1.00							38	6	8	1	70	300					
1004	0252	HUDSON, EDWARD			2		1.00												6										
1004	0253	HATHAWAY, JOSIAH			1		1.00												6										
1004	0254	HATHAWAY, JOHN			1		1.00												8										
1004	0255	HATHAWAY, BENJAMIN			3		1.00												6	13	4	1							
1004	0256	HATHAWAY, RUTH				3	1.00												1	6	8								
1004	0257	HAWS, SAMUEL				1	1.50												4										
1004	0301	HATHAWAY, SETH			1		1.00												2	18									
1004	0302	HATHAWAY, HANNAH					1.00			1.00									3	6	8								
1004	0303	HATHAWAY, THOMAS II			3		1.00			1.00									9	18									
1004	0304	HANDY, THOMAS			1		1.00												4	18									
1004	0305	HANDY, THOMAS JR				1	1.00												2	10									
1004	0306	HOWARD, MATHEW			2		1.00												4	15									
1004	0307	HAMMOND, SETH			3		1.00												4	10									
1004	0308	HAMMOND, DAVID			1		1.00													6	8								
1004	0309	HATHAWAY, JACOB			1	1	1.00												4										
1004	0310	HITCH, GEORGE			2		1.00												1			1							
1004	0311	HAMMOND, JEDUTHAN			1		1.00												1	6									
1004	0312	HAMMOND, BARNABAS			1		1.00												1										
1004	0313	HATHAWAY, OBED			1		1.00			1.00									5	13	4								
1004	0314	HUDDLESTONE, PELEG			1		2.00												5										
1004	0315	HOWLAND, ELIZABETH					1.00			1.00									4	12									
1004	0316	HAWS, SHUBEL			1		.50												1	10									
1004	0317	HACK, GEORGE				1	1.00												1	8	6								
1004	0318	JENNE, CORNELIUS			2	1	2.00												8	10									
1004	0319	JENNE, CALEB			1		1.00												4	10									
1004	0320	JABER, JEDUTHAN			1		1.00												4	10									
1004	0321	JENNE, JABEZ			2		1.00												4										
1004	0322	JENNE, JETHRO			1		1.00												2	13	4								
1004	0323	JENNE, CORNELIUS JR			1														1	13	4								
1004	0324	JENNE, BENJAMIN			1																								
1004	0325	JENNE, +HAZIEL			1																		10						
1004	0326	JENNE, NATHANIEL			1		1.00			1.00									5										
1004	0327	JENNE, SAMUEL			2		1.00												5										
1004	0328	JENNE, THOMAS			1		1.00												3										
1004	0329	JENNE, JOHN			2		1.00												10	10									
1004	0330	JENNE, EPHRAIM			2		1.00												4	6	8								
1004	0331	JENNE, ISAAC			1														1										
1004	0332	JENNE, HIX			1	1	1.00												10	10									
1004	0333	JENNE, JOB			1		.40												8										
1004	0334	JENNE, SAMUEL			1		.60												4										
1004	0335	JENNE, SETH			1		1.00												5	12									
1004	0336	JENNE, TUCKER			1		1.00												3										
1004	0337	INGRAHAM, TIMOTHY			2		1.00			1.00									12								65		
1004	0338	INGRAHAM, PAUL			1		1.00												3										
1004	0339	JENNE, GEORGE				1	1.00												2										
1004	0340	JOY, SAMUEL				1	1.00												1										
1004	0341	JENKENS, SAMUEL			1																		10						
1004	0342	KINNEY, THOMAS			1	1	1.00												5	6	8								
1004	0343	KINNEY, SAMUEL			1		1.00												2	10									
1004	0344	KEMPTON, WILLIAM			2	1	1.00			1.00													6						
1004	0345	KEMPTON, EPHRAIM			2		1.00												6										
1004	0346	KEMPTON, JOSEPH			1		1.00												3	19									
1004	0347	KEMPTON, MANASETH			1		1.00												4										
1004	0348	KEMPTON, BENJAMIN			1		1.00												3										
1004	0349	KEMPTON, STEPHEN			1																								
1004	0350	KEMPTON, THOMAS+EPHRAIM II			2		1.00												10	3	4								
1004	0351	KEIR, EBENEZAR			1	1	1.00												7	6	5								
1004	0352	KERBEY, THOMAS				1	1.00												3										
1004	0353	KILLEY, WILLIAM			1		.33												1	10									
1004	0401	LOUDEN, JOHN			2		1.00			1.00			1.00						10			1	30						
1004	0402	MORTEN, SETH			2		1.00			1.00									6	12	4								
1004	0403	MONDOL, SAMUEL			1		1.00												6	6	8		4						
1004	0404	MERIHEW, PRESERVED			1	1	1.00												1	6	8								
1004	0405	MITCHEL, WILLIAM			2		1.00												11	10									
1004	0406	MCPHERSON, JOHN			1					2.00			1.00	5,980					7				118						
1004	0407	MOSHER, MAXEN			1		1.00												2										
1004	0408	MARSHEL, THOMAS			1																								
1004	0409	MOCHE, MICHAEL			1		.33												1	10			8						
1004	0410	MAXFIELD, PATRICK			2		1.00												3				33						

£	s	d	HORSES	OXEN	CATTLE	GOATS AND SHEEP	SWINE	ACRES OF PASTURE	NUMBER OF COWS PASTURE WILL KEEP	ACRES OF TILLAGE	BUSHELS OF GRAIN PRODUCED PER YEAR	BARRELS OF CIDER PRODUCED PER YEAR	ACRES OF SALT MARSH	TONS OF SALT MARSH HAY PRODUCED PER YR	ACRES OF ENGLISH AND UPLAND MOWING LAND	TONS OF ENGLISH AND UPLAND HAY PER YEAR	ACRES OF FRESH MEADOW	TONS OF FRESH MEAD-OW HAY PER YEAR	NOTES	TOWN ID	INDIVIDUAL ID
			1		1.0														00	1004	0221
30			1		1.0														00	1004	0222
							1												00	1004	0223
							1													1004	0224
																				1004	0225
					1.0			2.0	1.0	1.00	15				4.0	1.0				1004	0226
					1.0					2.50	30				2.0	.8				1004	0227
20			1		1.0	9.0	1	12.0	3.0	3.00	30		2.0	2.0	10.0	3.0				1004	0228
					1.0		1													1004	0229
					2.0		1	4.0	1.0			2			4.0	2.0				1004	0230
				2				15.0	3.0	3.00	30				12.0	5.0				1004	0231
					1.0			4.0	1.0			1			7.0	2.0				1004	0232
					1.0		2												00	1004	0233
			1	3	4.0	14.0	1	10.0	4.0	6.00	80		5.0	1.2	14.0	9.0	5.0	4.0	00	1004	0234
					1.0	4.0	1	4.0	1.0	1.50	15	1			4.0	2.0				1004	0235
																				1004	0236
			1		1.0		1	2.0												1004	0237
																				1004	0238
																				1004	0239
																				1004	0240
150			3	2	4.0	15.0	1	35.0	8.0	6.00	80	3	16.0	7.0	12.0	5.0	1.0	1.0		1004	0241
			1		4.0	8.0	4	11.0	3.0	4.00	50				7.0	4.5				1004	0242
			2	4	7.0	25.0	3	35.0	8.0	7.00	90	3	8.0	6.0	18.0	9.0				1004	0243
			1	2	2.0	17.0	2	25.0	3.0	5.00	60	6	8.0	7.0	8.0	5.0			00	1004	0244
					1.0		1													1004	0245
60			1	2	3.0	18.0	1	6.0	3.0	4.00	32		6.0	4.0	9.0	5.0				1004	0246
			2	2	5.0	22.0	3	25.0	7.0	8.00	110		4.0	3.0	15.0	9.0				1004	0247
			2	2	3.0	18.0	3	20.0	3.0	6.00	50		3.0	3.0	6.0	5.0				1004	0248
120			1	4	4.0	27.0	1	20.0	7.0	9.00	90		3.0	2.0	26.0	17.0				1004	0249
				2	2.0	15.0		5.0	1.0				2.5	2.0	5.0	2.5				1004	0250
			1	2	1.0										5.0	4.0				1004	0251
							1													1004	0252
				2	2.0	21.0	2	10.0	2.0	3.00	36		2.0	1.0	7.0	4.0				1004	0253
				2	3.0	27.0	1	10.0	3.0	7.00	70	2	2.0	1.0	12.0	4.0				1004	0254
				4	3.0	40.0	3	6.0	3.0	6.00	60	3	2.5	2.5	12.0	5.0				1004	0255
							1	1.0												1004	0256
			1		1.0	2.0	1			2.00	20				2.0	.8				1004	0257
					2.0	7.0	1	4.0	1.0	3.00	27				3.0	1.5				1004	0301
					2.0								3.5	3.0	7.0	2.0				1004	0302
			1	2	4.0	25.0	2	18.0	4.0	2.00	30		2.0	2.0	24.0	6.0				1004	0303
7			1		2.0		1	3.0	1.0	.50	8	3			6.0	3.0				1004	0304
					1.0	1.0	3			2.00	25				8.0	3.0				1004	0305
				2	3.0	9.0	2	2.0	1.0	6.00	60		1.0	.5	10.0	4.0				1004	0306
			1	2	2.0	15.0	1			4.00	40				10.0	6.0				1004	0307
					1.0		1													1004	0308
			1	2	2.0	10.0	1	3.0	1.0	2.50	30				8.0	4.0				1004	0309
																				1004	0310
					1.0															1004	0311
				2	1.0		1			2.00	24				8.0	5.0				1004	0312
					3.0	11.0		8.0	2.0	1.50	25				.8	.5				1004	0313
																				1004	0314
					2.0		1	12.0	2.0	3.00	30	2			8.0	2.5				1004	0315
					1.0			4.0	1.0						1.0	.5				1004	0316
					2.0	7.0	1			2.00	20				4.0	1.0				1004	0317
			1	4	3.0	20.0	2	10.0	3.0	8.00	80		3.0	3.0	15.0	6.0	3.5	4.0		1004	0318
				2	2.0	17.0	2	6.0	2.0	4.00	36	1	1.5	1.5	5.0	3.0	1.0	2.0		1004	0319
				2	2.0	17.0	2	6.0	2.0	4.00	36	1	2.0	2.0	4.0	2.0	2.0	2.0		1004	0320
				2	2.0		2	2.0	1.0	3.00	36				8.0	3.0				1004	0321
					2.0		1			2.00	25				2.5	1.5				1004	0322
					1.0		1			1.00	16				2.0	1.0				1004	0323
																				1004	0324
																				1004	0325
20				2	4.0	20.0	2			5.00	50		1.0	1.0	8.0	4.0				1004	0326
			1	2	3.0	10.0	1	5.0	1.0	6.00	60		3.0	2.5	8.0	3.0	1.0	.8		1004	0327
			1	2	2.0	6.0	1			5.00	40		3.0	2.0	7.0	3.0				1004	0328
			1	2	3.0	12.0	2	12.0	3.0	5.00	70		3.0	3.0	8.0	8.0				1004	0329
			1	2	2.0		2	5.0	2.0	4.00	45	4			7.0	3.0				1004	0330
					1.0	1.0	1	4.0							2.0	.8				1004	0331
			1	2	3.0	30.0	3	20.0	9.0	4.50	50	3	3.0	2.0	20.0	9.0				1004	0332
			1		1.0	3.0	2	13.0	4.0	5.00	50		2.0	2.0	12.0	6.0	2.0	1.0		1004	0333
					2.0	2.0		5.0	1.0						4.0	3.0				1004	0334
				2	7.0	18.0	3	7.0	2.0	5.00	30				8.0	3.0				1004	0335
					1.0	1.0				3.00	10				6.0	2.0				1004	0336
			1		1.0		1													1004	0337
																				1004	0338
								3.0	1.0	2.00	20				5.0	2.0	3.0	1.0		1004	0339
								3.0												1004	0340
				2	2.0	12.0			3.0	2.00	20	2			6.0	3.0	1.5	1.0		1004	0341
					1.0		2	8.0	2.0	1.00	15				2.0	1.0				1004	0342
			2	2	4.0	18.0	1	16.0	6.0	6.00	68		15.0	12.0	7.0	5.0				1004	0343
			1	2	2.0	15.0	4	19.0	3.0	3.00	33				6.0	5.0				1004	0344
						12.0	1	5.0	1.0	1.50	14									1004	0345
					2.0	11.0	1													1004	0346
					1.0															1004	0347
					1.0															1004	0348
							1													1004	0349
			2	7	4.0	32.0		25.0	4.0	4.00	50		14.0	8.5	6.0	4.0				1004	0350
			1	2	3.0	27.0	4	5.0	2.0	7.00	70				12.0	6.0	2.0	1.0		1004	0351
					1.0										4.0	1.5				1004	0352
																			00	1004	0353
			1		1.0		1								1.2	.8				1004	0401
				2	3.0	8.0	4	6.0	2.0	4.00	50		3.0	1.5	12.0	6.0				1004	0402
				2	2.0	13.0	4	6.0	2.0	4.00	50		1.5	.8	3.0	1.0	2.0	1.0		1004	0403
					2.0	18.0	1			1.00	15				3.0	1.0				1004	0404
			2	2	4.0	21.0	2	12.0	5.0	5.00	60				16.0	9.0				1004	0405
															.5	.2				1004	0406
																				1004	0407
							1													1004	0408
																				1004	0409
																				1004	0410

TOWN ID	INDIVIDUAL ID	NAME	TITLE	STATUS	POLLS RATEABLE	POLLS NOT RATEABLE	HOUSES AND SHOPS ADJOINING	SHOPS ADJOINING	TWN MKS DISTINCTION	TANHOUSES, ETC.	TANHOUSES: TYPE	STILLHOUSES	WAREHOUSES	SUPERFICIAL FEET OF WHARF	MILLS	MILLS: TYPE	IRONWORKS, ETC.	IRONWORKS: TYPE
1004	0411	MAXFIELD, LADOCK			1													
1004	0412	NYE, THOMAS			2		2.00			1.00								
1004	0413	NYE, THOMAS JR			1		1.00			1.00			.25	500				
1004	0414	NYE, STEPHEN			1									250				
1004	0415	NYE, OBED			1								.25	500				
1004	0416	NASH, SIMEON			2													
1004	0417	NORTON, ELIJAH			1													
1004	0418	OMAN, PETER + SIMEON			1	1	1.00			1.00								
1004	0419	POPE, SETH			3		1.00											
1004	0420	POPE, SAMUEL			1		2.00											
1004	0421	POPE, LUEN			1		1.00			1.00								
1004	0422	POPE, JOSEPH			1		1.00											
1004	0423	POPE, THOMAS			3		1.00			1.00								
1004	0424	POPE, ISAAC			1		1.00											
1004	0425	POPE, ELNATHAN			1	1	1.00											
1004	0426	POPE, ELNATHAN JR				1	1.00											
1004	0427	POPE, EDWARD			1		1.00											
1004	0428	PECKHAM, JOHN			2	1	2.00											
1004	0429	PECKHAM, JOANNA	1				1.00											
1004	0430	PECKHAM, MARY	1															
1004	0431	PECKHAM, RICHARD			1		1.00											
1004	0432	PECKHAM, ISAIAH			4		1.00											
1004	0433	PECKENS, JOHN			1								.25	500				
1004	0434	PARKER, ELISHAI			1					1.00								
1004	0435	PIERCE, CALEB				1	1.00											
1004	0436	PRICE, SIMEON			1		1.00											
1004	0437	POPE, LEMUEL			2		1.00			1.00								
1004	0438	PARKER, MILES				1												
1004	0439	PARKER, MICAH			1		2.00											
1004	0440	PERREY, SAMUEL			1		1.00											
1004	0441	PARKER, AVERY			1		1.00											
1004	0442	PHILLIPS, PETER			1	1	1.00											
1004	0443	RUSSEL, JOSEPH			3		3.00			1.50	23		1.00	1.300	1.00			
1004	0444	RUSSEL, WILLIAM			2		1.00											
1004	0445	REA, URIEL			1					1.00								
1004	0446	RECKETSON, DANIEL			1		.50											
1004	0447	RUSSEL, JOHN			1		1.00			1.00								
1004	0448	RUSSEL, STEPHEN			1		1.00											
1004	0449	RUSSEL, SETH			1		1.00											
1004	0450	ROTCH, JOSEPH + SONS			4		1.00			1.00	11		3.00	14.924				
1004	0451	ROTCH, JOSEPH	23		1		1.00			1.00								
1004	0452	READ, ABRAHAM			2	1	1.00			2.00								
1004	0453	RALF, NATHANIEL			1		1.00											
1004	0454	ROBBINS, JOHN			1	1												
1004	0455	ROUSE, GEORGE				1	1.00											
1004	0501	SPOONER, SAMUEL				1	1.00											
1004	0502	SPOONER, SETH				1	1.00											
1004	0503	SPOONER, WALTER			2		1.00											
1004	0504	SPOONER, ISAAC			2		2.00											
1004	0505	SPOONER, NATHANIEL			3		1.00											
1004	0506	SHERMAN, ABRAHAM			1													
1004	0507	SPOONER, SAMUEL II			2	1	1.00											
1004	0508	SPOONER, JOHN	3		1		1.00								.25			
1004	0509	SHAW, WILLIAM			3		1.00											
1004	0510	SAMSON, JOSEPH			2		1.00											
1004	0511	SAMSON, JUDAH			1		1.00											
1004	0512	SAMSON, ELNATHAN			2		1.00			1.00								
1004	0513	SWIFT, JIREH			2		1.00											
1004	0514	SWIFT, JIREH JR			2		3.00			3.00					.25			
1004	0515	SWIFT, SILAS			1		1.00								.50			
1004	0516	SPENCER, DANIEL			1		1.00											
1004	0517	SELLERS, JAMES			2		1.00											
1004	0518	SUMMERTON, DANIEL			1		1.00			1.00								
1004	0519	SPOONER, ELEAZAR			1		1.00								.50			
1004	0520	SPOONER, BENJAMIN			1		1.00											
1004	0521	SPOONER, BARNABAS				1	1.00											
1004	0522	HAMMOND, SAMUEL				1	1.00											
1004	0523	SMITH, DANIEL			3		1.00			1.00								
1004	0524	SMITH, ABRAHAM			1		.50			1.00								
1004	0525	STEVENS, JOHN			1		1.00			1.00								
1004	0526	SEVERENCE, JOSEPH			1		1.00			1.00								
1004	0527	SMITH, JAMES			1		1.00			1.00								
1004	0528	SPENCER, THOMAS			1		1.00											
1004	0529	SPENCER, HENRY				1	1.00			2.00								
1004	0530	SHEPHERD, DAVID			2		1.00			1.00								
1004	0531	SPOONER, GRACE			1		1.00											
1004	0532	TABER, JACOB				1	1.00			2.00								
1004	0533	TABER, BARTH'O			1		1.00							500				
1004	0534	TABER, BENJAMIN				2												
1004	0535	TABER, JOHN	13		2		1.00			1.00					.25			
1004	0536	TABER, JOSEPH			1	1	1.00											
1004	0537	TABER, WILLIAM			2													
1004	0538	TABER, JACOB JR			2		1.00			1.00								
1004	0539	TABER, BENJAMIN			5		1.00			1.00								
1004	0540	TOBEY, ELISHAI			3		1.00			1.00								
1004	0541	TENKWIN, JOHN			2		1.00											
1004	0542	TABER, THOMAS	24		1		.50			3.00								
1004	0543	TABER, JONATHAN			1		.50			2.00								
1004	0544	TRIPP, SAMUEL			1		1.00											
1004	0545	TERRY, BENJAMIN			3		1.00											
1004	0546	TOBEY, ZACCHEUS JR			1		2.00								.60			
1004	0547	TOBEY, LOT			2		1.00											
1004	0548	TABER, AMAZIAH			1	1	1.00								1.00			
1004	0549	TABER, JABEZ			1		1.00			3.00								
1004	0550	TABER, THOMAS			1		1.00											
1004	0551	TABER, THOMAS			1										.12			
1004	0552	TABER, THOMAS	13		2		1.00			1.00					.12			
1004	0553	TABER, PETER			2		1.00			1.00					.12		.12	
1004	0601	TABER, JETHRO			1		1.00								.12			
1004	0602	TABER, ANTIPAS			1		1.00											

TOWN ID	INDIVIDUAL ID	NAME	ANNUAL WORTH OF THE WHOLE REAL ESTATE £	s	d	SERVANTS FOR LIFE	TONS OF VESSELS	VALUE OF MERCHANDISE £	s	d	VALUE OF FACTORAGE, COMMISSIONS £	s	d
1004	0411	MAXFIELD, LADOCK	22	18			8						
1004	0412	NYE, THOMAS	7				40						
1004	0413	NYE, THOMAS JR		10			105						
1004	0414	NYE, STEPHEN					9						
1004	0415	NYE, OBED	2	10			64						
1004	0416	NASH, SIMEON					15						
1004	0417	NORTON, ELIJAH											
1004	0418	OMAN, PETER + SIMEON	1	10									
1004	0419	POPE, SETH	1	10			10						
1004	0420	POPE, SAMUEL	16	8									
1004	0421	POPE, LUEN	18										
1004	0422	POPE, JOSEPH	7	10									
1004	0423	POPE, THOMAS	15										
1004	0424	POPE, ISAAC	11										
1004	0425	POPE, ELNATHAN	8	10									
1004	0426	POPE, ELNATHAN JR	5	13	4								
1004	0427	POPE, EDWARD	7										
1004	0428	PECKHAM, JOHN	13	15									
1004	0429	PECKHAM, JOANNA	6	10									
1004	0430	PECKHAM, MARY											
1004	0431	PECKHAM, RICHARD	4	10									
1004	0432	PECKHAM, ISAIAH	7	12									
1004	0433	PECKENS, JOHN	2	10			4	75	6				
1004	0434	PARKER, ELISHAI		15									
1004	0435	PIERCE, CALEB	1	13	4								
1004	0436	PRICE, SIMEON	1	10									
1004	0437	POPE, LEMUEL	8										
1004	0438	PARKER, MILES	1										
1004	0439	PARKER, MICAH	3	10									
1004	0440	PERREY, SAMUEL	10										
1004	0441	PARKER, AVERY	4	10									
1004	0442	PHILLIPS, PETER		15									
1004	0443	RUSSEL, JOSEPH	60			2	320	1.500					
1004	0444	RUSSEL, WILLIAM	6				4	180					
1004	0445	REA, URIEL	8										
1004	0446	RECKETSON, DANIEL	4										
1004	0447	RUSSEL, JOHN	10										
1004	0448	RUSSEL, STEPHEN	4										
1004	0449	RUSSEL, SETH	13	10			34						
1004	0450	ROTCH, JOSEPH + SONS	95				683	1.000					
1004	0451	ROTCH, JOSEPH	4										
1004	0452	READ, ABRAHAM	6					266	13	4			
1004	0453	RALF, NATHANIEL	2										
1004	0454	ROBBINS, JOHN	5	10									
1004	0455	ROUSE, GEORGE		15									
1004	0501	SPOONER, SAMUEL	7										
1004	0502	SPOONER, SETH	13										
1004	0503	SPOONER, WALTER	19	13	4								
1004	0504	SPOONER, ISAAC	6										
1004	0505	SPOONER, NATHANIEL	12										
1004	0506	SHERMAN, ABRAHAM	6				9						
1004	0507	SPOONER, SAMUEL II	3				70						
1004	0508	SPOONER, JOHN											
1004	0509	SHAW, WILLIAM	21	10		1							
1004	0510	SAMSON, JOSEPH	20										
1004	0511	SAMSON, JUDAH	4										
1004	0512	SAMSON, ELNATHAN	10	10			16						
1004	0513	SWIFT, JIREH	13	10									
1004	0514	SWIFT, JIREH JR	9	10									
1004	0515	SWIFT, SILAS	4	10									
1004	0516	SPENCER, DANIEL	6					418	10				
1004	0517	SELLERS, JAMES	3	10			62	220					
1004	0518	SUMMERTON, DANIEL	10				8						
1004	0519	SPOONER, ELEAZAR	7	13	4								
1004	0520	SPOONER, BENJAMIN	2										
1004	0521	SPOONER, BARNABAS	2										
1004	0522	HAMMOND, SAMUEL	6	13	4								
1004	0523	SMITH, DANIEL	7				4						
1004	0524	SMITH, ABRAHAM	4	10									
1004	0525	STEVENS, JOHN	2	10									
1004	0526	SEVERENCE, JOSEPH	3	13	4								
1004	0527	SMITH, JAMES	2	10									
1004	0528	SPENCER, THOMAS		15									
1004	0529	SPENCER, HENRY	6	10			25	700					
1004	0530	SHEPHERD, DAVID	9				45						
1004	0531	SPOONER, GRACE	3	13	4								
1004	0532	TABER, JACOB	18										
1004	0533	TABER, BARTH'O	4	10									
1004	0534	TABER, BENJAMIN	6	13	4								
1004	0535	TABER, JOHN	5	13	4								
1004	0536	TABER, JOSEPH	12										
1004	0537	TABER, WILLIAM	6										
1004	0538	TABER, JACOB JR	14										
1004	0539	TABER, BENJAMIN	8	10			8						
1004	0540	TOBEY, ELISHAI	10										
1004	0541	TENKWIN, JOHN	13	6	8		27						
1004	0542	TABER, THOMAS	10										
1004	0543	TABER, JONATHAN	7	6	8		9						
1004	0544	TRIPP, SAMUEL	6										
1004	0545	TERRY, BENJAMIN	14										
1004	0546	TOBEY, ZACCHEUS JR	12	13	4								
1004	0547	TOBEY, LOT	8										
1004	0548	TABER, AMAZIAH	8	10			17						
1004	0549	TABER, JABEZ	6										
1004	0550	TABER, THOMAS											
1004	0551	TABER, THOMAS		10									
1004	0552	TABER, THOMAS	3										
1004	0553	TABER, PETER	6	10									
1004	0601	TABER, JETHRO	4	10									
1004	0602	TABER, ANTIPAS	4										

Value of Money Lent at Interest £	s	d	Horses	Oxen	Cattle	Goats and Sheep	Swine	Acres of Pasture	Number of Cows Pasture Will Keep	Acres of Tillage	Bushels of Grain Produced Per Year	Barrels of Cider Produced Per Year	Acres of Salt Marsh	Tons of Salt Marsh Hay Produced Per Yr	Acres of English and Upland Mowing Land	Tons of English and Upland Hay Per Year	Acres of Fresh Meadow	Tons of Fresh Meadow Hay Per Year	Notes	Town ID	Individual ID
			2	4	6.0	36.0	4	30.0	8.0	6.00	70	15	10.0	8.0	20.0	10.0				1004	0411
					1.0		2													1004	0412
							3													1004	0413
							4													1004	0414
																				1004	0415
																				1004	0416
					1.0		1													1004	0417
					1.0	8.0	2													1004	0418
			2	2	2.0	20.0	1	12.0	4.0	6.00	60		12.0	5.0	13.0	6.0				1004	0419
			1	3	4.0	17.0	3	19.0	4.0	6.00	90		11.0	7.0	9.5	8.5	5.0	4.0		1004	0420
			2	4	5.0	10.0	4	24.0	7.0	6.00	75	6	9.0	6.0	23.0	13.0				1004	0421
			1		1.0		1	16.0	4.0	3.00	25		7.0	4.0	4.0	2.5	2.0	1.0		1004	0422
			2	2	4.0	25.0	2	15.0	4.0	5.00	55	4	11.0	11.0	8.0	7.0				1004	0423
			1	2	3.0	28.0	6	12.0	3.0	7.00	75	12	8.0	5.0	10.0	7.0				1004	0424
			1	2	3.0		3	12.0	2.0	4.00	56		4.0	3.5	11.0	6.0				1004	0425
				2	2.0	6.0	2	14.0	3.0	5.00	50		1.5	1.0	6.0	3.5				1004	0426
			1																	1004	0427
			1	2	3.0	39.0	4	14.0	5.0	6.00	70	15	6.0	5.0	18.0	8.0				1004	0428
					1.0	10.0	1	8.0	2.0	3.00	30				5.0	5.0				1004	0429
					3.0		1													1004	0430
20				2	1.0		1	15.0	3.0	3.00	39		.8	.5	6.0	3.0				1004	0431
			1	2	3.0	7.0	1	8.0	2.0	4.00	39	6	8.0	5.0	4.0	3.0				1004	0432
							1													1004	0433
															1.0	1.0				1004	0434
					2.0															1004	0435
																				1004	0436
			1	2	3.0	4.0	2	18.0	3.0	6.00	60		5.0	5.0	13.0	3.0	4.0	4.0	00	1004	0437
					1.0					3.00	40				1.0	.2				1004	0438
				2	1.0	15.0		3.0	1.0	4.00	48				5.0	3.0				1004	0439
			2		2.0	20.0	2	10.0	4.0	2.00	30		2.5	2.5	15.0	6.0				1004	0440
					1.0		1													1004	0441
					1.0	5.0	1			1.00	7				.8	.5				1004	0442
			4	6	9.0	11.0	8	50.0	10.0	10.00	100	5	12.0	10.0	40.0	20.0				1004	0443
			1																	1004	0444
					1.0															1004	0445
																				1004	0446
			2	2	2.0	18.0	1	20.0	5.0	4.00	60		2.5	1.2	16.0	7.0				1004	0447
					2.0	4.0	2	4.0	1.0	4.00	50				4.0	2.0				1004	0448
					2.0	10.0	1	20.0	4.0				1.0	.5	7.0	3.0				1004	0449
1,500			4		2.0		1	18.0	4.0						11.0	5.0				1004	0450
																				1004	0451
			3		1.0		1	2.0	1.0											1004	0452
			1				1													1004	0453
					2.0	14.0	2	8.0	2.0	5.00	55				10.0	4.5				1004	0454
					1.0					1.00	10				2.0	1.0				1004	0455
					4.0	16.0	3	15.0	3.0	4.00	40	2	5.0	3.0	11.0	6.0				1004	0501
			1	4	3.0	19.0	1	25.0	6.0	4.00	50	6	1.0	.8	13.0	12.0				1004	0502
			2	2	6.0	20.0	1	45.0	10.0	3.00	40	4			20.0	18.0				1004	0503
			1	2	3.0	17.0	1	9.0	3.0	4.00	30				4.0	3.0				1004	0504
			1	4	2.0	39.0	4	13.0	5.0	8.00	100		4.0	1.5	23.0	8.0	2.0	1.0		1004	0505
13	6	8	1	2	2.0	19.0	2	12.0	3.0	6.00	45		3.0	2.2	9.0	5.0				1004	0506
					1.0		1	8.0	1.0											1004	0507
																				1004	0508
			2	4	6.0	30.0	4	35.0	10.0	6.00	120	10	7.0	6.0	22.0	14.0				1004	0509
200			1	4	8.0	18.0	3	40.0	8.0	8.00	125	4			25.0	16.0				1004	0510
					2.0	8.0	1	3.0	1.0	1.00	20				6.0	5.0				1004	0511
			1		1.0		1	2.0	1.0						4.0	3.5				1004	0512
150			1	2	4.0	30.0	3	15.0	5.0	8.00	80	2	7.0	4.0	10.0	5.0	4.0	3.0		1004	0513
60			1		3.0	18.0	2	8.0	2.0	1.00	10		2.0	1.8	6.0	3.0				1004	0514
			1	2	1.0	14.0	1													1004	0515
			1																	1004	0516
			1																	1004	0517
100				2	3.0	20.0	2	18.0	4.0	1.50	20				9.0	3.0	4.0	3.0		1004	0518
			1		1.0		1	7.0	2.0	5.00	55				9.0	3.0	4.0	3.0		1004	0519
					1.0		1	4.0		2.00	20				1.0	.5				1004	0520
					2.0	14.0				2.00	15				6.0	2.0	3.0	1.5		1004	0521
				2	2.0	18.0	2	7.0	2.0	5.00	55				11.0	6.0				1004	0522
					1.0															1004	0523
							1													1004	0524
					1.0	13.0		4.5	1.0	2.00	20				1.0	.5				1004	0525
					2.0	11.0	1	6.0	1.0	2.00	30				1.5	1.0	2.0	3.0		1004	0526
																				1004	0527
																				1004	0528
			1		1.0			2.0	1.0						2.0	1.0				1004	0529
			1		1.0		1	3.0	1.0				1.5	1.0	3.0	1.0				1004	0530
					1.0		1	6.0	1.0	2.00	20		2.0	1.5	4.0	2.0				1004	0531
				2	4.0	24.0	3	40.0	7.0	6.00	90	50	7.0	5.0	16.0	9.0	4.0	2.0		1004	0532
50			1	2																1004	0533
			1		3.0	19.0	3	10.0	2.0	7.00	70		1.0	.8	10.0	4.0	6.0	3.0		1004	0534
					1.0															1004	0535
			1	2	4.0	23.0	3	28.0	4.0	10.00	130	3	8.0	5.0	14.0	6.0	3.0	2.0		1004	0536
			1		2.0	10.0		4.0	1.0	3.00	40		1.0	.5	9.0	5.0				1004	0537
13	6	8	1	2	5.0	39.0	5	30.0	7.0	6.00	80				10.0	8.0	6.0	5.0		1004	0538
					1.0		1													1004	0539
			2	2	2.0	15.0	3	20.0	4.0	4.00	40				10.0	6.0	5.0	3.0		1004	0540
			1	4	6.0	22.0		35.0	6.0	6.00	72	10	10.0	6.0	12.0	6.0				1004	0541
			1		2.0	8.0	2	20.0	4.0	2.00	20	6	2.0	1.0	11.0	6.0	3.0	1.5		1004	0542
			1	2	1.0	11.0	1	10.0	2.0	2.50	25	7	4.0	2.0	10.0	5.0				1004	0543
			1	2	4.0	14.0	3	6.0	2.0	3.00	45	2			8.0	4.0	2.0	1.0		1004	0544
			1	4	3.0	40.0	9	15.0	6.0	6.00	100	2	4.5	1.0	12.0	12.0				1004	0545
			2	2	3.0	9.0	3	8.0	4.0	8.00	100				25.0	7.0	12.0	6.0		1004	0546
			1		2.0	10.0	1	12.0	2.0	4.00	36				6.0	2.0	2.0	1.0		1004	0547
			1	2	2.0	16.0	1	16.0	3.0	5.00	45	2	1.0	.5	7.0	3.5	5.0	2.5		1004	0548
				2	4.0	16.0		15.0	3.0	6.00	40	3	1.0	.5	5.0	4.0	5.0	2.5		1004	0549
			1		2.0	12.0	2	15.0	3.0	8.00	64				5.0	3.0	1.0	1.0		1004	0550
							1								2.0	1.0	1.5	1.0		1004	0551
					1.0		1	2.0												1004	0552
			1	2	3.0	17.0	4	6.0	1.0	8.00	45		.8	.5	6.0	3.5	3.0	1.5		1004	0553
					1.0		1													1004	0601
					3.0	8.0	1	11.0	1.0	3.00	30				8.0	3.5				1004	0602

TOWN ID	INDIVIDUAL ID	NAME	TITLE	STATUS	POLLS RATEABLE	POLLS NOT RATEABLE	HOUSES AND SHOPS ADJOINING	SHOPS ADJOINING	TWN MKS DISTINCTION	TANHOUSES, ETC.	TANHOUSES: TYPE	STILLHOUSES	WAREHOUSES	SUPERFICIAL FEET OF WHARF	MILLS	MILLS: TYPE	IRONWORKS, ETC.	IRONWORKS: TYPE	ANNUAL WORTH £	s	d	SERVANTS FOR LIFE	TONS OF VESSELS	MERCH £	s	d	FACTORAGE £	s	d
1004	0603	TOBEY, ZACCHEUS			4		1.00													12	10			20						
1004	0604	TOBEY, JONATHAN			1	2	1.00													6	10									
1004	0605	TABER, PARDON			1		1.00													1	10									
1004	0606	TABER, LEWIS			2		1.00				1.00									2	10									
1004	0607	TABER, PRINCE			2															2										
1004	0608	TALLMAN, WESSON			1	1	2.50				1.00									11	10									
1004	0609	TABER, STEPHEN			3		2.33				1.00					1.76				34				32						
1004	0610	TABER, THOMAS			1		1.00													5										
1004	0611	THOMAS, EBENEZAR			1		1.00													6										
1004	0612	TOBEY, JOHN			1		2.00													7										
1004	0613	TOBEY, ELNATHAN			1		1.00				1.00									13										
1004	0614	TALLMAN, WILLIAM			1		3.00				2.00									20				40	80					
1004	0615	TABER, TRUMAN			1		1.00													10	10		1							
1004	0616	TRIPP, JOSEPH			1	1	1.00													3										
1004	0617	TRIPP, JOSEPH JR			2																			20						
1004	0618	TURNER, SAMUEL				1	1.00													3										
1004	0619	VINCENT, ISAAC			1		1.00													12	10			8						
1004	0620	WOOD, WILLIAM			1	1	2.00													17				17						
1004	0621	WOOD, ZERAIAH			1		1.00											1.00		8	10									
1004	0622	WING, BARNABAS	5		3		1.00								600	.60				5				27	4					
1004	0623	WEST, BARTHOLOMEW			1	1	1.00													20										
1004	0624	WEST, JOHN			2	1	2.00													25				22						
1004	0625	WEST, SAMUEL			2		1.00													11	5									
1004	0626	WEST, STEPHEN			1		2.00													13	10									
1004	0627	WINSLOW, JOB			1															5	15									
1004	0628	WINSLOW, EZRA			1		1.00													7										
1004	0629	WING, DANIEL + BARNABAS			2		2.00													15										
1004	0630	WING, JOSEPH			3		1.00				1.00									14										
1004	0631	WEST, BARTHOLOMEW II			2		1.00													15	10									
1004	0632	WILLIS, JIREH			1		1.00													4	6	8								
1004	0633	WILLIS, EBENEZER			1		1.00									.84				10	5									
1004	0634	WESTON, ISAAC			2	1	1.00				1.00									5										
1004	0635	WESTON, JOHN			1															1	10									
1004	0636	WESTON, GEORGE			1	1	1.00													3	10									
1004	0637	WILLIAMS, JOHN			2		.33				1.00									3	10									
1004	0638	WALKER, JOHN			2		1.00				1.00									3										
1004	0639	WRIGHTETON, HENRY			1		1.00													3	10									
1004	0640	WILLCOX, WILLIAM				1															12									
1004	0641	WHITE, ELIZABETH					1.00													7	10									
1004	0642	WASHBURN, MOSES JR			1		1.00													1	14									
1004	0643	WRIGHTENTON, THOMAS			2		1.00				1.00									7										
1004	0644	WASHBURN, MOSES			1	1	1.00													2	10									
1004	0645	WASHBURN, BAZALEL			1		1.00													1	5									
1004	0646	WEST, ELI			1		.66									.25				3	5									
1004	0647	WEST, HANNAH	1		1	1	1.00				1.00									9										
1004	0648	WHITE, WILLIAM			2		1.00													9	10									
1004	0649	WILLIAMS, LEMUEL			1		1.00				1.00									3	6	8		100	400					
1004	0650	WEEDEN, JOHN			1		1.00													2										
1004	0651	RUSSELL, CALEB			4	1	2.00				2.00				1,300	1.00		1.00		36				61	400					
1004	0652	SHERMAN, JOHN			1		1.00													1										
1004	0653	WING, JABEZ			2		1.00													3	13	4								
1004	0701	MACUMBER, ZEBUDEE			1		1.00				1.00									2										
1004	0702	SLOCUM, HOLDER			2		1.00														10									
1004	0703	ALLEN, ZEBULON			1		2.00													8	16									
1004	0704	TUCKER, HENRY			2		1.00													10										
1004	0705	CASE, JOHN			1		1.00													2	6	8								
1004	0706	WING, EDWARD			3		2.00													35										
1004	0707	ALLEN, PRINCE			3		2.00													12										
1004	0708	WILBUR, JONATHAN			2		1.00																							
1004	0709	SHEARMAN, THOMAS			1															2	10									
1004	0710	ALLEN, SETH			1		1.00													15										
1004	0711	RUSSELL, ABRAHAM			1		1.00													2	6	8								
1004	0712	TUCKER, JOSEPH JR			1		2.00													13										
1004	0713	TUCKER, JOHN			1		1.00													16										
1004	0714	WOOD, WILLIAM	5		1		1.00				1.00									7	10			21						
1004	0715	WOOD, JESIAH			2		1.00				1.00									6										
1004	0716	WOOD, LUTHAN			1																			15						
1004	0717	SLOCUM, REBECCA																					3							
1004	0718	HOWLAND, BENJ'A			2	1	1.00													13										
1004	0719	HOWLAND, WILLIAM				1	1.00													1	10									
1004	0720	MOSHER, ROGER			1	1	1.00													1	3	4								
1004	0721	WILBUR, DAVID			1		1.00													2	3	4								
1004	0722	HOWLAND, ABRAHAM			1		1.00				1.00													8						
1004	0723	SMITH, BENJ'A			2	1	1.00													14										
1004	0724	SMITH, SAMUEL			1		1.00													6										
1004	0725	RUSSELL, JOHN			1		2.00				2.00									25										
1004	0726	RUSSELL, ELIJAH			1		1.00													6	13	4								
1004	0727	HOWLAND, GIDEON			1		1.00													9	13	4								
1004	0728	EARL, BARNABAS				1	1.00													17										
1004	0729	GIFFORD, PELEG			1		1.00													9										
1004	0730	GIFFORD, ABIAL			1		1.00				1.00									3	6	8								
1004	0731	POTTER, STOTEN			2																									
1004	0732	CRAW, JOHN			1		1.00													4	10									
1004	0733	HART, ARCHIPPUS			1		1.00													4	10									
1004	0734	ALLEN, JOSEPH			1		1.00													4	10									
1004	0735	FANCE, NATHANIEL			1		1.00													1	10									
1004	0736	CASWELL, JOSEPH			1		1.00													1	10									
1004	0737	BLACKMER, STEPHEN			1	1	1.00													1	10									
1004	0738	GIFFORD, DAVID			2		1.00				1.00									5										
1004	0739	RIDER, WILLIAM			1	1	1.00				1.00									9	13	4								
1004	0740	RIDER, SAMUEL			1		1.00													7										
1004	0741	RIDER, BENJAMIN			1		1.00													7										
1004	0742	ALLEN, JONATHAN			1		1.00													5										
1004	0743	MOSHER, CONSTANT			2	2	4.00													6										
1004	0744	WINSLOW, JONATHAN			2																	5									
1004	0745	WINSLOW, BENJ'A	1		2		1.00													2										
1004	0746	CASWELL, THOMAS			1		1.00													2										
1004	0747	WASHBURN, PETER			1	1	1.00									1.75				2										
1004	0748	WILBUR, HENRY			1		1.00													5										
1004	0801	LUDY, EZERIAH			1		1.00													3										

Columns under **VALUE OF MONEY LENT AT INTEREST** are £ (l) / s / d.

£	s	d	HORSES	OXEN	CATTLE	GOATS AND SHEEP	SWINE	ACRES OF PASTURE	NUMBER OF COWS PASTURE WILL KEEP	ACRES OF TILLAGE	BUSHELS OF GRAIN PRODUCED PER YEAR	BARRELS OF CIDER PRODUCED PER YEAR	ACRES OF SALT MARSH	TONS OF SALT MARSH HAY PRODUCED PER YR	ACRES OF ENGLISH AND UPLAND MOWING LAND	TONS OF ENGLISH AND UPLAND HAY PER YEAR	ACRES OF FRESH MEADOW	TONS OF FRESH MEADOW HAY PER YEAR	NOTES	TOWN ID	INDIVIDUAL ID
			2	1	5.0	37.0	4	12.0	5.0	6.00	70	2	3.0	2.0	20.0	11.0				1004	0603
			1	2	4.0	20.0	3	10.0	3.0	9.00	95		4.0	1.5	18.0	4.5				1004	0604
															1.0	.5				1004	0605
																				1004	0606
																				1004	0607
				2	2.0	12.0		14.0	4.0	4.50	45		1.0	.8	21.0	8.5				1004	0608
			?	9	6.0	45.0	6	30.0	14.0	25.00	170				50.0	22.0	10.0	6.0		1004	0609
				4	2.0	12.0	2	4.0	2.0	8.00	40				12.0	9.0			00	1004	0610
				2	3.0		1	8.0	3.0	2.00	20	2	5.0	4.0	11.0	4.0				1004	0611
			1	3	2.0	9.0	1	4.0	2.0	5.00	50				10.0	5.0	1.0	1.0		1004	0612
			1	2	4.0	17.0	4	20.0	5.0	8.00	100				20.0	10.0	5.0	4.0		1004	0613
			1	2	4.0	20.0	2	8.0	4.0	2.00	20	3			18.0	8.0	3.0	1.5		1004	0614
			1	2	4.0	16.0	2	17.0	4.0	6.00	70	4	2.0	1.0	20.0	8.0				1004	0615
																				1004	0616
																				1004	0617
																				1004	0618
50			1	2	4.0	28.0	2	10.0	4.0	9.00	120		3.0	1.0	16.0	10.0				1004	0619
			2	2	7.0	19.0	4	24.0	6.0	6.00	90	8	10.0	6.0	10.0	7.5	3.0	2.0		1004	0620
			1	2	2.0	15.0	1	12.0	3.0	6.00	65		6.0	4.0	8.0	4.0				1004	0621
					1.0	3.0	1													1004	0622
			1	4	4.0	3.0	7	50.0	8.0	6.00	70	10	22.0	16.0	20.0	10.0				1004	0623
			2	4	9.0	80.0	4	70.0	16.0	8.00	92	2	50.0	25.0	6.0	4.0				1004	0624
			1	2	3.0	19.0	2	11.0	3.0	5.00	60		15.5	12.0	5.5	4.0				1004	0625
			1	4	5.0	40.0	2	15.0	6.0	3.00	25		23.0	15.0	7.0	6.0				1004	0626
			1		2.0	8.0	2	7.0	3.0	3.00	36	4	2.0	2.0	7.0	4.5				1004	0627
				2	2.0	8.0	3	13.0	3.0	3.00	36	4			4.0	4.0				1004	0628
40			2		6.0	18.0	2	24.0	6.0	3.50	66	3			18.0	11.0				1004	0629
			1		6.0	22.0	3	27.0	6.0	6.50	90	6	2.0	1.8	20.0	12.0				1004	0630
			1	2	5.0	30.0	2	35.0	5.0	6.00	60	5	17.0	13.0	7.0	5.0	1.5	1.5		1004	0631
			1	2	2.0	5.0	2	5.0	2.0	3.00	30		1.0	.5	5.0	2.0				1004	0632
			2	4	3.0	35.0	3	18.0	6.0	6.00	60		2.0	2.0	9.0	4.0				1004	0633
			1		1.0	10.0	2	2.0	2.0	4.00	46				8.0	3.5				1004	0634
				2	1.0					1.50	10				5.0	2.0				1004	0635
																				1004	0636
					1.0															1004	0637
			2		2.0	11.0	2			2.00	25				4.0	4.0				1004	0638
				2	2.0	12.0	2	15.0	2.0	3.00	30		3.0	2.0	3.0	1.0				1004	0639
							1													1004	0640
			1		4.0			15.0	4.0	4.00	45				12.0	8.0				1004	0641
				2	2.0		3	2.0		2.00	30				4.0	2.0				1004	0642
				2	3.0	24.0	1	10.0	3.0	7.00	60		3.0	2.0	7.0	4.5				1004	0643
				2	2.0	20.0	2	3.0	1.0	3.00	25				6.0	2.0				1004	0644
					1.0		1			2.00	15				3.0	1.0				1004	0645
				2	1.0		2	1.0							3.0	1.0				1004	0646
			1	3	3.0	15.0		14.0	3.0	3.00	40	2			12.0	6.0				1004	0647
			1	3	4.0	25.0	2	16.0	4.0	6.00	80	1	4.0	4.0	16.0	6.0				1004	0648
			1																	1004	0649
					1.0			2.0							2.5	.8				1004	0650
			4	8	5.0	40.0	7	36.0	9.0	6.00	100	20	6.0	4.0	15.0	12.0	5.0	5.0		1004	0651
																				1004	0652
				2	2.0	15.0	2	2.0	1.0	2.00	25				3.0	2.0				1004	0653
					1.0		2	2.0	1.0						2.0	1.0				1004	0701
																				1004	0702
			1		2.0		2	8.0	2.0	2.00	30		6.0	3.0	12.0	6.0				1004	0703
			1	2	2.0	10.0	1	25.0	4.0	4.00	50				30.0	12.0				1004	0704
					1.0			3.0	1.0	1.00	10				2.0	1.0				1004	0705
			3	2	15.0	20.0	1	75.0	16.0	8.00	100	3	20.0	10.0	46.0	30.0				1004	0706
			1	2	8.0		1	15.0	5.0	5.00	55		4.0	3.0	15.0	9.0				1004	0707
					2.0	10.0	1	2.0		1.00	10				4.0	1.5				1004	0708
					1.0				1.0	1.75	15				7.0	3.0				1004	0709
			1	2	5.0	12.0	2	6.0	4.0	4.00	50		12.0	8.0	8.0	1.0				1004	0710
					1.0		1	4.0	1.0	1.00	15				1.0	1.0				1004	0711
			1	3	6.0	26.0	6	8.0	4.0	6.00	74	5	8.0	5.0	24.0	8.0				1004	0712
			2	3	8.0	20.0	5	14.0	6.0	8.00	80	4	15.0	7.0	10.0	7.0	10.0	7.0		1004	0713
			1	1	2.0		2	6.0	3.0	7.00	50		3.0	2.0	5.0	2.0	7.0	3.0		1004	0714
30			1		3.0		3	1.0	1.0	3.00	20	5			5.0	2.0	2.0	1.0		1004	0715
				3																1004	0716
120			3		4.0															1004	0717
			1		8.0	22.0		25.0	5.0	5.00	60		9.0	7.0	10.0	6.0				1004	0718
					1.0		1	2.0	1.0						2.0	1.0				1004	0719
					2.0				1.0	5.00					2.0	1.0				1004	0720
					1.0					1.00	10									1004	0721
			1		3.0	2.0	1	10.0	3.0	3.00	40		9.0	5.0	5.0	3.0				1004	0722
			2	2	4.0		2	20.0	5.0	5.00	70	2	16.0	10.0	20.0	10.0				1004	0723
			1	2	4.0	3.0	1	10.0	3.0	3.00	40		9.0	5.0	10.0	4.0				1004	0724
			4	4	6.0		1	50.0	10.0	8.00	110		14.0	8.0	30.0	10.0				1004	0725
			1	2	3.0		1	14.0	3.0	1.00	18				13.0	5.0				1004	0726
			1		5.0	40.0	2	10.0	3.0	7.00	70		10.0	7.0	6.0	4.0				1004	0727
			2	2	7.0	30.0	2	25.0	3.0	3.00	50	4	15.0	12.0	15.0	12.0				1004	0728
			1	2	4.0	15.0	1	8.0	4.0	2.00	20	2	1.0	.8	12.0	4.5				1004	0729
					4.0	4.0	1	15.0	3.0	3.00	30				7.0	3.0	3.0	1.5		1004	0730
			1		2.0	8.0	2												00	1004	0731
					1.0	5.0	1	2.0	1.0	3.00	25				8.0	4.0				1004	0732
					3.0	12.0	2	4.0	2.0	1.00	20		1.5	.5	4.0	4.0			00	1004	0733
				1	2.0	20.0		6.0	2.0						6.5	6.0				1004	0734
					1.0															1004	0735
																				1004	0736
					2.0	5.0	1	2.0	1.0						2.0	1.0				1004	0737
					2.0	2.0	1	4.0	2.0	1.25	20		1.5	1.0	7.0	3.0				1004	0738
			1	1	4.0	16.0	2	25.0	4.0	4.00	50				26.0	8.0				1004	0739
			1	2	4.0	9.0	3	5.0	3.0	4.00	60				7.0	5.0				1004	0740
					4.0	10.0	1	6.0	3.0	2.50	35				9.0	5.0				1004	0741
					2.0		1	5.0	2.0	3.00	20	3			7.0	3.0				1004	0742
					5.0	5.0	1	3.0	1.0	3.50	30				3.0	2.0				1004	0743
					1.0					1.00	10									1004	0744
					1.0	10.0	1	6.0	2.0	3.00	25				3.0	1.5				1004	0745
										3.50	50				2.5	2.0				1004	0746
										3.00	25						3.0	2.0		1004	0747
			1	4	3.0	20.0	1													1004	0748
				2	2.0		1			3.00	50				1.5	1.0			no	1004	0801

Dotted cells (···) reproduce rows printed entirely as clusters of dots in the source.

TOWN ID	INDIVIDUAL ID	NAME	TITLE	STATUS	POLLS RATEABLE	POLLS NOT RATEABLE	HOUSES AND SHOPS ADJOINING	SHOPS ADJOINING	TWN MKS DISTINCTION	TANHOUSES, ETC.	TANHOUSES: TYPE	STILLHOUSES	WAREHOUSES	SUPERFICIAL FEET OF WHARF	MILLS	MILLS: TYPE	IRONWORKS, ETC.	IRONWORKS: TYPE
1004	0802	THURBER, EDWARD			1		1.00											
1004	0803	COMMINGS, RANSON				1	1.00											
1004	0804	RUSSELL, DINAH	1		2		1.00			1.00					.25			
1004	0805	COOK, JOB			1		1.00											
1004	0806	HAYWARD, NATHAN				2	1.00			1.00								
1004	0807	ALLEN, SILVENAS			1		1.00			1.00								
1004	0808	ALLEN, JETHRO				1												
1004	0809	LOUS, DEMERANVILL				5	4.00											
1004	0810	PETTIS, ABRAHAM				4	1.00											
1004	0811	BOOTH, ANTHONY				1	1.00											
1004	0812	GIFFORD, BENJAMIN II			1		2.00											
1004	0813	SOBLE, JOSEPH	29		1		1.00											
1004	0814	SHEARMAN, ISRAEL				1	1.00			2.00								
1004	0815	MOSHER, BENJ'A				1	1.00											
1004	0816	MOSHER, JOANNA					1.00											
1004	0817	WOODMANEY, THOMAS				2	1.00											
1004	0818	BEDON, RICHARD				1	1.00											
1004	0819	REED, THOMAS				1	1.00											
1004	0820	CHASE, JACOB			1													
1004	0821	CHASE, BENJAMIN			1		1.00											
1004	0822	CHASE, DAVID			1		1.00											
1004	0823	CHASE, EZEKIEL			2		1.00											
1004	0824	RUSSELL, DAVID			1		1.00											
1004	0825	PETTIS, EBENEZER			1		1.00											
1004	0826	GIFFORD, ICHABOD			1													
1004	0827	COHEN, ZENUS			1		1.00											
1004	0828	CORNEL, ISRAEL			3		2.00											
1004	0829	PRATT, PAUL			1		1.00								1.00			
1004	0830	TALLMAN, JAMES			1	1	1.00											
1004	0831	SMITH, WIDOW + SON	1		1		1.00											
1004	0832	WILCOX, STEPHEN JR			1	1	1.00											
1004	0833	BENTLEY, ROBERT			1													
1005		**DIGHTON**																
1005	0101	···	···	···	···	···	···	···	···	···	···	···	···	···	···	···	···	···
1005	0102	···	···	···	···	···	···	···	···	···	···	···	···	···	···	···	···	···
1005	0103	···	···	···	···	···	···	···	···	···	···	···	···	···	···	···	···	···
1005	0104	···	···	···	···	···	···	···	···	···	···	···	···	···	···	···	···	···
1005	0105	···	···	···	···	···	···	···	···	···	···	···	···	···	···	···	···	···
1005	0106	···	···	···	···	···	···	···	···	···	···	···	···	···	···	···	···	···
1005	0107	···	···	···	···	···	···	···	···	···	···	···	···	···	···	···	···	···
1005	0108	···	···	···	···	···	···	···	···	···	···	···	···	···	···	···	···	···
1005	0109	···	···	···	···	···	···	···	···	···	···	···	···	···	···	···	···	···
1005	0110	···	···	···	···	···	···	···	···	···	···	···	···	···	···	···	···	···
1005	0111	···	···	···	···	···	···	···	···	···	···	···	···	···	···	···	···	···
1005	0112	···	···	···	···	···	···	···	···	···	···	···	···	···	···	···	···	···
1005	0113	···	···	···	···	···	···	···	···	···	···	···	···	···	···	···	···	···
1005	0114	···	···	···	···	···	···	···	···	···	···	···	···	···	···	···	···	···
1005	0115	···	···	···	···	···	···	···	···	···	···	···	···	···	···	···	···	···
1005	0116	···	···	···	···	···	···	···	···	···	···	···	···	···	···	···	···	···
1005	0117	···	···	···	···	···	···	···	···	···	···	···	···	···	···	···	···	···
1005	0118	···	···	···	···	···	···	···	···	···	···	···	···	···	···	···	···	···
1005	0119	···	···	···	···	···	···	···	···	···	···	···	···	···	···	···	···	···
1005	0120	···	···	···	···	···	···	···	···	···	···	···	···	···	···	···	···	···
1005	0121	···	···	···	···	···	···	···	···	···	···	···	···	···	···	···	···	···
1005	0122	···	···	···	···	···	···	···	···	···	···	···	···	···	···	···	···	···
1005	0123	···	···	···	···	···	···	···	···	···	···	···	···	···	···	···	···	···
1005	0124	···	···	···	···	···	···	···	···	···	···	···	···	···	···	···	···	···
1005	0125	···	···	···	···	···	···	···	···	···	···	···	···	···	···	···	···	···
1005	0126	···	···	···	···	···	···	···	···	···	···	···	···	···	···	···	···	···
1005	0127	···	···	···	···	···	···	···	···	···	···	···	···	···	···	···	···	···
1005	0128	***, NOAH			1		···			···		···	···	···	···		···	
1005	0129	BURT, GORDEN			1		1.00											
1005	0130	WHITMARSH, ROUFUS			1													
1005	0131	FISHER, JEREMIAH			1													
1005	0132	WINSLOW, JEREMIAH			1		1.00											
1005	0133	WINSLOW, PELEG			2													
1005	0134	PEIRCE, JABEZ			2		1.00											
1005	0135	CAREY, SETH			1													
1005	0136	FRANCIS, PELEG			1		1.00											
1005	0137	BABBIT, RUTH	1		1													
1005	0138	ATWOOD, EPHARIM JR			1		1.00											
1005	0139	POOL, SAMUEL			2		1.00											
1005	0140	POOL, EBENEZER			1		1.00											
1005	0141	POOL, ISAAC			2		1.00											
1005	0142	BRIGGS, JAMES			1		.50											
1005	0143	BRIGGS, ANN	1		1		.50											
1005	0144	GODDING, MATTHEW			1		1.00											
1005	0145	ATWOOD, EPHARIM				1												
1005	0146	BRIGGS, ELIKAIM			2		1.00								1.00			
1005	0147	BRIGGS, JOTHAM			1		1.00											
1005	0148	REED, SAMUEL			2		1.00											
1005	0149	BRIGGS, EBENEZER			2		1.00											
1005	0150	BARTLIT, SARAH	1		1		1.00											
1005	0151	BARTLIT, EDWARD			1													
1005	0152	WARL, LYDIA	1				1.00											
1005	0153	TRAFFORN, BENJAMIN			1		1.00											
1005	0154	WRIGHT, AMOS			3		1.00											
1005	0155	FISH, BENJAMIN			1													
1005	0156	HELDING, ZEBEDEE			1		1.00											
1005	0157	JACOB, JOSEPH JR			1		1.00											
1005	0158	PHILLIPS, JOHN I			1		1.00											
1005	0159	PHILLIPS, SETH			1													
1005	0160	BROWN, WILLIAM			2		1.00							1.00					
1005	0161	GODDING, JOSEPH			1		1.00											
1005	0162	TALBOT, ZEPHANIAH			1													
1005	0163	GOODING, JOB			2													
1005	0164	ATWOOD, SILVESTER			1		1.00											

TOWN ID	INDIVIDUAL ID	NAME	ANNUAL WORTH £	ANNUAL WORTH s	ANNUAL WORTH d	SERVANTS FOR LIFE	TONS OF VESSELS	MERCHANDISE £	MERCHANDISE s	MERCHANDISE d	FACTORAGE £	FACTORAGE s	FACTORAGE d
1004	0802	THURBER, EDWARD	5										
1004	0803	COMMINGS, RANSON	1	6	8								
1004	0804	RUSSELL, DINAH	14										
1004	0805	COOK, JOB	2										
1004	0806	HAYWARD, NATHAN	1										
1004	0807	ALLEN, SILVENAS	5	10									
1004	0808	ALLEN, JETHRO											
1004	0809	LOUS, DEMERANVILL	5	13									
1004	0810	PETTIS, ABRAHAM	1	10									
1004	0811	BOOTH, ANTHONY		10									
1004	0812	GIFFORD, BENJAMIN II	4										
1004	0813	SOBLE, JOSEPH	4										
1004	0814	SHEARMAN, ISRAEL	2	10									
1004	0815	MOSHER, BENJ'A											
1004	0816	MOSHER, JOANNA	2	3	4								
1004	0817	WOODMANEY, THOMAS	1	10									
1004	0818	BEDON, RICHARD	1										
1004	0819	REED, THOMAS	2										
1004	0820	CHASE, JACOB	1										
1004	0821	CHASE, BENJAMIN	1	10									
1004	0822	CHASE, DAVID	3										
1004	0823	CHASE, EZEKIEL	5										
1004	0824	RUSSELL, DAVID	4										
1004	0825	PETTIS, EBENEZER	3										
1004	0826	GIFFORD, ICHABOD											
1004	0827	COHEN, ZENUS	1	10									
1004	0828	CORNEL, ISRAEL	6	13	4								
1004	0829	PRATT, PAUL	4										
1004	0830	TALLMAN, JAMES	5	13	4								
1004	0831	SMITH, WIDOW + SON	8										
1004	0832	WILCOX, STEPHEN JR	11										
1004	0833	BENTLEY, ROBERT	1	10									
1005		**DIGHTON**											
1005	0101	···	···	···	···	···							
1005	0102	···	···	···	···	···							
1005	0103	···	···	···	···	···							
1005	0104	···	···	···	···	···							
1005	0105	···	···	···	···	···							
1005	0106	···	···	···	···	···							
1005	0107	···	···	···	···	···							
1005	0108	···	···	···	···	···							
1005	0109	···	···	···	···	···							
1005	0110	···	···	···	···	···							
1005	0111	···	···	···	···	···	28						
1005	0112	···	···	···	···	···							
1005	0113	···	···	···	···	···							
1005	0114	···	···	···	···	···							
1005	0115	···	···	···	···	···							
1005	0116	···	···	···	···	···							
1005	0117	···	···	···	···	···							
1005	0118	···	···	···	···	···							
1005	0119	···	···	···	···	···							
1005	0120	···	···	···	···	···							
1005	0121	···	···	···	···	···							
1005	0122	···	···	···	···	···							
1005	0123	···	···	···	···	···							
1005	0124	···	···	···	···	···	30						
1005	0125	···	···	···	···	···							
1005	0126	···	···	···	···	···							
1005	0127	···	···	···	···	···							
1005	0128	***, NOAH	···	···	···	···							
1005	0129	BURT, GORDEN		10									
1005	0130	WHITMARSH, ROUFUS	70	10			11						
1005	0131	FISHER, JEREMIAH											
1005	0132	WINSLOW, JEREMIAH	6	10									
1005	0133	WINSLOW, PELEG					13						
1005	0134	PEIRCE, JABEZ	13										
1005	0135	CAREY, SETH											
1005	0136	FRANCIS, PELEG	9										
1005	0137	BABBIT, RUTH	5										
1005	0138	ATWOOD, EPHARIM JR	8										
1005	0139	POOL, SAMUEL	4										
1005	0140	POOL, EBENEZER	6	10									
1005	0141	POOL, ISAAC	6										
1005	0142	BRIGGS, JAMES	9										
1005	0143	BRIGGS, ANN	9										
1005	0144	GODDING, MATTHEW	4	10									
1005	0145	ATWOOD, EPHARIM				1							
1005	0146	BRIGGS, ELIKAIM	5										
1005	0147	BRIGGS, JOTHAM	2	10									
1005	0148	REED, SAMUEL	8	10									
1005	0149	BRIGGS, EBENEZER	5										
1005	0150	BARTLIT, SARAH		10									
1005	0151	BARTLIT, EDWARD											
1005	0152	WARL, LYDIA	1			1							
1005	0153	TRAFFORN, BENJAMIN	1	10									
1005	0154	WRIGHT, AMOS	3										
1005	0155	FISH, BENJAMIN											
1005	0156	HELDING, ZEBEDEE	1	10									
1005	0157	JACOB, JOSEPH JR	4	10			14						
1005	0158	PHILLIPS, JOHN I	1	10									
1005	0159	PHILLIPS, SETH	1	6	8								
1005	0160	BROWN, WILLIAM	5	10		1	100	133					
1005	0161	GODDING, JOSEPH	14				30						
1005	0162	TALBOT, ZEPHANIAH											
1005	0163	GOODING, JOB					30						
1005	0164	ATWOOD, SILVESTER	18										

£	s	d	Horses	Oxen	Cattle	Goats and Sheep	Swine	Acres of Pasture	Number of Cows Pasture Will Keep	Acres of Tillage	Bushels of Grain Produced per Year	Barrels of Cider Produced per Year	Acres of Salt Marsh	Tons of Salt Marsh Hay Produced per Yr	Acres of English and Upland Mowing Land	Tons of English and Upland Hay per Year	Acres of Fresh Meadow	Tons of Fresh Meadow Hay per Year	Notes	Town ID	Individual ID
				2	2.0	5.0	5	10.0	2.0	6.00	80				10.0	5.0				1004	0802
					1.0					4.00	40									1004	0803
120			1	2	3.0	25.0	3	10.0	5.0	4.00	40	4			12.0	8.0				1004	0804
					1.0	6.0	2			2.00	20				1.0	1.0				1004	0805
					1.0		1													1004	0806
			1	2	1.0	15.0	1	10.0	3.0	4.00	32				7.0	2.5				1004	0807
			1	2	2.0		1													1004	0808
30				4	3.0	10.0	3			4.00	40				10.0	6.0			00	1004	0809
					1.0		1			2.00	20				2.0	1.0				1004	0810
					1.0														00	1004	0811
				2	2.0	8.0	1	6.0	2.0	2.00	25				6.0	2.0				1004	0812
			1		2.0		1	2.0	1.0	2.00	20		2.0	1.0	6.0	2.0			00	1004	0813
					1.0			6.0	1.0	2.00	20				2.0	1.0				1004	0814
																				1004	0815
45					1.0		1	2.0	1.0	.75	6				3.0	1.0				1004	0816
				2	1.0					3.00	30									1004	0817
										1.00	10						1.5	1.0		1004	0818
				2	1.0					2.00	20				2.0	1.0				1004	0819
					1.0		1								2.0	1.0				1004	0820
					1.0					1.50	15				1.5	.5				1004	0821
					1.0			6.0	1.0						6.0	2.0				1004	0822
				2	2.0		1	6.0	1.0	8.00	60				6.0	4.0				1004	0823
				2	1.0	14.0	2	6.0	1.0	2.00	20				6.0	2.0				1004	0824
			1	1	1.0		2	3.0	2.0	4.00	30				6.0	3.0				1004	0825
				1	1.0															1004	0826
					1.0	4.0				1.00	4				2.0	1.0				1004	0827
19			1	2	3.0	4.0	1	2.0	1.0	6.00	70				9.0	5.0				1004	0828
																				1004	0829
			1	2	2.0		2	5.0	2.0	3.00	30				6.0	4.0				1004	0830
			1	1	3.0	20.0	2	15.0	3.0	3.00	40	6			10.0	5.0				1004	0831
			1	2	2.0	20.0	2	20.0	4.0	4.00	50		3.0	2.0	12.0	6.0				1004	0832
																				1004	0833
75			1	2	5.0	29.0	1	26.0	10.0	10.00	145	6			8.0	8.0	5.0	3.0		1005	0101
			1	2	1.0															1005	0102
					1.0	5.0	1	6.0	1.0	4.00	30									1005	0103
			1	4	2.0	11.0	1	10.0	6.0	5.00	50	15			20.0	8.0				1005	0104
				1	1.0	7.0	1	2.0	1.0	1.00	10	3			2.0	1.0				1005	0105
			1		3.0	6.0	3	10.0	3.0	5.00	40	10			5.0	5.0	4.0	2.0		1005	0106
				3	2.0	6.0	2	1.0	1.0	4.00	30	8			5.0	3.0	3.5	2.5		1005	0107
			1	2	2.0	11.0	1	4.0	3.0	6.00	75	2			6.0	5.0				1005	0108
				2	1.0		1	5.0	1.0	4.00	30	16			7.0	5.0	2.0	1.5		1005	0109
			2	2	2.0		3	10.0	9.0	8.00	80	8	12.0	9.0	10.0	5.0				1005	0110
15								4.0	2.0			3			4.0	2.0				1005	0111
4	10																			1005	0112
			1	4	5.0	20.0	4	10.0	6.0	9.00	120	10	1.5	1.0	15.0	8.0	6.0	4.0		1005	0113
				2	2.0		3	12.0	5.0	6.00	30		4.0	4.0	5.0	2.0	3.0	2.0		1005	0114
9																				1005	0115
37	15		2	4	3.0	15.0	2	5.0	6.0	6.00	50		2.0	1.5	6.0	4.0	2.0	1.5		1005	0116
			1	2	2.0	80.0	1	30.0	10.0	3.00	30		2.5	1.8	3.0	2.0				1005	0117
				2	1.0	4.0	2	2.5	1.0			3								1005	0118
				2	5.0	20.0	4	20.0	6.0	6.00	60	20			20.0	12.0	4.0	2.5		1005	0119
25				1	1.0		1	6.0	2.0			8								1005	0120
			2	4	4.0	7.0	7	3.0	5.0	4.00	40	30			2.0	1.0	10.0	7.0		1005	0121
					1.0		2	3.0	1.0	1.00	16									1005	0122
					3.0		1	8.0	3.0	1.00	15									1005	0123
15			1		2.0	7.0		2.0	1.0	1.00	15				1.0	1.5				1005	0124
													4.0	3.0						1005	0125
					1.0															1005	0126
																				1005	0127
																				1005	0128
																				1005	0129
				2				3.0	2.0	5.00	40									1005	0130
																				1005	0131
			1		1.0		1	1.0	2.0	3.00	25				2.0	1.5	6.0	4.0		1005	0132
			1		1.0		1													1005	0133
			1		1.0			4.0	4.0	5.00	60		6.0	6.0	6.0	3.5	7.0	3.0		1005	0134
5					2.0	5.0	1	6.0	3.0	4.00	50				7.0	3.0				1005	0135
					1.0	3.0	2													1005	0136
			1		2.0	10.0		5.0	3.0	4.00	40				4.0	2.0				1005	0137
																				1005	0138
																				1005	0139
					3.0		1	1.0		2.00	20				4.0	2.0	1.5	1.5		1005	0140
					3.0		1	5.0	3.0	3.00	30				3.0	2.5	3.0	2.5		1005	0141
				2	2.0		2	4.0	4.0	3.00	30	8			2.0	1.0	4.0	2.5		1005	0142
					3.0	8.0	2	4.0	4.0	3.00	30	8			2.0	1.0	4.0	2.5		1005	0143
			1	1	2.0	12.0	3	1.0	1.0	2.50	25				4.0	4.0				1005	0144
																				1005	0145
					2.0		1	1.0	1.0			5			4.0	2.0	2.0	1.0		1005	0146
			1		1.0	7.0	1	1.0	1.0	2.00	20	1			2.0	1.0				1005	0147
					4.0	9.0	1	3.0	3.0	3.00	35	8			4.0	3.0	3.0	2.0		1005	0148
					2.0	9.0	3	3.0	3.0	4.00	40				3.0	3.0	2.0	2.0		1005	0149
										1.00	5						1.0	1.0	00	1005	0150
																			00	1005	0151
10					1.0		1										2.0	1.0		1005	0152
					1.0		2			1.00	15									1005	0153
					1.0		1			2.00	10									1005	0154
					1.0															1005	0155
			1		1.0		4													1005	0156
					1.0		2	1.0	1.0			4								1005	0157
										1.00	8									1005	0158
					1.0			3.0	1.0						1.0	1.0				1005	0159
					2.0					1.00	10									1005	0160
100			1	1	3.0	4.0	3	12.0	4.0	7.00	80	5			18.0	8.0				1005	0161
60																				1005	0162
																				1005	0163
			1	2	5.0	20.0	1	3.0	5.0	6.00	50	6			5.0	3.0	8.0	7.0		1005	0164

BRISTOL COUNTY—Continued.

DARTMOUTH TOWN.

Name of head of family	Free white males of 16 years and upward, including heads of families	Free white males under 16 years	Free white females, including heads of families	All other free persons	Slaves
Gidley, Henry	2		5		
Macomber, Elijah	1	1	1		
Briggs, Caleb	1	1	2		
Gidley, Samuel	1	3	2		
Rickerson, John	2	2	6		
Packard, Eliphalet	1	1	2		
Packard, Noah	2		2		
Russell, Stephen	1		2		
Fisher, James	2	2	2		
Gifford, Ichabod	1	2	2		
Gifford, Benjamin	1		2		
Gifford, James	1	3	2		
Gifford, Jonathan, 2d	1	2	1		
Slocum, Jonathan	1	1	3		
Grinnell, Remington	2	1	4		
Gifford, Stephen	1	4	3		
Lawton, Abraham				4	
Dick, Silas				4	
Cornell, Peleg	4		3		
Russell, Benjamin	2		2	1	
Gifford, Abraham	3	2	4		
Cushman, Ichabod	1	1	3		
Gifford, Thomas	1		3		
Wood, Josias	2	2	5		
Wood, Luthern	3		3		
Wood, Alice	1		1		
Hathaway, Elizabeth		1	4		
Peirce, Clothier	1		1		
Russell, Jonathan	2		1		
Lawrence, Isaa	1	4	5		
Howland, Cook	1	2	2		
Briggs, Phebe			2		
Howland, Jonathan	1	2	3		
Howland, Timothy	2	1	4		
Allen, James	2	1	3		
Estes, Joseph	2	3	4		
Rickerson, Joseph	2	3			
Russell, Giles	3		2		
Packard, Joel	1	1	2		
Howland, Benjamin, 3d	2	1	5		
Russell, Barnabas	2	1	5		
Smith, Peleg	4	1	5		
Smith, Collins	1	2	2		
Smith, Benjamin	3	2	3		
Howland, Abraham	4		2		
Smith, Samuel	3	1	4		
Howland, Benjamin, 2d	3	1	3		
Howland, John	2	1	2		
Anthony, William	2	2	2		
Howland, Benjamin	1		3		
Howland, Isaac	1	2	3		
Brightman, Johnson	1		4		
Briggs, Cornelius	3	2			
Smith, Hannah	1		2		
Kirbee, Weston	1		4		
Smith, George	3	1	2		
Briggs, Daniel	1		2		
Howland, Katharine	1		1		
Hicks, Thomas	2		4		
Howland, William	1	1	4		
Howland, Joseph, 2d	1		2		
Wilbore, David	3	2	3		
Allen, Ebenezer	3		2		
Howland, Joseph, 1st	1	1	2		
Akin, William	1		2		
Smith, Eleazer	1		2		
Sherman, Barnabas	1	2	4		
Howland, Olivia	2		3		
Russell, David	2		2		
Russell, Stephen	1	2	2		
Orlat, John	1	2	2		

DARTMOUTH TOWN—continued.

Name of head of family	Free white males of 16 years and upward, including heads of families	Free white males under 16 years	Free white females, including heads of families	All other free persons	Slaves
Winslow, Church	1	1	3		
Russell, Noah	1		3		
Lapham, Nicholas	3	1	2		
Lapham, Humphry	1	1	2		
Shaw, Barnabas	2	1	3		
Sherman, Benjamin	1		3		
Smith, Reuben	1		4		
Howland, Henry	2	4	2		
Russell, Isaac	2	1	3		
Russell, Joseph	2	1	3	1	
Potter, William	2	2	2		
Smith, George, 2d	2	2	3	1	
Russell, Henry	2	3	3		
Quoniwell, Peter				7	
Trafford, Phillip	1	1	4		
Moshier, Ebenezer	2	1	3		
Moshier, Benjamin	1		1		
Hatch, Ichabod	1	1	6		
Trafford, Joseph	1	1	3		
Hicks, Thomas	2		2		
Smith, Henry	1	1	3		
Quawn, Joseph				3	
Sherman, William	2		2		
Sherman, Peleg	4	3	3		
Sherman, Humphrey	2	2	4		
Russell, Thomas	2	2	4		
Macomber, Anson	1		2		
Sherman, Benjamin, 2d	1	1	2		
Johnson, James	1	1	3		
Briggs, Weston	1		1		
Sherman, Shadrach	1	1	4		
Rickerson, Anna	1		4		
Tucker, Henry	1	3	2	2	
Beard, John	1		1		
Beard, Obediah	1	2	2		
Smith, David	2		2		
Russell, Humphry	3	2	5		
Wilcox, Sarah			2		
Smith, Benjamin, 2d	1	1	2		
Sherman, Jedediah	3	1	3		
Chace, Benjamin	1	3	7		
Shepard, John	3	2	4		
Akin, Benjamin	1				
Akin, Job	1	3	1		
Smith, Jerusha			2		
Swift, Foster	1	1	3	1	
Wilcox, Thomas	2	2	4		
Sanford, William, 1st	1	1	3	2	
Sanford, George	2	1	2		
Slocum, Paul	1	1	6		
Sanford, Elisha	1	1	2		
Sanford, Richard	1		1		
Sanford, Peleg	1	1	1		
Sanford, William, 2d	1	1	2		
Gifford, Elihu	3	5	4		
Talman, William	1	2	6		
Sanford, John	3	1	4		
Wood, John	2	4	6		
Wady, John	2		2		
Cushman, Ebenezer	1	1	2		
Howland, Warren	1		2		
Wait, Daniel	1	3	7		
Sherman, Tisdale	2	2	2		
Sherman, Phillip	4	1	3		
Russell, Elijah	2		10		
Russell, Ezra	1	1	5		
Cushman, Obed	1	1	5		
Akin, John	2	1	5		
Almy, Joseph	2	1	5		
Almy, Anthony	1	1	4		
Almy, Christopher	1	1	2		
Almy, Peleg	1	2	1		
Lawton, David	1	2	3		
Macomber, Peregrine	2		3		
Almy, Giles	1		4		
Howland, Thomas, Jun	1	2	2		
Allen, Reuben	1	2	2		
Case, Adam	1		4		
Allen, Margaret			4		
Allen, Thomas, 2d	1	3	4		
Sisson, William	1	3	5		
Gifford, Samuel	1	2	4		
Macomber, Constant	1		3		
Cornell, Gideon	7		4		
Slocum, Jonas		2	4		
Gifford, Caleb	1	1	3		
Tucker, Henry	1	2	4		
Case, Rachael		2	1		
Russell, Joseph, 2d	2	1	3		
Allen, Thomas, 1st	2	1	3		
Slocum, Peleg, 1st	4	1	5	1	
Case, Isaiah	1	2	2		
Russell, Noah, 2d	1	2	2		
Slocum, Christopher	3		2		
Howland, Daniel	1		2	1	

DARTMOUTH TOWN—continued.

Name of head of family	Free white males of 16 years and upward, including heads of families	Free white males under 16 years	Free white females, including heads of families	All other free persons	Slaves
Slocum, Peleg, 2d	4	1	2		
Slocum, Giles	1	1	2		
Butts, Stephen	1	3	5		
Butts, Abraham	2	2	4		
Cornell, Timothy	1		3		
Brightman, Henry	1		5		
Brightman, Ellis	1	1	2		
Brightman, Wanton	1	2	5		
Allen, Jedediah	1		5		
Wood, Thomas	1		6		
Allen, Benjamin	1	1	6		
Reed, Thomas	1		1		
Drinkwater, Ama		2	2		
Sowle, Elizabeth		1	2		
Barker, John	2	4	3		
Gifford, Peleg, Jun	1	2	3		
Gifford, Abial	4	2	3		
Gifford, Peleg	3	1	3		
Barker, William	3	1	3		
Barker, William, Jun	1		5		
Tucker, Joseph	1		3		
Lawton, Jonathan	1	1	3		
Eddy, Zephaniah	2	2	2	1	
Tucker, John	3	2	2		
Slade, Edward	2	4	5	1	
Tucker, Benjamin	1	2	4	1	
Tucker, Abraham	1		2		
Tucker, Barzilla	1		2		
Wady, Humphry	1	2	2		
Russell, Josiah	2	2	2		
Howland, Wing	1	1	4		
Sanford, David	1		2		
Akin, Timothy	1	1	2		
Akin, Jonathan	1	1	3		
Nelson, William	1	1	3		
Sherman, Caleb	1	2	4		
Rickerson, John	3		4		
Akin, Elihu	3	3	4		
Sherman, Mary		1	3		
Rickerson, William	2	3	3		
Moshier, Stephen	1		2		
Akin, James	2	1	1		
Tripp, John	1		3		
Akin, Richard	1		4		
Wait, Henry	1	2	2		
Akin, Jacob	1	1	2		
Russell, Michael	2		3		
Howland, Jonathan	1	1	3		
Eason, Walter	1	2	6		
Howland, John	4	3	5		
Bliss, Arnold	1	1	5		
Howland, Timothy, 2d	1	4	1		
Quash, Anthony				7	
Quash, Abraham				2	
Davis, Edmund	1		4		
Sherman, Paul	3		4		
Sherman, Jonathan	3	1	3		
Sherman, Butler	2	1	3		
Sherman, Prince		1			
Sherman, Zoath	1	1			
Coggeshall, Pero				8	
Howland, Pero				2	1
Slocum, Holder	3		2	1	
Gifford, Joseph	1		4		
Russell, Pero				6	
Sherman, Timothy	4		3		
Smith, Lorey	1	1	2		
Sherman, Edward	1	2	4		
Maxfield, Edmund	3	2	3		
Gifford, David	2	3	3		
Hammond, Hannah		1	4		
Pettis, Simpson	1	3	4		
Howland, Gideon	1	4	3	1	
Sherman, Jonathan	1		4		
Collins, John	2		2		
Mitchel, Elkanah	1	2	4		
Badcock, John	1	2	4		
Peckham, Isaiah	3		4		
Devol, David		4	4		
Smith, Benjamin	1	2	4		
Winslow, Weston	1	2	3		
Mirick, Deborah			1		
Hoskins, George	2	2	6		
Peckham, Caleb			2		
Russell, Cornelius	1		4		
Maxfield, Timothy, Jun	2	1	1		
Badcock, Benjamin	1		1		
Strange, Sarah			3		
Sherman, Bathsheba			2		
Allen, Jethro	2	1	2		
Allen, Silvanus		2	4		
Vance, Nathaniel	4	1	6		
Allen, Joseph	2		2		
Chandler, Phebe		1	2		
Sheldon, John	1	1	4		

DARTMOUTH TOWN—continued.

NAME OF HEAD OF FAMILY.	Free white males of 16 years and upward, including heads of families.	Free white males under 16 years.	Free white females, including heads of families.	All other free persons.	Slaves.
Hart, Archippus	1		3		
Handy, John	1	3	3		
Joy, Samuel	1	1	3		
Bowdish, William	2	1	2		
Russell, Allen	1	3	4		
Cook, Andros	2		5		
Hicks, Daniel	1		3		
Washburn, Peter	1		3		
Russell, Stephen, Junr	1		1		
Russell, Clark	1	2	1		
Rogers, John	1		1		
Russell, Stephen	1	3	4		
Booth, Isaiah	1		2		
Booth, Benjamin	1		3		
Knap, Ebenezer	1		2		
Upham, Burnett	1		1		
Hathaway, Jethro	1	2	3		
Wing, Primus				4	
Davis, John	1		1		
Hathaway, Paul	1	2	4		
Winslow, Edward	3		3		
Simmonds, Isaac				3	
Hathaway, Meletiah	3	1	8		
Potter, Holliday	1	2	4		
Maxfield, Timothy	1		1		
Sherman, Daniel	1		2		
Maxfield, John	1	1	4		
Maxfield, Abraham	1	1	4		
Devol, Abner	1	3	3		
Smith, Elishub	1	1	4		
Howard, Daniel	2	2	5		
Smith, John	2		6		
Moshier, Barnabas	1	3	2		
Wood, William	1	1	2		
Russell, Elizabeth	1		3		
Solomon, James				3	
Russell, Michael	1		6	2	
Handy, George	2	2	2		
Russell, Elisha	3	3	4		
Barker, Jabez	2		4		
Allen, Thomas, 1st	2	3	3	1	
Stratton, Oder	1		1		
Stratton, Benjamin	1		1		
Tripp, Ephraim	1	1	2		
Chace, John	3		3		
Chace, Nathaniel	1	3	3		
Howland, Joshua	1		2		
Chace, Abner	3	1	4		
Howland, Caleb	1	2	2		
Howland, Daniel, Senr	1	1	2		
Wood, John	1		2		
Wood, Benjamin	1	2	3		
Howland, Luther	3	1	1		
Perkins, Benjamin	2		2		
Anthony, Jacob	1	1	2		
Barker, Joseph	2		4		
Smith, Increase	1	1	1		
Howland, Sarah	1		3		
Barker, Stephen	1	4	2		
Russell, Joshua	1	4	3		
Peabody, Daniel	1		3		
Gifford, Silas	1	1	4		
Sowle, Jethro	1	1	1		
Harrison, Francis	1	1	2		
Mott, Thomas	3		3		
Russell, Jethro	1	3	3		
Wing, Primus, 2d				3	
Fish, Thomas	1		2		
Potter, Joshua	2	2	7		
Potter, Humphry	1	5	2		
Gifford, Jonathan, 1st	3	2	4		
Sherman, George	1	3	4		
Devol, Joseph	1	3	5		
Gifford, Daniel	1		2		
Gifford, Gideon	1	1	3		
Potter, Prince	3	4	6		
Tripp, William	2		4		
Devol, John	1	2	3		
Devol, Job	2	2	4		
Sherman, Israel	2		4		
Moshier, George	2	1	3		
Wood, Enos	1	1	2		
Wheating, Daniel	1	1	5		
Moshier, Michael	1	4	1		
Wheating, Joseph	1		2		
Moshier, Jesse	1	1	2		
Sherman, Reuben, Junr	1	2	4		
West, Samuel	1	2	4		
Beaden, Benjamin	1	2	2		
Beaden, Henry	1		2		
Beaden, Richard	1	1	2		
Beaden, Stephen	2		3		
Woodmansee, Thomas	2		1		
Woodmansee, Gideon	1	2	1		
Reed, Thomas, Junr	1	2	4		
Reed, Elijah	1		1		
Reed, Lemuel	2	1	2		
Pettis, Abraham	1		3		
Pettis, David	1		2		
Howland, John	1	3	2		
Kurbee, Thomas	2		3		
Allen, Benjamin	1	2	2		
Allen, Thomas	1	2	3		
Allen, Judah	1	1	2		
Rogers, Gideon	1	1	3		
Rogers, Daniel	1		3		
Rogers, Stephen	1	2	1		
Moshier, Constant	1		2		
Wait, Reuben	1	3	3		
Shepard, Abner	1	2	1		
Washburn, Ira	1		2		
Chace, Ebenezer	1	2	3		
Peck, Bristol				4	
Gifford, James	1	1	2		
Gillat, John	1		2		
Wilson, Luther	1	1	3		
Andrews, John	1	3	5		
Kurbee, Silas	1	3	3		
Kurbee, William	1		1		
Babcock, Peleg	1	3	2		
Chace, Jared	1	3	2		
Cornell, John	1	2	3		
Cornell, Amos	2		2		
Cornell, Susannah			2		
Baker, James	1		2		
Cowen, Zenas	1		2		
Cowen, Ebenezer	2	2	2		
Cowen, Joshua	2		3		
Chace, Simeon	2	4	1		
Biggs, William	2	1	3		
Chace, David	2	1	1		
Peirce, Clothier	1	1	3		
Blackman, Ebenezer	1	3	4		
Moshier, John	2	6	5		
Reed, Benjamin	1		3		
Reed, Benjamin, Junr	1	3	1		
Reed, William	1		2		
Reed, John	1	1	1		
Moshier, Roger	3		3		
Chace, Ezekiel	2		4		
Wilkey, Peter	2	2	4		
Pettis, William	1		5		
Wait, Abner	1	1	5		
Crank, George				4	
West, Hope			2		
Russell, William	1		1		
Craw, Sherman	1	1	4		
Cummings, Benjamin	3		6		
Winslow, John	1		2		
Winslow, Abigail			1		
Gifford, David	2		1		
Gifford, Archippus	1	1	5		
Gifford, William	1	3	1		
Harrison, Joseph	1		5		
Smith, Thomas	1	1	3		
Moshier, Lemuel	1	2	3		
Moshier, Elihu	1	2	4		
Hart, Jonathan	1	1	3		
Hart, Seth	1		4		
Hart, Luke	1		2		
Hart, William	3	3	2		
Moshier, Hannah			2		
Tucker, Jonathan	1	2	4		
Moshier, Barnabas	1		1		
Rider, William	1		2		
Rider, William, Junr	1	4	3		
Rider, Samuel	2	4	3		
Rider, Benjamin	2	3	3		
Armitage, John	1		1		
Wilbore, Henry	3		3	1	
Washburn, Beraliel	1	4	5		
Pettis, James	1	3	3		
Andrews, Stephen	1	2	4		
Mott, Adam	2		1		
Phillips, Nathaniel	2		2		
Peirce, Samuel	1	1	2		
Fisher, William	1	1	3		
Phillips, Ira	2		3		
Collins, William	2		2		
Collins, Jonathan	2	2	4		
Bennett, John	2	1	2		
D'Meranville, Sherman	2	1	4		
Hathaway, Abraham	2	3	3	1	
Howland, Gideon	4	1	3		
Anthony, Gideon	1		2		
Knap, Axel	1		2		
Sherman, Reuben	6		3		

BRISTOL COUNTY—Continued.

Name of head of family	Free white males of 16 years and upward, including heads of families	Free white males under 16 years	Free white females, including heads of families	All other free persons	Slaves
DARTMOUTH TOWN.					
Gidley, Henry	2		5		
Macomber, Elijah	1	1	5		
Briggs, Caleb	1	1	2		
Gidley, Samuel	1	3	2		
Rickerson, John	2	2	6		
Packard, Eliphalet	2	1	2		
Packard, Noah	2		2		
Russell, Stephen	1		2		
Fisher, James	2	2	2		
Gifford, Ichabod	1	2	2		
Gifford, Benjamin	1		2		
Gifford, James	1	3	2		
Gifford, Jonathan, 2d	1	2	3		
Slocum, Jonathan	1	1	3		
Grinnell, Remington	2	1	4		
Gifford, Stephen	1	4	3		
Lawton, Abraham				4	
Dick, Silas				4	
Cornell, Peleg	4		3		
Russell, Benjamin	2		2	1	
Gifford, Abraham	3	2	4		
Cushman, Ichabod	1	1	2		
Gifford, Thomas			2		
Wood, Josias	2	2	5		
Wood, Luthern	3		3		
Wood, Alice	1		2		
Hathaway, Elizabeth		1	4		
Peirce, Clothier	1		1		
Russell, Jonathan	2		2		
Lawrence, Isaa	1	4	5		
Howland, Cook	1	2	2		
Briggs, Phebe			2		
Howland, Jonathan	1	2	3		
Howland, Timothy	2	1	4		
Allen, James	2	1	3		
Estes, Joseph	2		4		
Rickerson, Joseph	2	3	1		
Russell, Giles	3		2		
Packard, Joel	1	1	2		
Howland, Benjamin, 3d	2	1	1		
Russell, Barnabas	2	1	3		
Smith, Peleg	4	1	5		
Smith, Collins	1	2	2		
Smith, Benjamin	3	2	3		
Howland, Abraham	4		4		
Smith, Samuel		1	4		
Howland, Benjamin, 2d	3	1	3		
Howland, John	1	2	2		
Anthony, William	2	2	2		
Howland, Benjamin			1		
Howland, Isaac	1	2	3		
Brightman, Johnson	1	2	4		
Briggs, Cornelius	3	2	5		
Smith, Hannah	1		2		
Kurbee, Weston	2		1		
Smith, George	3	1	2		
Briggs, Daniel	1	1	1		
Howland, Katharine		1	2		
Hicks, Thomas	2		4		
Howlant, William	1	1	4		
Howland, Joseph, 2d	1	1	1		
Wilborn, David	3	1	3		
Allen, Ebenezer	2		2		
Howland, Joseph, 1st	3		3		
Akin, William	1	1	2		
Smith, Eleazer	1		2		
Sherman, Barnabas	1	3	4		
Howland, Olivia	1	2	3		
Russell, David	2		3		
Russell, Stephen	1	2	2		
Orlat, John	1	2	2		
DARTMOUTH TOWN—continued.					
Winslow, Church	1	1	3		
Russell, Noah	1		1		
Lapham, Nicholas	3	1	2		
Lapham, Humphry	1	1	2		
Shaw, Barnabas	2	1	3		
Sherman, Benjamin	1		2		
Smith, Reuben	1		2		
Howland, Henry	2	4	3		
Russell, Isaac	2	1	3		
Russell, Joseph	2	1	3	1	
Potter, William	2	2	3		
Smith, George, 2d	2	3	3	1	
Russell, Henry	3	3			
Quoniwell, Peter				7	
Trafford, Phillip	1	1	4		
Moshier, Ebenezer	2	1	3		
Moshier, Benjamin	1		3		
Hatch, Ichabod	1	1	6		
Trafford, Joseph	1	4	3		
Hicks, Thomas	2		2		
Smith, Henry	1	1	3		
Quawn, Joseph				3	
Sherman, William	2	1	2		
Sherman, Peleg	4	3	3		
Sherman, Humphrey	1	3	3		
Russell, Thomas	1	2	4		
Macomber, Anson	1	4	2		
Sherman, Benjamin, 2d	2	1	2		
Johnson, James	2	1	3		
Briggs, Weston	1	1	2		
Sherman, Shadrach	1	1	4		
Rickerson, Anna	1		1		
Tucker, Henry	1	3	2	2	
Beard, John	1		1		
Beard, Obediah	1	2	2		
Smith, David	2	1	2		
Russell, Humphry	3	2	5		
Wilcox, Sarah			2		
Smith, Benjamin, 2d	1	1	2		
Sherman, Jedediah	3	1	3		
Chace, Benjamin	1	3	7		
Shepard, John	3	2	4		
Akin, Benjamin	1				
Akin, Job	1	3	1		
Smith, Jerusha			2		
Swift, Foster	1	1	3	1	
Wilcox, Thomas	2	2	4		
Sanford, William, 1st	1	1	3	2	
Sanford, George	2	1	3		
Slocum, Paul	1	1	6		
Sanford, Elisha	1	1	2		
Sanford, Richard	1		1		
Sanford, Peleg	1	1	1		
Sanford, William, 2d	1	1	4		
Gifford, Elihu	3	5	4		
Talman, William	1	2	6		
Sanford, John	3		3		
Wood, John	2	4	6		
Wady, John	2		1		
Cushman, Ebenezer	1	1	2		
Howland, Warren	1	3	2		
Wait, Daniel	1	3	7		
Sherman, Tisdale	2	3	2		
Sherman, Phillip	4	1	3		
Russell, Elijah	2		10		
Russell, Ezra	1		1		
Cushman, Obed	1	1	5		
Akin, John	2	1	5		
Almy, Joseph	2	1	5		
Almy, Anthony	1		4		
Almy, Christopher	5	1	2		
Almy, Peleg	1	1	1		
Lawton, David	1	2	3		
Macomber, Peregrine	2		3		
Almy, Giles	1		4		
Howland, Thomas, Junr	2	2	4		
Allen, Reuben	1	2	2		
Case, Adam	1	1	3		
Allen, Margaret		1	4		
Allen, Thomas, 2d	1		2		
Sisson, William	1	3	1		
Gifford, Samuel	1	2	5		
Macomber, Constant	1	4	3		
Cornell, Gideon	7		2		
Slocum, Jonas		2	4		
Gifford, Caleb	1	1	2		
Tucker, Henry	2		1		
Case, Rachael	1	2	3		
Russell, Joseph, 2d	2	1	5		
Allen, Thomas, 1st	4	1	1		
Slocum, Peleg, 1st	4	1	5	1	
Case, Isaiah	1	2	1		
Russell, Noah, 2d	1	2	2		
Slocum, Christopher	3		2		
Howland, Daniel	1	1	2	1	
DARTMOUTH TOWN—continued.					
Slocum, Peleg, 2d	4	1	2		
Slocum, Giles	1	1	2		
Butts, Stephen	1	3	5		
Butts, Abraham	2	2	4		
Cornell, Timothy	1		3		
Brightman, Henry	1		5		
Brightman, Ellis	1	1	1		
Brightman, Wanton	1	2	2		
Allen, Jedediah	1	2	5		
Wood, Thomas	1		2		
Allen, Benjamin	1	1	6		
Reed, Thomas	1		1		
Drinkwater, Ama		2	1		
Sowle, Elizabeth		1	2		
Barker, John	2	4	3		
Gifford, Peleg, Junr	1	2	3		
Gifford, Abiel	4	2	3		
Gifford, Peleg	1	1	1		
Barker, William	3	1	3		
Barker, William, Junr	1	1	5		
Tucker, Joseph	3		3		
Lawton, Jonathan	1	1	5		
Eddy, Zepheniah	2	1	3		
Tucker, John	3	2	5	1	
Slade, Edward	2	4	5		
Tucker, Benjamin	1	2	4	1	
Tucker, Abraham	1		1		
Tucker, Barzilla	1	1	2		
Wady, Humphry	1	2	3		
Russell, Josiah	2	2	2		
Howland, Wing	1	3	4		
Sanford, David	1	1	1		
Akin, Timothy	1	1	2		
Akin, Jonathan	1	1	2		
Nelson, William	1	1	3		
Sherman, Caleb	1	2	4		
Rickerson, John	3		2		
Akin, Elihu	3	3	4		
Sherman, Mary		1	3		
Rickerson, William	2	3	3		
Moshier, Stephen	1		2		
Akin, James	2	1	1		
Tripp, John	1		3		
Akin, Richard	1		3		
Wait, Henry	1	2	4		
Akin, Jacob	1	1	2		
Russell, Michael	2		2		
Howland, Jonathan	1	1	3		
Eason, Walter	1	2	3		
Howland, John	4	3	6		
Bliss, Arnold	1	1	5		
Howland, Timothy, 2d	1	4	1		
Quash, Anthony				7	
Quash, Abraham				2	
Davis, Edmund	1		1		
Sherman, Paul	3		4		
Sherman, Jonathan	3	1	3		
Sherman, Butler	3	1	3		
Sherman, Prince	2	1	2		
Sherman, Zoath	1	1	1		
Coggeshall, Pero				8	
Howland, Pero				2	
Slocum, Holder	3		2	1	
Gifford, Joseph	1		4		
Russell, Pero				6	
Sherman, Timothy	4		3		
Smith, Lorey	1	1	2		
Sherman, Edward	1	1	4		
Maxfield, Edmund	3	2	3		
Gifford, David	2	3	3		
Hammond, Hannah			1		
Pettis, Simpson	1	3	4		
Howland, Gideon	1	4	3	1	
Sherman, Jonathan	1		4		
Collins, John	2		2		
Mitchel, Elkanah	1	2	4		
Badcock, John	1	2	4		
Peckham, Isaiah	3		4		
Devol, David	1	4	4		
Smith, Benjamin	1	2	4		
Winslow, Weston	1	2	3		
Mirick, Deborah			3		
Hoskins, George	2	2	6		
Peckham, Caleb	1	2	1		
Russell, Cornelius	1	1	4		
Maxfield, Timothy, Junr	1		1		
Babcock, Benjamin	2		3		
Strange, Sarah	1		2		
Sherman, Battesheba	2	1	3		
Allen, Jethro	2	1	2		
Allen, Silvanus	3	1	4		
Vance, Nathaniel	4	1	6		
Allen, Joseph	2		2		
Chandler, Phebe	1	2	5		
Sheldon, John	1	1	4		

DARTMOUTH TOWN—continued.

NAME OF HEAD OF FAMILY.	Free white males of 16 years and upward, including heads of families.	Free white males under 16 years.	Free white females, including heads of families.	All other free persons.	Slaves.
Heart, Archippus	1		3		
Handy, John	1	3	3		
Joy, Samuel	1	1	3		
Bowdish, William	3	1	7		
Russell, Allen	1	3	4		
Cook, Audera	2		8		
Hicks, Daniel	2		3		
Washburn, Peter	1		3		
Russell, Stephen, Jun	1		1		
Russell, Clark	1	2	1		
Rogers, John	1		1		
Russell, Stephen	1	3	4		
Booth, Isaiah	1		3		
Booth, Benjamin	1		2		
Knap, Ebenezer	1		2		
Upham, Burnett	1		2		
Hathaway, Jethro	1	2	3		
Wing, Primus				4	
Davis, John	1		1		
Hathaway, Paul	1	2	4		
Winslow, Edward	3		3		
Simmonds, Isaac				3	
Hathaway, Meletiah	3	1	8		
Potter, Holiday	3	2	4		
Maxfield, Timothy	1		1		
Sherman, Daniel	1		2		
Maxfield, John	1	1	4		
Maxfield, Abraham	1	1	4		
Devol, Abner	1	3	3		
Smith, Elishub	1	1	4		
Howard, Daniel	2	2	5		
Smith, John	2		6		
Moshier, Barnabas	1	3	2		
Wood, William	1	1	2		
Russell, Elizabeth	1		3		
Solomon, James				3	
Russell, Michael	1		6	2	
Hindy, George	2	2	2		
Russell, Elisha	3	3	4		
Barker, Jabez	2		4		
Allen, Thomas, 1st	2	3	3	1	
Stratton, Oder	1		1		
Stratton, Benjamin	1		1		
Tripp, Ephraim	1	1	2		
Chace, John	3		3		
Chace, Nathaniel	1	3	3		
Howland, Joshua	1		2		
Chace, Abner	3	1	4		
Howland, Caleb	1	2	2		
Howland, Daniel, Sen	1	1	2		
Wood, John	1		2		
Wood, Benjamin	1	2	3		
Howland, Luther	3	1	1		
Perkins, Benjamin	2		2		
Anthony, Jacob	1	1	2		
Barker, Joseph	2		4		
Smith, Increase	1	1	3		
Howland, Sarah	1		3		
Barker, Stephen	1	4	2		
Russell, Joshua	1	3	2		
Peabody, Daniel	1	4	3		
Gifford, Silas	1	1	4		
Sowle, Jethro	1	1	2		
Harrison, Francis	1	1	2		
Mott, Thomas	3		3		
Russell, Jethro	1	3	3		
Wing, Primus, 2d				3	
Fish, Thomas			2		
Potter, Joshua	2	2	7		
Potter, Humphry	1	5	2		
Gifford, Jonathan, 1st	3	2	4		
Sherman, George	1	3	4		
Devol, Joseph	1	3	5		
Gifford, Daniel	1		2		
Gifford, Gideon	1	1	3		
Potter, Prince	3	4	6		
Tripp, William	2		4		
Devol, John	1		3		
Devol, Job	1	2	1		
Sherman, Israel	2		4		
Moshier, George	2	1	3		
Wood, Enos	1		2		
Wheating, Daniel	1	1	5		
Moshier, Michael	1	4	1		
Wheating, Joseph	1		1		
Moshier, Jesse	1		2		
Sherman, Reuben, Jun	1		2		
West, Samuel	1	2	4		
Beaden, Benjamin	2		3		
Beaden, Henry	1		2		
Beaden, Richard	1		3		
Beaden, Stephen	2		1		
Woodmansee, Thomas	2		1		
Woodmansee, Gideon	1	2	1		

DARTMOUTH TOWN—continued.

NAME OF HEAD OF FAMILY.	Free white males of 16 years and upward, including heads of families.	Free white males under 16 years.	Free white females, including heads of families.	All other free persons.	Slaves.
Reed, Thomas, Jun	1	2	4		
Reed, Elijah	1		4		
Reed, Lemuel	1	2	1		
Pettis, Abraham	1		3		
Pettis, David	1		2		
Howland, John	1	1	3		
Kurbee, Thomas	1		2		
Allen, Benjamin	1		2		
Allen, Thomas		2	3		
Allen, Judah		2	1		
Rogers, Gideon	1		3		
Rogers, Daniel	1		2		
Rogers, Stephen	1	2	3		
Moshier, Constant	1		3		
Wait, Reuben	1	3	2		
Shepard, Abner	1	2	3		
Washburn, Ira	1	2	3		
Chace, Ebenezer	1		3	4	
Peck, Bristol			2		
Gifford, James	1	1	2		
Gillat, John	1		2		
Wilson, Luther	1	1	3		
Andrews, John	1		5		
Kurbee, Silas	1	3	3		
Kurbee, William	1		2		
Babcock, Peleg	1	3	2		
Chace, Jared	1	1	2		
Cornell, John	1		3		
Cornell, Amos	2		2		
Cornell, Susannah	1		2		
Baker, James		2	2		
Cowen, Zenas	2		2		
Cowen, Ebenezer	2	2	3		
Cowen, Joshua	2		1		
Chace, Simeon	2	4	3		
Biggs, William			1	3	
Chace, David	2	1	3		
Peirce, Clothier	1	1	4		
Blackman, Ebenezer	1		5		
Moshier, John	2	8	5		
Reed, Benjamin	1		3		
Reed, Benjamin, Jun	1	3	3		
Reed, William	1		1		
Reed, John	1	1	2		
Moshier, Roger	3		1		
Chace, Ezekiel	1	1	3		
Wilkey, Peter	2	2	4		
Pettis, William	1		4		
Wait, Abner	1	1	5		
Crank, George				4	
West, Hope			2		
Russell, William	1	1	2		
Craw, Sherman	1	1	4		
Cummings, Benjamin	3	1	6		
Winslow, John	1		2		
Winslow, Abigail	1		2		
Gifford, David	2		1		
Gifford, Archippus	1	1	5		
Gifford, William	1	3	5		
Harrison, Joseph	1	1	3		
Smith, Thomas	1	3	3		
Moshier, Lemuel	1	2	3		
Moshier, Elihu	1	2	3		
Hart, Jonathan	1	1	4		
Hart, Seth	1	3	4		
Hart, Luke	1	3	3		
Hart, William	3	3	2		
Moshier, Hannah			2		
Tucker, Jonathan	1	2	4		
Moshier, Barnabas	1		1		
Rider, William	1		2		
Rider, William, Jun	1	4	3		
Rider, Samuel	2	4	3		
Rider, Benjamin	2	3	3		
Armitage, John	1		4		
Wilbore, Henry	3		3	1	
Washburn, Beraliel	1	4	5		
Pettis, James	1	3	4		
Andrews, Stephen	1		3		
Mott, Adam	1	2	4		
Phillips, Nathaniel	2		1		
Peirce, Samuel	2	1	2		
Fisher, William	2	1	2		
Phillips, Ira	1	2	3		
Collins, William	1		2		
Collins, Jonathan	2	2	3		
Bennett, John	2	1	2		
D'Meranville, Sherman	4	1	4		
Hathaway, Abraham	2	3	3		
Howland, Gideon	4	1	3	1	
Anthony, Gideon	1		2		
Knap, Axel	1		3		
Sherman, Reuten	6		3		

BRISTOL COUNTY—Continued.

NEW BEDFORD TOWN.

Name of head of family	Free white males of 16 years and upward, including heads of families	Free white males under 16 years	Free white females, including heads of families	All other free persons	Slaves
Allen, Benjamin	4	1	3		
Allen, David	2	2	5		
Butler, Benjamin	2	1	4		
Butler, Obed	2	1	1		
Butler, Benjamin, Jr	1	1	1	1	
Allen, Peleg	1	1	1	1	1
Kempton, David	1	1	3	2	
Russell, Caleb, Jun	1	3	2		
Russell, Caleb	3		2		
Kenley, Ambros	3		2		
Sherman, Butler	1	1	3		
Allen, James	1	3	5		
Tripp, Samuel	1	1	4		
Moshier, Samuel	1	1	1		
Tripp, Samuel, Jun	1	1	1		
Robinson, William	1	1	4		
Russell, Joseph	1		4		
Russell, Abraham	1	1	3	4	
Kempton, Ephraim	1	1	4		
Green, Caleb	1	1	4		
Howland, Matthew	2	4	2		
Pope, Edward	1	3	3	2	
Babcock, Eastland	3	2	4		
Haskell, Roger	2	1	3		
Howland, Humphrey	1	5	3		
Grinnell, Moses	1	2	5		
Howland, Isaac	3		4		
West, Elisha	2	1	3		
Howland, James	1	1	3		
Howland, Isaac, Jun	1		3		
Mathew, Jeremiah	2	2	2	1	
Akin, John	2		3		
Cannon, John	3	2	4		
Toby, William	3	2	5		
Russell, Barnabas	1	4	3		
Hazard, Thomas	1	4	3		
NEW BEDFORD TOWN—continued.					
Rotch, William	2	1	3	2	
Perry, Ebenezer	1	1	3	1	
Ingraham, Timothy	1	2	3		
Coggeshall, John	3	3	2		
Akin, Thomas	3	1	2		
Parker, Avery	2	2	2		
Hayden, James	1		2		
Ricketson, Daniel	3		2	1	
Hammond, Thomas	1				
Russell, Gilbert	2		3		
Austin, Joseph	3		2		
Bennett, Daniel	1		5		
Davis, James	2	3	5		
Hatchsett, Sarah		1	1		
Moshier, Anna			1		
Phillips, Selina			1		
Arter, Lydia			2		
Ingraham, Paul	3	1	3		
Moshier, Benjamin	2		1		
Rickettson, Abraham	1		1		
Gordon, William	2		2		
Ross, William	1		2		
Sampson, Abigail			2		
Nash, Simeon	3	2	4		
Davis, Abraham	2		3		
Hyers, Elizabeth		2	2		
Tabor, Benjamin	2	1	2		
Congdon, Caleb	1		1		
Proud, John	1	2	8	1	
Sherman, Ichabod	2	2	4	1	
Hill, Benjamin	3	1	6		
Howland, Benjamin	2		1		
Shepard, Elizabeth	1	1	3		
Claghorne, William	2	1	3		
Church, Charles	4	1	4		
Barney, Griffin	3		4	1	
Osborne, Samuel	1		1		
Smith, Daniel	2	1	3		
Fish, Henry	1		1		
Grinnell, Cornelius	1	2	2		
Howland, Cornelius	1		3		
Tabor, Benjamin, Junr	2	1	3		
Tabor, Daniel	3	1	1		
Rotch, Joseph	1		3		
Whippy, George	1	2	4		
Russell, William	3	1	3		
Russell, William, Junr	1		2		
Dunbar, Elisha	1	2	2		
Gerrish, John	2		4		
Howland, Peleg	1	1	3		
Russell, Seth	4		3	1	
Ayres, Joseph	1	2	3		
Dunham, Dinah		1	3		
Farr, Nathaniel	1	2	3		
Douglas, William	1	2	1		
Smith, Abraham	5	1	6		
Gedord, Jonathan	2	1	2		
Cook, Sarah		1	2		
Brightman, Susannah					
Meader, William	1		2		
Kempton, Menapah	4	2	4		
Langworthy, John	4		3		
Kempton, Sarah	1		4		
Eyres, Edward	1		3		
Beetle, Henry	1	1	2		
Price, Oliver	1	2	3		
Blossom, Elisha	1	1	2		
Cannon, Phillip	1	3	2		
Henshaw, William	1	2	3		
Claghorne, George	1	6	8		
Smith, Jonathan	3		6		
Potter, Stephen	2	1	3		
Russell, Jonathan	2		3		
Maxfield, Patrick	2		2		
Maxfield, Zadock	2	3	2		
East, George	3		5		
Hammond, Jabez	3		5		
Fuller, Francis	2		2		
Sherman, John	2	6	4		
Hillman, Zachariah	2	2	4		
Sillings, John	2	5	4		
Delano, Nathaniel, Junr	1		2		
Smith, Deborah	1	2	4		
Wilkey, Alden	1		2		
Babcock, Jethro	1	5	4		
Hoskins, William	2		4		
Hathaway, John	1		3		
Hathaway, Abner	2	3	3		
Kempton, Ephraim, Junr	2	2	4		
Stowell, Daniel	1		3		
Sherman, Asa	2		3		
Hempton, Thomas	2		3		
Hatch, James	1	1	3		
Willis, Ebenezer	2		3		

BRISTOL COUNTY—Continued.

NAME OF HEAD OF FAMILY.	Free white males of 16 years and upward, including heads of families.	Free white males under 16 years.	Free white females, including heads of families.	All other free persons.	Slaves.
NEW BEDFORD TOWN—continued.					
Potter, Thurston	1	2	2		
Coggeshall, Gideon	1		2		
Kempton, Obed	1	2	2		
Kempton, Elijah	1		3		
Willis, Jirah	2		1		
Kempton, Ephraim	1		1		
Allen, Francis	1	1	3		
Allen, Robert	1	3	5		
Bowdish, James	1		2		
Peckham, Mercy	1		2		
Peckham, John	1		2	1	
Peckham, Johannah	1	1	1		
Case, Job	1		1		
Peckham, Mary	2	1	3		
Hathaway, Richard	2	3	3		
Ridington, Robert	2	3	3		
West, Samuel	1		2		
West, Stephen	1		1		
Babcock, Spooner	1		2		
West, Elnathan	1	1	2		
Winslow, Benjamin	3	2	5		
Talman, William	4		4	2	
Peckham, Mary			2		
Tabor, Freeman	1	1	3		
Russell, William	1		5		
Hathaway, John	3	1	3		
Hathaway, Josiah	3		3		
Hathaway, Lemuel	1	1	4		
Mendall, Thomas	1		4		
Ridington, Mary	1		2		
Adams, Walley	3	2	2		
Bates, Worth	1	3	4		
Hathaway, Jabez	1	1	1		
Chafee, John	2		1		
Sherman, Abisha	2		4		
Hathaway, Jonathan	3		2		
Tallman, Weston	1	1	4		
Perry, Samuel, Sen	2		4	1	
Cushman, Towle	1	2	6		
Swift, Paul	1		2		
Swift, Jirah	3		3	2	
Kempton, Joseph	2	1	6		
Blackwell, John	2		2		
Stetson, Charles	2	3	2		
Drew, Josiah	2	2	7		
Hart, Simpson	2		2		
Spooner, Simpson	1	2	2		
Hathaway, Humphrey	1	1	2		
Dillingham, Benjamin	2	3	2		
Dillingham, Cornelius	1		2		
Mendall, Lemuel	1		4		
Terry, Isaac	3	2	2		
Somerton, Daniel	1	1	1		
Crandon, Thomas	2		2		
West, Bartholomew	1	4	4		
West, Anna			1		
Hitch, Elgit	2		4		
Hitch, Samuel	2	4	4		
Doane, Joshua	1	2	3		
Allen, Silvanus	1		1		
Allen, Silvanus, Jun	1	1	1		
Allen, Jethro, 2d	2	2	3		
Allen, Paul	2	3	3		
Delano, Thomas	1	3	4		
Church, Joseph	2	3	5		
Wood, Isaac	2	1	9		
Tabor, Pardon	5		4		
Drew, Isaac	2	2	3		
Drew, Joshua	1	5	3		
Sleuman, John	1	1	4		
Tripp, Job	1	1	7		
Stevens, William	3		2		
Tabor, John	4	3	5	1	
Jenne, Jethro, Jun	2	1	8		
Childs, Aaron				5	
Pope, Yetseth	2		2		
Parker, Lydia	1		2		
Hammond, Barnabas	2	3	2		
Hitch, George	2		6		
Williams, Lemuel	1	1	4		
Norton, Hannah		2	4		
Hathaway, Robert	1	2	4		
Jenne, Levi	1	5	4		
Merrthew, Reuba					
Procter, Samuel	3	3	2	2	
Hammond, Richard	2	2	2		
Jenne, Sarah					
Alden, John	2	3	5	1	
Loring, Innocent	3	2	3		
Allen, Elisha	1	3	4		
Weston, Samuel	3	1	6		
Crandon, James	1	3	3		
Stoddard, Noah	1	1	1		
Stoddard, Ichabod	2		3		
Stott, Leven	1	3	4		

NAME OF HEAD OF FAMILY.	Free white males of 16 years and upward, including heads of families.	Free white males under 16 years.	Free white females, including heads of families.	All other free persons.	Slaves.
NEW BEDFORD TOWN—continued.					
Sherman, John	1	1	3		
Hathaway, Elkanah	1	1	4		
Delano, Calvin	1	1	4		
Sherman, Isaac	2	2	5		
Allen, Jethro	2	2	3		
Church, Benjamin	2		3		
Procter, Samuel, Jun	2		3		
Stutson, Charles	3		4		
Stutson, Thaddeus	1	1	4		
Eldridge, Edward	1	4	4		
Paddock, Eunice			2	1	
Frederick, Joseph	1	3	3		
Grinnel, Benjamin		3	2		
Stoddard, Nicholas	1		2		
Delano, Joseph	1	3	2		
Hathaway, Arthur	1	2	3		
Hathaway, Nathaniel	1		3		
Jenne, Lydia		1	3		
Blosson, Benjamin	1		3		
Blosson, Joseph	1		1		
Blossom, Benjamin, Jun					
Copeland, Elisha	1		2		
Clark, Susannah	2	1	2		
Allen, Rufus	1	5	2		
Delano, John	2		3		
Delano, Richard	4		4		
Delano, Richard, Jun	1		2		
Tabor, Thomas	2		4		
Delano, Ephraim	1	1	6		
Weeden, John	3	1	4		
Nelson, Abner	1		4		
Hammond, Selathial	1		4		
Delano, Reuben	1	2	5		
Pope, Lemuel	1	1	3		
Pope, Samuel	3	1	2		
Smith, Henry, Jun	1		2		
Sisson, Akus	1	2	2		
Chace, Ebeneser	2	2	4		
Pope, Edmund	1	3	6		
Hathaway, Samuel	3	1	6		
Hathaway, Jethro	1				
Hathaway, Clark		2	3		
Allen, George	3	3	3		
Delano, Nathan	1	4	4		
Eldridge, John	1		2	1	
Freeman, Obed	4	3	3		
Delano, Joshua	1		3		
Fuller, Peter	1	2	3		
Ellis, Malicha	1	3	4		
Pope, Seth	2		2		
Damon, Joseph	3	1	8		
Tabor, Jeduthun	1	4	5		
Blankenship, William	1	1	2		
Handy, Gemaliel	1	1	1		
Delano, Nathaniel	4	4	4		
Peckham, Prince	1	2	3		
Peckham, Isaiah	1		3		
Peckham, Peleg	1	1	2		
Shaw, John	1	3	5		
Shaw, William	1		1		
Shaw, William, Jun	1	4	4		
Pease, Dorcas		1	4		
Jenne, Caleb	2	6	5		
Rider, Ezekiel	1	3	4		
Tupper, Samuel	1	4	3		
Stetson, Nathaniel	2	4	3		
Mitchel, William	1				
Mitchel, David	2		2		
Jenne, Jabez	2	1	4		
Allen, Noah	1				
Allen, Noah, Jun	2		3		
Burges, Joseph	4	1	2		
Kempton, James	1	5	6		
Eldridge, Isaiah	3	1	2		
Kempton, Stephen	3	5	5		
Tinkum, John	2	3	2		
Trip, Thomas	4	3	4		
Trip, Ephraim	1		1		
Tinkum, Mary	1	2	5		
Kempton, William	1	6	3		
Kinney, Jacob	1	3	3		
Kinney, Samuel	2	1	3		
Jenne, Jethro	3	2	3		
House, Abel	1		1		
Jenne, Henry	2	2	3		
Jenne, Jonathan	1	4	1		
Jenne, Patience	1		3		
Jenne, Abner	1	1	3		
Jenne, Nathaniel	2	1	3		
Jenne, Israel	1	1	4		
Hammond, Seth	1	1	3		
Hammond, Seth, Jun	1	1	6		
Annable, Isaac	3	2	4		
Handy, Thomas	2		1		

NAME OF HEAD OF FAMILY.	Free white males of 16 years and upward, including heads of families.	Free white males under 16 years.	Free white females, including heads of families.	All other free persons.	Slaves.
NEW BEDFORD TOWN—continued.					
Handy, David	1	4	1		
Handy, Thomas, Jun	2		2		
Cornish, Patience			3		
Lawrence, Ebeneser	1		1		
Morton, Seth	1		3		
Morton, Jethro	1	1	2		
Dexter, William	1	1	5		
Howard, Abner	1	4	3		
Stevens, Elisha	1	0	3		
Bennett, Amos	1	1	3		
Phillips, Peter	1		1		
Holmes, Joseph	1		2		
Wright, Lucy			2		
Jenne, Elizabeth	1		2		
Hammond, Asa	1		2		
Smith, Henry	2		1		
Hathaway, Jacob	3	1	3		
West, Edward	1		2		
Hathaway, Micah	3	4	3		
Hathaway, Gemaliel	1		1		
Kempton, Jonathan	1	2	4		
Hathaway, Stephen	4	1	10		
Nye, Obed	4	1	6		
Spooner, Caleb	2		7		
Pope, Alice			2	1	
West, William	2	4	3		
Burges, Reuben	1		3		
Nye, Jonathan	1	4	3		
Nye, Obed, Jun	1		3		
Akin, Bartholimew	2	2	3		
Tabor, Bartholimew	1	3	3		
Hudelston, Peleg	3		3		
Nye, Thomas	2		4		
Tabor, Nicholas	3	1	4		
Jenne, Reuben	2		2		
Spooner, Benjamin	3		3		
Tabor, Lewis	1	1	3		
Peckins, John	2	1	1		
Bennett, Robert, 2d	3	4	3		
Wilkey, Cornel	2	3	3		
Marshall, Phebe		1	2		
Whitefield, Joseph	3	2	3		
Tobey, Seth	1	3	3		
Allen, Eleaser	1	4	4		
Diminick, Bradock	2	2	3		
Crowel, John	2	6	3		
Sisson, Benjamin	2	2	3		
Allen, Ebeneser	1	1	3		
Delano, Gideon	1		1		
Clark, David	1	3	4		
Spooner, Grace			2		
Killey, Amos	2	2	4		
Bennett, Joseph	1	1	2		
Joseph, Christopher	1	1	3		
Eldridge, Selathial	2		3		
Wood, Gideon	1	1	1		
Wood, Zeruiah	2		2		
Wood, Elihu	1	2	3		
Nye, Stephen	1	1	3		
Nye, Stephen, Jun	1		3		
Bryant, Gemaliel	1		2	1	
Padleford, Bathsheba	1		1		
Tompkins, Christopher	1		2		
Parker, William	1	4	1		
Ridington, John	2	2	4		
Harvey, Louis			3		
Tobey, Lemuel	3	3	3		
Tobey, Elisha	1	1	2		
Blackmore, John	1		2		
Omens, Jonathan	1	1	1		
Washburn, Lettis	1	3	2		
Cushman, Miel	1	2	1		
Swift, Silas	2		9		
Hammond, Christopher	1	2	3		
Omen, Simeon	3		3		
Hammond, Mary			3		
Peirce, Joseph	1	3	4		
Spooner, Barnabas	2		1		
Tabor, Elizabeth			2		
D'Meranville, Robin	1		2		
Tabor, Jacob	1	2	3		
D'Meranville, Simeon	1	1	4		
Tabor, Stephen	1	1	2		
Spooner, David	1	1	3		
Bennett, Thomas	1	1	3		
Tabor, Stephen, Jun	1	2	5		
Nye, Nathan	1	1	3		
White, Benjamin	1	2	4		
Severance, Thomas	2		3		
Severance, Joseph	1		1		
Bennett, Jeremiah	4		3		
Tobey, John	1		2		
Mason, Rueben	1	1	6		
Tabor, William	2		3		

BRISTOL COUNTY—Continued.

NEW BEDFORD TOWN—continued.

Name of head of family.	Free white males of 16 years and upward, including heads of families.	Free white males under 16 years.	Free white females, including heads of families.	All other free persons.	Slaves.
Tabor, Edward	1	2	4		
White, William	3	1	2		
White, William, Junr	1	3	2		
Parker, Micah	1	2	1		
Rounseville, Abner	1		2		
Tobey, Jonathan, Junr	1	3	2		
Hathaway, Elihu	1		1		
Hathaway, Joseph	1	3	4		
Hathaway, Edward	1	4	2		
Hathaway, Seth	4	2	2		
Tobey, Jonathan	2	2	3		
Ralph, Michael	3	1	3		
Washburn, Bezaliel	1		3		
Burden, Lemuel	1		4		
Easterbrooks, Benjamin	1	1	2		
Andrews, William	1		2		
Weston, George	2	1	3		
Weston, Isaac	1				
Fuller, Jeremiah	1	1	1		
Weston, John	1	2	5		
Blackmore, Salisbury	1	5	2		
Weston, Elnathan	1		2		
Perkins, Henry	1	1	7		
Fuller, Simeon	1	1	3		
Spooner, Micah	1	1	7		
Reynolds, William	1	3	2		
Kersey, Joseph	1	3	4		
Gifford, Thomas	2		1		
Sherman, Henry	1	1	4		
Sherman, Job	1	4	4		
Washburn, Moses	3		2		
Spooner, Nathaniel, Junr	1	4	5		
Jenne, Beulah			1		
Spooner, Nathaniel	1		2		
Spooner, Philip	1	2	2		
Fuller, Mary	1		3		
Hathaway, Hannah	1		2		
Winslow, Ezra	1	3	2		
White, Simpson					
Spooner, Isaac	2		4		
Shokley, Samuel	1	2	2		
Spooner, Samuel	1		2		
Spooner, William	1	2	4		
Spooner, Elnathan	3		3		
Hathaway, Eleazer	2	3	5		
Wing, Jabez	1		1		
Wing, Shearjashub	1	1	3		
Cornish, Hananiah	1	1	3		
Ellis, Joseph	4		2		
Wing, Paul	2	3	7		
Howard, Solomon	1	2	4		
Atwood, Joseph	1	2	3		
Tobey, Zacheus	2		6		
Tobey, Zoah	1		5		
Rouse, John	1		3		
Tobey, Lot	2		4		
West, William	2	4	4		
Cook, Thomas	1	2	3		
Jenne, Seth	2	3	2		
Jenne, Job	1	3	5		
Perry, Lemuel	2	2	7		
Bennett, Robert	1		4		
Bennett, Gilbert	1		3		
West, Samuel	2		3		
Cushman, Elisha	3		2		
Cushman, Elisha, Junr	1	1	2		
Cushman, James	1		1		
Cushman, Jonathan	1	2	1		
Allen, William	1		2		
Chaddock, John	1	1	4		
Tabor, Archalus	1		6		
Cushman, Seth	1		2		
Tabor, Elnathan	1	1	2		
Fuller, Ziba	1	1	3		
Pratt, James	1	1	1		
Sampson, Jude	1		3		
Holmes, William	1	1	1		
Tabor, Humphrey	1	3	2		
Tabor, Abraham	1	1	2		
Tabor, William	3	2	4		
Tabor, Mary			2		
Tabor, Joseph	2	1	5		
Holmes, James	2		3		
Tabor, Ruth	1		3		
Tabor, Antipus	1		2		
Gifford, Lewis	1	2	4		
Tabor, Peter	1		1		
Tabor, Joshua	2	1	2		
Tabor, Amos	1	2	6		
Weeden, Hannah			2		
Skiff, John	1	2	4		
Pope, Isaac	2	1	7		
Vincent, Isaac	3		3		
Vincent, Abner	1		2		
Terry, Benjamin	2	3	5		
Terry, Thomas	2	1	6		
Tabor, Prince	2	1	2		
Sprague, Samuel	1		4	2	
Ingraham, Thomas	1	2	3		
Gifford, Thomas	1	2	5		
Foster, Chillingworth	1	2	5		
Foster, Elnathan	1	1	3		
Skiff, John, Junr	1	1	4		
Manchester, Job	1	1	2		
Smith, Worton	1		3		
Sweet, Silas	2	4	5		
Dillingham, John	2	2	5		
Shepard, David	1		4		
Bennett, Desire			2		
Bennett, William	1	2	3		
Bennett, Edward	3	4	6		
Gray, John	2		3		
Sampson, Joseph	3		10		
Allen, Ebenezer	4		7		
Fitzsimmons, Amos	3	3	2	1	
Hammett, Barnabas	2	1	5		
Davis, Nicholas	4	4	6		
Davis, Timothy	2	2	7		
Wilcox, Job	1		1		
Tabor, Richard	1	1	4		
Cook, Pardon	2	1	5		
Cook, Paul	2		2		
Cook, Joseph	1	3	8		
Borman, Samuel	1		3		
Hathaway, Elnathan	1		1		
Hathaway, Samuel	1	2	5		
Hathaway, Silas	2	1	5		
Davis, Nathan, Junr	2	1	4		
Davis, Nathan	1		2		
Davis, Richard	1		2		
Russell, John	1		2		
Wing, Daniel	1		2		
Wing, William	1	2	2		
Wing, Barnabas	1	1	2		
Tripp, Samuel	1		1		
Tripp, Stephen	1	1	3		
Hathaway, Lot	1	1	9		
Hathaway, Obed	1		5		
Howland, Abraham	1	1	2		
Spooner, Alden	2	1	5	1	
Spooner, Walter	1	1	4		
Spooner, Seth	1	3	4		
Keen, Ebenezer	1				
Keen, Ebenezer, Junr	2		5		
Keen, Jesse	1	3	3		
Allen, Abraham	1	1	1		
Tabor, Amariah	1		2		
Eldridge, Amos	1	1	2		
Sherman, Johannah			2		
Tabor, Jabez	3		2		

BRISTOL COUNTY—Continued.

The five numeric columns in each panel are, in order:
1. Free white males of 16 years and upward, including heads of families.
2. Free white males under 16 years.
3. Free white females, including heads of families.
4. All other free persons.
5. Slaves.

WESTPORT TOWN.

NAME OF HEAD OF FAMILY.	1	2	3	4	5
Wilcox, John	3		2		
Davis, Jonathan	3		3	2	
Tabor, Phillip	3	1	3	4	
Corey, Benjamin	1	2	3	3	
Corey, Thomas	3			2	
Almy, William	1	3	5	5	
Brightman, Henry	3	2	5	3	
Brightman, Israel	2		4	3	
Earl, Christopher	1			4	
Earl, George	1			2	
Macomber, Wanton	1			2	
Brightman, Joseph	1			1	
Wilcox, William	1		2	2	
Brightman, Thomas	1	1	2	2	
Cogshell, Daniel	1		2	4	
Hicks, William	3			2	
Hicks, John	1		1	3	
Brownill, Paul	1		1	2	
Tabor, Mary				2	
Sherman, Preserved	2		1	7	

WESTPORT TOWN—con. (continued)

NAME OF HEAD OF FAMILY.	1	2	3	4	5
Sherman, Robert	1		1	3	
Sherman, Levi	1	1	5	3	
Sherman, Gideon	1		1	3	
Macomber, Ruth			1	3	
Macomber, William, 3d	4		1	4	
Macomber, Timothy	2	1	1	3	
Sowle, Oliver	1		3	1	
Sowle, Benjamin, 2d	1				
Richmond, London (a Negro)					
Hart, Job (a Negro)				4	
Dick, Exeter				6	
Earl, John					
Earl, William	3		3	4	
Earl, Paul	2		2	2	
Davis, William	1	3		4	
Davis, Phillip	3			2	
Earl, Robert	3			7	
Hicks, Barnabas	1	1		2	
Hicks, Thomas	1	1	1	4	
Cornell, Christopher	2	1	1	7	
Macomber, William	1	2	1		
Sowle, Weston	2		1		
Brightman, William	2		2		
Macomber, Phillip	1		1		
Macomber, Humphry			3	2	
Macomber, Abiel	1			2	
Brightman, John				2	
Gifford, George	3		3	4	
Gifford, Christopher	1		2	2	
Gifford, Jonathan	1			4	
Watkins, William	1	1		2	
Brownill, Abner	1	2		3	
Brownill, George, 3d	1			5	
Springer, Samuel	1	2		3	
Howland, Prince	2	3		5	
Brightman, George	2	2		5	
Mayhew, Hillyard	3			4	
Gardner, Thomas	1	1		2	
Drane, Micah	1				
Davis, Benjamin	2	1		2	1
Allen, Joseph	2			3	
Earl, Stephen	1			1	
Tabor, Jonathan	1	1		1	
Tabor, Thomas	1			2	
Knight, John	1			2	
Cadman, Hannah				3	
Wilbour, John				4	
Gifford, Abraham	1		3	3	
Corey, Isaac	1		1	8	
Davis, Stephen	3		3	4	
Wood, Israel	1		1	2	
Potter, Elijah	3		2	4	
Church, Gideon	3		1	6	
Cornell, Gideon	1		2	1	
Cornell, Stephen	1		1	2	
Cornell, Daniel	1		1	2	
Devol, Abner	1		1	2	
Sowle, James	1		2	3	
Sowle, Henry	2			4	
Davis, Job	2			2	
Davis, Pardon	1			2	
Davis, John	1		4	3	
Eddy, Ichabod	1			1	
Eddy, Ebenezer	1		1	6	
Davis, Gideon	2		1	3	
Robinson, William	3		1	3	
Tripp, Daniel	3			2	
Wait, Gideon	1		1	1	
Davis, Nathan	1		2	2	
Tripp, Elizabeth				1	
Sowle, Lemuel	1		1	2	
Sowle, Joseph	2			2	
Sowle, Isaac	2			5	
Sowle, David	1			2	
Cuff, Paul					7
Wilcox, Silvanus	1		4	1	
Sowle, Benjamin	1			1	
Sowle, Jacob	1			1	
Allen, Daniel	2			3	
Case, Wanton			3	2	
Case, Moses	1		3	2	
Case, Ama			1	3	
Kirbee, William	1		2	3	
Allen, Humphry	1		3	3	
Gifford, William, jun.	1			3	
Porter, Peleg	1		2	3	
Porter, Noah	1			1	
Gifford, Joseph	1		4	6	
Wilcox, Culbert	1		1		
White, Humphry	1		1	3	
Hammond, David	2		1	3	
Potter, Phillip	1			2	
Potter, Rebecca			2		

WESTPORT TOWN—con. (continued)

NAME OF HEAD OF FAMILY.	1	2	3	4	5
Gifford, William	2	1		2	1
Gifford, Richard	1		1	3	
Macomber, Nathaniel				3	
Macomber, Mercy				3	
Potter, Nathaniel	2	1	2	4	
Gifford, Caleb	1	4	1	5	
Potter, Ichabod	2	1	4	5	
Kirbee, Nathaniel	1		1	4	
Brownill, Benjamin	2			3	
Tabor, Job	1			2	
Tabor, Gideon			2	3	
Tripp, John	2			1	
Wood, William	2			3	
Wood, William, jun.	1			1	
Manchester, Lemuel	1		3	7	
Manchester, James	1		3	2	
Tripp, David	2			3	
Tripp, David, jun.	1			5	
Wood, John	1		2	3	
Briggs, Job	1		3	3	
Manchester, Archer	1		1	5	
Manchester, Thomas	2		3	5	
Snell, Benjamin				3	
Dyer, Preserved	1		1	3	
Brownill, Jonathan	1		1	4	
Dyer, Zacheus	2		2	4	
Dyer, John	2			5	
Dyer, John	1			3	
Head, Joseph	2			3	
Manchester, Elizabeth			1	3	
Browning, George, jun.	1		5	2	
Browning, George	1			6	
Browning, Samuel	3		1	6	
Church, Constant	1		3	1	
Tompkins, Gilbert	2		2	4	
Brownill, Pardon	1		4	5	
Richmond, Peres	1			3	
Coggeshall, Jonathan	2			3	
Davenport, Jonathan	1			3	
Devol, Benjamin	1		4	2	
Palmer, John	2		2	1	
Palmer, Perez	1			2	
Head, John	1		2	3	
Shaw, Zebedee	1		1	1	
Brownill, Silvester	1			2	
Rickard, William	3		5	3	1
Underwood, Nicholas	1		2	3	
Hazard, Oliver	1		3	4	
Moshier, Edmund	1		2	5	1
Sisson, Constant	1			4	
Dennis, Joseph	1		1	3	
Moshier, Joshua	1			3	
Brownill, Benjamin, jun.	1		1	2	
Potter, Thomas	1		1	3	
Devol, Seth	1		2	4	
Hart, Eber	1		2	2	
Hart, George	1		2	4	
Macomber, Job, 2d	1		1	2	
Wait, Shadrach	1		2	2	
Tabor, Ruth				3	
Weeden, John	1			3	
Potter, Ama			1	3	
Brownill, Prince	1			3	
Clawson, Joseph	1			3	
Potter, Abner	2		2	4	
Potter, Stokes	1		4	5	
Potter, Ichabod, 2d	1		1	4	
Almy, Job	2			5	
Kirbee, Richard	3		1	1	2
Gifford, Daniel	1		2	6	
Gifford, Timothy	4		3	7	
Kirbee, Nathaniel, 1st	1			2	
Kirbee, Robert	1			3	
Allen, Abraham	1		3	1	
Davis, Ezekiel	1			2	
Barker, Robert	2			3	
Allen, Thomas	3			2	
Allen, Mary				3	
Cornell, Robert	1			1	
Allen, George	2		2	1	4
Acker, Joseph					
Freeborn, Cuff					3
Amos, Dick					6
Brightman, Gardner	1		1	5	
Wilcox, William	1	2		2	1
Fisher, Job	1		5		
Fisher, Arthur	1			2	
Tolman, Ezekiel	1				
Wing, Edward	1		4		
Wing, Joseph	2		2	2	
Macomber, Samuel	2		3		
Tolman, Jonathan	2	4	3		
Tolman, Gideon	1	3	1		
Briggs, David	2		7	3	
Cornell, Elihu	1		2	3	

BRISTOL COUNTY—Continued.

WESTPORT TOWN—con.

Name of head of family	Free white males of 16 years and upward, including heads of families	Free white males under 16 years	Free white females, including heads of families	All other free persons	Slaves
Gifford, Elijah	2	1	4		
Gifford, Sarah			1		
Allen, Williams	1	1	4		
Allen, Ebenezer	1	2	4		
Wilcox, Benjamin	3	1	3		
Wilcox, Samuel	2	1	3		
Gifford, Mariam	2		3		
Wing, Edward, junr	1	3	2		
Wing, David	1	2	5		
Potter, John	1		2		
Wing, Prince	1	2	4		
Howland, Charles	1	1	2		
White, Sibel			1		
Cornell, Peleg	1		1	1	
Cornell, John	1		1		
Cornell, Peleg, junr	1	2	3		
Cornell, Holden	1		1		
Almey, Mary			3		
Wing, John	2	2	6		
Cook, Bennett	2	4	4		
Fisher, John	1		3		
Cornell, Abraham	2		2		
Cornell, Thomas	2		3		
Tripp, Jacob	2		2		
Brownell, Cornelius	2		5		
Devol, Pardon	1		1		
Sisson, Wilson	1	1	1		
Talman, Jedediah	1		1		
Howland, Thomas	1		2		
Howland, John	1	4	1		
White, Roger	1		4		
Wilcox, Abner	3	1	2		
Wilcox, David	2	1	3		
White, George	2		2		
Kurbee, Robert	1		1		
Kurbee, John	2	1	3		
Sisson, Jonathan	4	2	3		
Sisson, Gideon	1	1	2		
Tippett, John	1		2		
Howland, Lydia		1	1		
Brownill, Thomas	3		3		
Milk, Lemuel	1	2	3		
Howland, Reuben	1		3		
Tripp, Giles	1		2		
Tripp, Charles	1	1	1		
Sowle, David	1		1		
Brownill, Thomas, junr	1	1	2		
Sowle, Joseph	2	1	3		
Howland, Phillip	1		1		
Howland, Isaac	1	1	1		
Russell, Sebiah	2		6		
Slade, Buffom	1	1	5		
Howland, Wesbon	2	1	3		
Buffington, Stephen	2	1	2		
Wood, David	1	1	3		
Gifford, Benjamin	1		2		
Cuff, John				5	
Kurbee, Stephen	2	1	5		
Russell, David	1	1	2		
Tripp, Joshua	1	1	3		
Tripp, Caleb	1		3		
Kurbee, Justice	3		4		
Kurbee, Weston	2	1	2		
Kurbee, Elihu	1	1	1		
Kurbee, Jonathan	1	1	2		
Tripp, Benjamin	1		1		
White, Jonathan	1	1	2		
White, Holder	1		2		
Brownill, Peleg	1		4		
Cornell, Stephen	1	1	4		
White, Silvanus	1	2	3		
White, Obed	1	1	4		
Earl, Joshua	2		8		
Tripp, Isaac	2	2	3		
Tripp, John	1		3		
Tripp, Frances	1		3		
Tripp, Peleg	1		3		
Tripp, Ebenezer	3	2	6		
Earl, Job	1	1	3		
Tripp, James	1	2	2		
Lyon, Thomas	1	1	2		
Sisson, Phillip	3		2		

WESTPORT TOWN—con.

Name of head of family	Free white males of 16 years and upward, including heads of families	Free white males under 16 years	Free white females, including heads of families	All other free persons	Slaves
Custineau, Raymond	1	2	3		
Sisson, James	1		4		
Sisson, Daniel	2	1	3		
Devol, Barnabas	1	3	4		
Potter, John	1		1		
Wait, John	1	1	4		
Wait, Jeremiah	2	1	2		
Wait, Daniel	1		3		
Tripp, George	2		1		
Wilbore, Ebenezer	1		2		
Wilbore, Ichabod	1	1	1		
Tripp, Phillip	1		2		
Tripp, Edmund	1	4	2		
Tripp, Preserved	1		2		
Tripp, Stokes	1		2		
Tripp, Nathaniel	1		1		
Gifford, Isaac	1		8		
Moshier, Jonathan	2		4		
Kurbee, Ichabod	1		2		
Kurbee, David	1	1	2		
Tripp, Ichabod	1		1		
Tripp, Constant	1		1		
Pettis, Isaac	1	4	2		
Macomber, Pardon	1		4		
Snell, Peter	2		6		
Coggeshall, John	1	4	2		
Tripp, Anthony	1	4	1		
Macomber, George	1		1		
Lake, James	1		1		
Macomber, Noah	2		4		
Devol, John	1		2		
Devol, Samuel	1	1	2		
White, William	3	1	2		
Tripp, Thomas	3	1	5		
Moshier, John	1		3		
Devol, Charles	1	1	1		
Devol, David	2	1	3		
Devol, Joshua	1	1	1		
Wood, George	1		1		
Wood, George, junr	1	2	7		
Lawton, George	6	1	3		
Macomber, Job	1		4		
Case, Edmund	1	1	4		
Tripp, George, 2d	1	2	4		
Tripp, Perry	2				
Tabor, Jonathan	2	1	4		
Davis, Stephen	2	3	2		
Briggs, Thomas	1	1	3		
Davis, Aaron	2	1	6		
Wilcox, Ephraim	1	1	4		
Moshier, George	1		6		
Howland, John	1	1	3		
Cornell, Job	1	4	2		
Wood, Thomas	1		2		
Crocker, Robert	1	1	3		
Davis, Benjamin, 2d	1	3	5		
Davis, John, 1st	2		3		
Davis, Eber	1	1	6		
Peckham, Stephen	2				
Tippett, Henry	1	1	3		
Peckham, Jonathan	4		4		
Howland, Henry	4		4		
Howland, Henry, junr	1	1	2		
Sisson, Lemuel	1				
Sisson, Job			4		
Butts, Chase	1		3		
Milk, Job	1	1	2		
Butts, James	1	2	1		
Wood, Robert	1		2		
Allen, Adam	1	1	5		
Cornell, John	1	2	4		
Devol, Benjamin	2	2	5		
Tilson, Jacob	1		5		
Burdick, George	1	4	4		
Macomber, Joshua	1		3		
Brownill, Josias	1	2	3		
Tripp, Weston	1	1	3		
Tripp, Joseph	1		3		
Brownill, Robert	2	1	2		
Brownill, James	1	2	1		
Brownill, Joseph	1	3	1		
Tripp, Ichabod	1		1		

WESTPORT TOWN—con.

Name of head of family	Free white males of 16 years and upward, including heads of families	Free white males under 16 years	Free white females, including heads of families	All other free persons	Slaves
Tripp, Nathan	1	3	5		
Tripp, Jonathan	2		2		
Brownill, George, 2d	1	2	7		
Anthony, Job	2		4		
Tripp, Peleg	2	1	2		
Little, Barker	3	4	4		
Devol, Daniel	1		1		
Gifford, Stephen, 2d	3	2	1		
Cornell, Charles	1		3		
Devol, Barjonah	1		4		
Tripp, James, 1st	2	3	4		
Macomber, Timothy	1	4	3		
Potter, Edmund	1	5	4		
Potter, David	1	3	4		
Devol, Abner	1	1	4		
Baker, Ebenezer	1	3	1		
Baker, Mehetable	3	1	3		
Moshier, Job	1	1	3		
Howland, Humphry	1	3	1		
Chace, Jacob	3	2	3		
Chace, John	1		3		
Potter, Ephraim	3		3		
Potter, Stephen	2	2	3		
Potter, Benjamin	1		2		
Chace, Benjamin	3	2	2		
Sherman, Thomas	2	3	4		
Chace, Joseph	1	2	6		
Gifford, John	1	2	6		
Macomber, Peter	1	1	3		
Cornell, David	1	3	1		
Tripp, Daniel	2		4		
Cornell, Benjamin	1		1		
Tripp, Culbert	1	1	3		
Gifford, William	1	3	3		
Gifford, John, 2d	1	5	5		
Briggs, Ephraim	1	2	2		
Briggs, Lovett	1		1		
Briggs, William	1	1	3		
Macomber, Abiel	4		5		
Macomber, Abner	1	3	4		
Capron, John	1		2		
Waddell, Thomas	1	1	4		
Cornell, George	1	4	2		
Davis, Abiel	2		3		
Davis, Abiel, junr	1		3		
Bazemore, John	1	2	3		
Peckham, Stephen, 2d	2	2	3		
Waddell, Burden	2	5	4		
Gifford, Benjamin	2		1		
Boomer, Matthew	1	4	2		
Boomer, Matthew, junr	1		1		
Boomer, Benjamin	1	1	1		
Boomer, Edward	1	1	3		
Sherman, Job	1		2		
Sherman, Samuel	1	1	1		
Boomer, Ephraim	1	2	2		
Woddell, Phinehas	1		3		
Warren, Perry	1	1	2		
Moshier, Weston	1	4	2		
Burden, Isaiah	1		3		
Gifford, Nathaniel	2	3	2		
Warren, Cornelius	3		5		
Pettis, Rebecca			3		
Crocker, Canaan	1	2	1		
Burden, Edward	2		3	1	
Burden, Gideon	1	3	4		
Sanford, Phillip	3	3	4		
Crocker, Stephen	1	2	5		
Pettis, Daniel	1		4		
Hart, Aaron	1	3	6		
Macomber, Weston	1		1		
Macomber, William	1				
Anthony, Winsor				5	
Brownill, Benjamin	2		3		
Brownill, Josiah	1	2	2		
Pettis, Nathan	1		2		
Pettis, Joshua	1	2	2		
Sandy, Silas	1	1	5		
Booth, George	1		3		
Weaver, Joseph	1	1	3		
Brownill, Ichabod	1	1	3		

<u>LETTER OF JAMES B. CONGDON, DATED DECEMBER 13, 1867</u>
<u>TO THE CHAIRMAN OF BRISTOL COUNTY COMMISSIONERS</u>
<u>EXPLAINING THE STATUS OF THE PROPRIETORS RECORDS</u>

By your request, I have examined the books called the "Proprietors Records" which are now in the possession of the City of New Bedford. These books purport to be the records of the proprietors of the land in the old town of Dartmouth, which was embraced in the purchase of William Bradford.

These records are of two kinds: 1st, the records of the corporation. By an act of the General Court, the proprietors of the land were constituted a corporation so that sales could be made and titles given through officers appointed for that purpose.

The Corporation Records are in one book and include the period from 1725/6 to 1821, the last record being made by Abner B. Gifford, Proprietor's Clerk.

The records of the sales and transfers of the lands of the Proprietary. These are in four books, and in them are found recorded all the lands which constitute the old town of Dartmouth.

The deed to William Bradford dated in 1654 and the sales and transfers of these lands was soon commenced. In what manner these sales were conducted and the titles verified does not appear.

In the year 1725 all the records of the Proprietary were destroyed by fire --- the records of the corporation and the records of the conveyances of land. This was a most unfortunate event. All was in confusion. Fortunately the Field Books of the old surveyor, Benjamin Crane, by whom a large part of the land had been surveyed, were saved. Books of a similar description, kept by two other surveyors are with them. There are, as near as I can judge [the covers being gone in some instances, makes it difficult to decide as to the exact number], twelve of these books.

After the burning, all there was remaining was these Field Notes, and the deeds, if any there were, in the hands of those who had purchased lands of the corporation.

All that we now have, the book of the records of the corporation and the four books of registration have been produced since the year 1725.

Soon after the destruction of the books, meetings were held by the proprietors, at which various methods were proposed to meet the exigency.

The measures taken at these meetings resulted in the re-production, from various sources, of the evidences of title, and their record in the books I have mentioned.

*Introduction, Dartmouth Proprietors, <u>Land Records</u>, 1867.

Previous to Crane's surveys, it would appear that the land was held and conveyed in the form of shares. Considerable space is devoted in one of the books to statements of the interests of sundry persons who had acquired titles through the original owners of the property who were thirty-five in number.

From the examination which I have been able to make of these records which begin by giving a copy of the deed from Wamsutta to Bradford in 1654 and a list of those who were interested with him in the purchase. I am unable to say from what source they were taken. It would appear as if any one who claimed to hold a portion of the land was allowed to have his claim recorded as he should state it. It is possible that a further investigation will disclose the source from whence these memoranda were derived. They were not copied into the book we now have until very much later than other records were made.

We now come to the records which were written out from Crane's Field-Books. He commenced his operations as a surveyor about 1710 or 1711. The records which were made after the fire, other than those of which I have already spoken, are,

1. Records written out from the brief field-notes made by Crane.
2. Records made of deeds which had been given previous to the fire, and which were brought in for registry after the fire.
3. Records made of deeds given for sales made after the fire.

It was not, I think, until many years after the fire, and long after the records of the descriptions 2 and 3 had been commenced and largely accumulated, that the attempt was made to recover from the brief and blind notes of Crane, the surveyor, a full description of the property conveyed by the corporation and surveyed by him. I have not had it in my power to form any judgment as to the extent to which this operation was required and accomplished. It seems to have been undertaken and carried on by virtue of the same authority and mainly by the same individual which produced the first records of which I have spoken. The probability is that a large-part of Crane's surveys of land conveyed by the company which had not been recorded from the deeds themselves after the fire, were written out and recorded under this arrangement. It would be, however, a labor of months, if not years, to ascertain this. And there is nothing in the circumstances of the case that calls for this. The Resolve of the General Court looks only to the preservation of the records as they are. Beyond this it does not go. The Field Books of Surveyor Crane, are, with two exceptions, in good order; and all that need be done in relation to them is to prevent further delapidation and keep them where they will be safe from fire.

The first records that were made after the fire were of conveyances made previous to it, the evidences of which were brought forward by the holders for registry, and it would appear that the records of this description were mixed up with those of the conveyances which continued to be made until there was no land to convey. A man would bring the evidence of his title to land, dated, say in 1711. That would be recorded in 1728. At the same time a deed might be brought of a conveyance just made by the company. The registry of the latter would follow the former; and so they would continue to be blended, until no more of the deeds given previous to the fire should be presented. A major part of the records are of this description.

From what has been stated you will be able to learn the character of these records. You will have seen that all there is contained in these books has been recorded since 1725. From whatever source the papers may have been obtained whose date is previous to 1725, there can be, I think, no doubt of their genuineness. These records have been, I believe, admitted as evidence in our courts.

Of the records of papers dated subsequent to the fire it is enough to say that they were made direct from the original conveyances.

It is clear that these books are of the character embraced in the Resolve of the Legislature. The Resolve authorizes the County Commissioners to have copies of such books of records of "proprietors, or town proprietaries, as in their judgement ought to be preserved and perpetuated."

Having decided that it is your duty to carry the resolve into effect as it regards these records, it will be for you to decide what portion of them it will be proper to have copied that they may "be preserved and perpetuated."

The Field-books, eleven or twelve in number, do not appear to come within the description of the Act of the General Court.

I do not consider that copies of these are required, either by the act or by the object which the legislature has in view. There can be no doubt that there has been transferred from them to the other records, all that there is in them of any importance in connection with the end to be attained.

I do not see that anything is to be gained by making a copy of what may be properly called the Corporation Records---that is, the records of the meetings of the proprietors. In the books which contains the account of the proceedings of the proprietors, there are no descriptions of the land conveyed. Nothing is there found but the records of the choice of officers and of the proceedings which took place when the fire had destroyed the proprietary records.

Setting this book one side, there remains FOUR BOOKS OF WHAT MAY BE PROPERLY CALLED "LAND RECORDS." IT IS TO THESE THAT THE ACT OF THE GENERAL COURT REFERS, AND IT IS THESE, I SUPPOSE THAT YOU WILL DECIDE TO HAVE COPIED.

This being decided upon it is then to be considered in what way it is to be accomplished so as to render the work of the greatest value to the people. This involves several considerations:

1. Shall there be a book for each book to be copied or shall all be copied into one book?
2. Shall the same arrangement of entries be made in the copies, or shall the copies be arranged chronologically?
3. Shall the orthography and abbreviations of the entries be adhered to, or shall the spelling be corrected and modernized?

I shall not, here, enter into an examination of these questions. When you shall call upon me, I shall be prepared to give you my views in relation to them.

It must, I think, be evident to you, that great care must be taken that this work may be so executed as to carry out in full, the intentions of the General Court.

The copies which you are authorized to have prepared are to be authenticated in the most conclusive manner; and when thus authenticated, they are to be received as evidence in our Courts of Justice.

These books are now in my hands, and I should be pleased to see you in relation to this work at any time it may suit your convenience to call.

With Much Regard,

James B. Congdon

MAP OF SOUTHERN BRISTOL COUNTY (1871)*

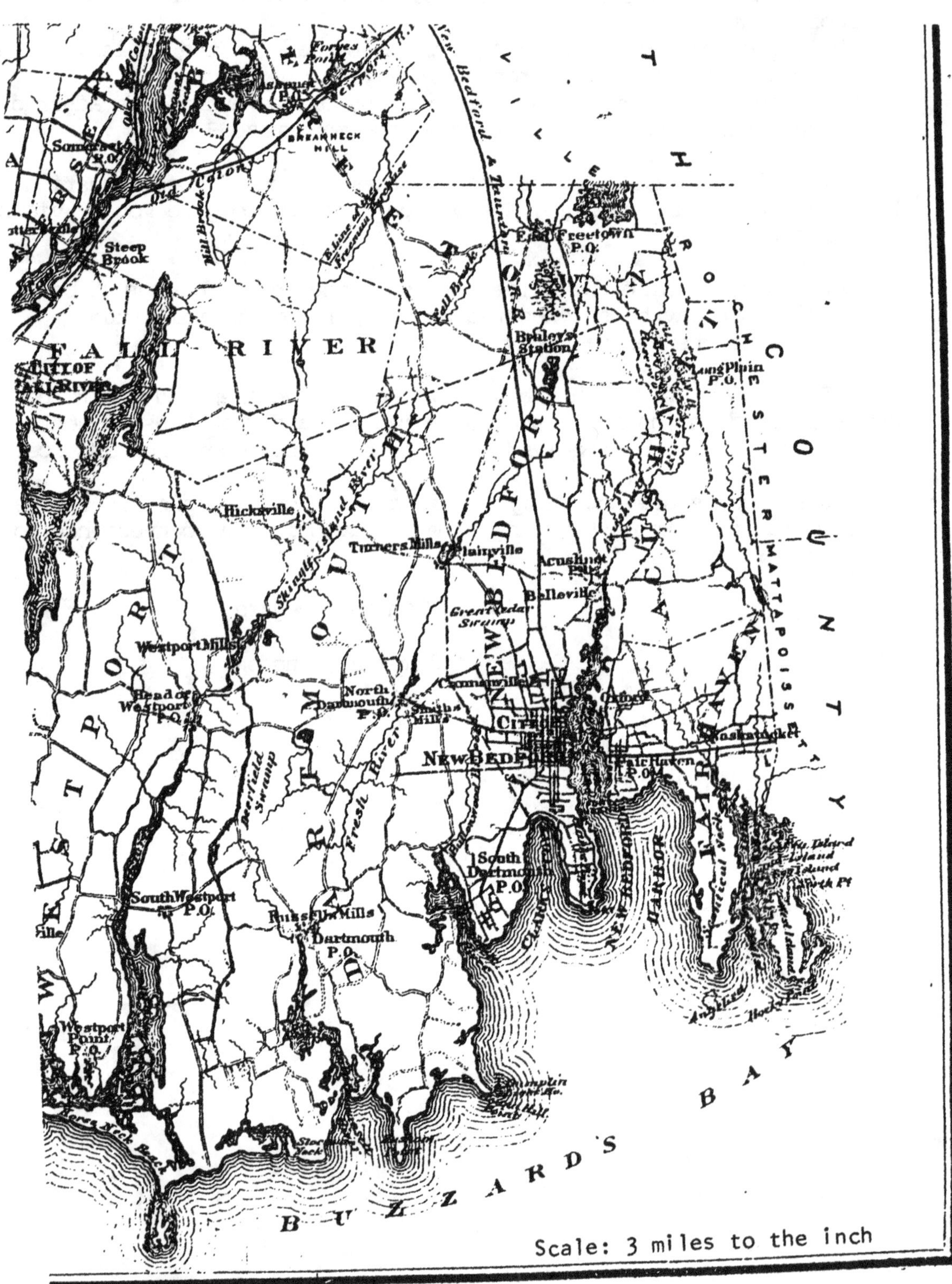

Scale: 3 miles to the inch

*Frederick W. Beers, <u>Atlas of Bristol County, Massachusetts,</u>
(New York: F.W. Beers & Co., 1871), p.7

www.ingramcontent.com/pod-product-compliance
Lightning Source LLC
Chambersburg PA
CBHW080450030726
47592CB00011B/3049